On Being
HUMAN

Essays in
Theological Anthropology

BY

RAY S. ANDERSON

GRAND RAPIDS
WILLIAM B. EERDMANS PUBLISHING COMPANY

Copyright © 1982 by William B. Eerdmans Publishing Company
255 Jefferson Ave. S.E., Grand Rapids, MI 49503
All rights reserved
Printed in the United States of America

Library of Congress Cataloging in Publication Data:

Anderson, Ray Sherman.
On being human.

Includes index.
1. Man (Christian theology) — Addresses, essays,
lectures. I. Title.
BT701.2.A52 1982   233   82-13940
ISBN 0-8028-1926-5

TABLE OF CONTENTS

PREFACE

M Y NEIGHBOR LOOKED AT ME QUIZZICALLY WHEN I REPLIED, TO HIS question why I was not driving in to the office as frequently as before, that I was writing a book. "Are you doing this because you have to," he asked, "or because you want to?"

I am not sure whether the answer to that question makes any difference to the reader or not, though I suspect that it does. Some books are written to advance or preserve the professional and academic life of the author. (For an untenured professor of theology, the alternatives may be publish or parish!) Other books are written as part of an ongoing dialogue in which teaching becomes learning and one's own contribution becomes part of a continuing quest. Every so often in this kind of conversation, one is impelled to call out, "Listen, everybody! I have something to say!" This is a book that I wanted to write.

This book had its inception when I was asked by a colleague at a Christian college to lecture to his psychology students about a theological perspective on human personality. Attempting to distinguish between human personality as a cluster of attributes manifested in behavior and the core of the human self as personal being created in the image of God, I chose to lecture on *personhood* rather than on personality. I argued for defining the self on an ontological as opposed to a phenomenological basis, and presented a case for integrating psychological concepts with the theological through the primacy of the ontic over the noetic. After class the psychology professor told me, "If I understand what you were saying at all, it appears that we couldn't be coming at the question of the human person from more opposite directions!" This experience, however, led us to explore together the nature of the self from a Christian perspective; and in several courses I pursued, with my students' help, what I then called a theology of personhood.

These explorations continued at the seminary where I now teach, both with graduate students in psychology and with theology students. Soon I came to see this as the very core of the theological curriculum. Although anthropology is one of the classical divisions or loci of theological study, in practice it has often been squeezed in between the doctrine of God and the doctrine of Christ. Pondering the significance of Karl Barth's remark that "theology has become anthropology since God became man," I began to see theological anthropology at the heart of the theological course of study.

The Westminster Catechism teaches that "the chief end of man is to glorify God and to enjoy him forever." One might go on to ask what is the chief end of God? What center could one find to the entire range of theology other than God's intention to create the human person as the crowning act of his creation and as the consummate act of his own ministry of reconciliation through the incarnation, resurrection, and glorification of the *man* Jesus Christ? It would be presumptuous to claim this, except for the insistence of God himself that this is precisely his purpose. Theological anthropology, therefore, must never settle for less, but it must never forget that its only basis for this claim is the crucified, risen, and glorified humanity of Jesus Christ.

This book was written to set forth the outlines of this larger agenda. Whereas Christology was the decisive issue for the early church, it may well be anthropology which is decisive for the church today. I shall argue that the implicit anthropological assumptions we bring to contemporary issues — whether sociological, psychological, or ethical — affect the theological conclusions we draw in the areas of soteriology and ecclesiology, not to mention the doctrines of justification and sanctification. More than any other modern theologian Karl Barth developed theological anthropology from this perspective, and I have formulated my approach on his insights — constructively though not uncritically, I trust.

I have tried to show that the caricature of Barth's theology as hopelessly constricted by christological and eschatological concerns, and thus left with no place for authentic human existence, is not entirely fair. Because Barth takes the humanity of Jesus Christ with absolute seriousness, he takes the concrete and creaturely humanity of all persons seriously. Setting aside questions some critics have raised about the philosophical intuitions which caused Barth to restrict divine revelation to the pure subjectivity of God's act, no one can fault him on the matter of taking the incarnation, and therefore the creation, with utter seriousness. I do not mean here either to defend Barth's theology or to demonstrate how he would have approached the issues I shall treat. What I write does depend on insights contributed through Barth's theological anthropology, but I am prepared to have my contribution measured by its faithfulness to the divine Word and the human situation.

I should be happy if this book were viewed more as a programmatic essay than a textbook in theological anthropology. Two objectives have been uppermost. In the first place, I am attempting to set an agenda for discussions in theological anthropology. The questions confronting the church today in the areas of human sexuality, marriage and family, abortion, and the "right to die," are first of all a matter of what we mean by "human," "human life," and "person." I offer these essays in theological anthropology as a proposed foundation for these discussions. Second, I am attempting to address contemporary issues from a pastoral perspective. Revealed truth cannot be abstracted from reconciling truth. The human situation has already been addressed and embraced by the Word of reconciliation. The theological task is no less a pastoral task than an academic profession. I hope that pastors will be encouraged in that task by a theological anthropology which liberates the human rather than merely lectures the sinner.

Finally, I express appreciation to my students, whose willingness to bear with obscurities of language and thought and whose keen interest in this material stimulated me to continue this exploration. Their names will not appear here, but many who have contributed to my own learning through questioning, challenging, and believing, are themselves now teaching and ministering the grace and truth of Christ. It is to these who have gone before and those who are taking up for the first time the question of what it means to be human that this book is dedicated. And if you should find some of them reading this book, you might ask them, "Are you reading this because you have to or because you want to?"

Pasadena, California   RAY S. ANDERSON
August 1982

PART ONE

THE FORM
OF THE HUMAN

CHAPTER ONE

TOWARD A
THEOLOGICAL ANTHROPOLOGY

E VERY DISCUSSION OF HUMANITY MUST TAKE NOTE OF THE CLASSIC
lament Job uttered against the Creator:

> Man that is born of woman is of few days, and full of trouble.
> He comes forth like a flower, and withers;
>   he flees like a shadow and continues not.
> And dost thou open thy eyes upon such a one
>   and bring him into judgment with thee?
> Who can bring a clean thing out of an unclean?
>   There is not one.
> Since his days are determined,
>   and the number of his months is with thee,
>   and thou hast appointed his bounds that he cannot pass,
> look away from him and desist,
>   that he may enjoy, like a hireling, his day (Job 14:1-6).[1]

In all of human literature no one has touched the pathos of the human
situation as keenly as Job. And no one has expressed such defiance of all that
seems to stand against this existence, even God himself, as this ancient Hebrew
author. While Job represents the Hebrew soul in its affliction, he also expresses
on behalf of the Hebrew a conviction that life, even under affliction, belongs
to the one who experiences it. Job seems to be saying, "My life is a torturous
and tormented existence, but it is mine, so leave me alone!"

Kierkegaard once told the parable of a typographical error which was
personified and given an existence of its own. It was then addressed in such
a way as to suggest that a correction would be necessary to change it into the
true form intended. It promptly protested, wrote Kierkegaard, because in this
case correction meant annihilation. Better to persist as an error than not to
have existence at all! But Job does not really admit that his existence is an
error. Rather he argues that his existence will be vindicated in the end as one
having its own purpose and even righteousness. Reaching into the depth of

---

1. All Scripture citations, unless otherwise indicated, are from the Revised Standard Version.

his own existence as that which was originally determined by God, he finds the courage to affirm that existence over against circumstances which seem to prove that the Creator has forgotten him.

Another Hebrew poet wrote of humanity in more elegant terms and possibly with a clearer vision.

> "When I look at thy heavens, the work of thy fingers,
> the moon and the stars which thou hast established,
> what is man that thou art mindful of him? . . .
> Yet thou hast made him little less than God
> and dost crown him with glory and honor" (Ps. 8:3-5).

Which is the more accurate portrayal? A little less than God, or not much better off than the beasts of the field? If the latter understates the value of our personal humanity, how can we be sure that the former does not overstate it? On what grounds could one convince a person for whom life appears to be unrelenting pain and meaningless frustration that he or she is the object of a Creator's love and as such "of more value" than all other creatures? We like to sing with the Psalmist of the exalted nature of "man," but we listen to the poet who speaks on behalf of those for whom there is neither strength nor reason to sing. Can we define the nature of human personhood without saying too little or too much, and thus failing to grasp the mystery which meets us in every face — and most unavoidably in our own?

WHAT IS A HUMAN PERSON?

The attempt of theology to speak of the uniqueness of human personhood has not been altogether successful. In trying to define the essence of humanity expressed as "human nature," theologians and philosophers come to grief over the inability of language to hold "being" in its grasp. Philosophers once optimistically posited "theory of being" (ontology) as the very core of "thinking about reality" (metaphysics). Because being was assumed to exist as an object of thought, rational thought could be assumed to be itself a structure of reality. "Human being" consequently became an object of thought before it became a description of existence. For the medieval philosopher, nature is the expression of being. Human nature is thus considered ontologically rather than phenomenologically; that is, human beings exist and have value because of who they are essentially, not (as a more modern concept would hold) because of what they do with their existence "existentially." Many have judged that classical metaphysics failed to sustain the assumption that being exists as an object of thought; and this failure explains a turning away from the so-called ontological approach to the human person in favor of a more concrete and dynamic concept in terms of *how* a person acts and reacts rather than *who* a person is.

We shall define phenomenology in this discussion in the broad sense of an attempt to discern the meaning of events and experiences through what can be perceived by the senses. Our interest is in the general abandonment of ontology as a basis for determining the nature of human personhood in favor of a more phenomenological approach, based on either existentialist or naturalist interpretations of human existence. What is of even more interest is that Hebrew anthropology, whether viewing the human situation from the heights of the Psalmist or the depths of Job, has no theory of being (ontology) nor does it surrender personal existence to the caprice of time and chance. We shall look more closely at this as we formulate the contours of a biblical anthropology and answer the question: what is a human person?

This question did not escape the attention of the earliest theologians of the church. Shortly after the New Testament period, they drew on Greek language and throught-forms in an attempt to develop a theological anthropology. Taking the word *hypostasis* from Greek middle Platonic thought, which was essentially Stoic, they put a face on it, a *prosopon*. This concept they designated as "person." Because the power of conceptual thought for the Greeks centered on the nature of things in terms of "essence" (*ousia*), they were more concerned with human nature as "substance" than with person as a dynamic function of existence. Their definition of human nature denoted a static, substantial entity rather than the dynamic attributes of personal existence. The Greek word *prosopon* — like the Latin *persona* — originally meant "mask," and then "face." The *prosopon* or "face" is not the personal reality, but discloses — and also hides — that reality which is the "essence" of the human.

The legacy of patristic anthropology to the medieval theologians was thus a somewhat static and highly abstract notion of human nature. In the early christological creeds the concept of "person" as an individual subsistence (or *hypostasis*) of humanity became the designation for the unity of the divine and human nature in Jesus. But this referred to Jesus' essential being, not to the particular "personality" he expressed as a first-century Palestinian Jew. On the other hand, trinitarian theologians could speak of God as "three persons" coinhering in a single divine essence. Here again, the word "person" is more a "face" through which the essence of being is revealed than a discrete entity with its own particular essence.

It is of interest to note that Augustine, the fifth-century theologian, was one of the first persons — if not the first — to "interiorize" his thoughts. In his *Confessions* Augustine set forth what we think of as a biography of the inner life, a self-conscious depiction of his own existence as a person. Today we take it for granted that persons are self-conscious personalities, with an interior life which is expressed as thoughts, feelings, and behavior; but for the Greeks, interior life was not the essential person. The interior life was unstable, unpredictable, and thus unreal.[2]

The medieval development of Christian anthropology, however, followed the more traditional Greek concept of person as an essence rather than a personal and historical existence. In the sixth century Boethius defined person as "an individual subsistence of a rational nature." This set the stage for the medieval scholastics, who continued to develop a concept of being as an object of thought. A person, therefore, exemplifies a particular quality of being which has a rational nature capable of reflecting on being. Drawing on Aristotelian metaphysics, Thomas Aquinas, in the thirteenth century, argued for a proportionality or analogy between human being and divine being. One could posit the existence of God as divine being on the basis of being able to ascertain the reality of human being. From the existence of human beings, one could argue by analogy for the existence of God. Nature, including human nature, seemed clear enough to Thomas as an object of knowledge; therefore, the nature of God could also be assumed as the presupposition on which human nature rests.

In following Boethius in his concept of person as individuated substance possessing rational faculties, Aquinas ignored a much more dynamic and hopeful concept of person set forth in the twelfth century by Richard of St. Victor, who taught that a person is "an incommunicable ex-sistence of an intellectual nature" (*persona est intellectualis naturae incommunicabilis exsistentia*). What is unique in Richard's definition is that the Latin *ex-sistentia*, from which our word "existence" comes, literally means "that which stands forth out of itself." This definition emphasizes that the human person does not merely "possess" an essence (nature), which has substance as an object of thought, but is a person who "stands out" of himself toward the source of being. Yet this "standing out" of oneself, as an existing person toward others, does not entail the loss of one's essential nature. There is something "incommunicable" about personal being, notwithstanding the openness of being to other being. The self is not exhausted in relation to others. Something finally incommunicable remains as the essence of being.[3]

Unfortunately, Western theology, both Roman Catholic and Protestant, followed Boethius rather than Richard of St. Victor. This tended to produce an atomistic concept of person which led to a strongly individualistic as well as

---

2. For a representative collection of patristic statements on theological anthropology (including Augustine) see J. Patout Burns (ed.), *Theological Anthropology* (Philadelphia: Fortress, 1981).

3. Heribert Mühlen shows how this concept of person was taken up by Johannes Duns Scotus and developed in terms of a doctrine of the Trinity; *Sein und Person nach Johannes Duns Scotus* (Werl, West Germany: Dietrich-Coelde-Verlag, 1954).

rational view of the human self. The result is a dualism between nature and grace on the one hand, and between nature and experience on the other. This was true for those who tried to understand the human person introspectively as an autonomous ethical agent (such as Tertullian, the Latin-Greek father of the third century) or as the ego of a psychological complex (Augustine) or as a substance possessing certain potencies (the medieval scholastics). No matter which of these modes prevailed, a dualism remained which drove a wedge between human being as nature and human person as either the object of divine grace or as the subject of personal experience (personality).

The first result of this dichotomy was the assertion following the Enlightenment of the autonomy of "natural man" over against "religious man." When human nature is set over against grace as a neutral substance, either a metaphysical principle or a sacramental act is required to relate natural being to supernatural being. The secularization of human thought in the Enlightenment (particularly following Kant) has made it difficult if not impossible for many modern thinkers to sustain a concept of human nature as an object of divine grace. And because the dogma undergirding the theology of the sacrament as an infusion of divine grace into human nature was built on Aristotelian metaphysics (Aquinas), modern theologians are equally hard pressed to assert the basic religious value of human nature.[4]

A second result of this dichotomy has become more pronounced since the advent of the behavioral sciences. We have seen that medieval ontology defined human nature as a non-physical "substance" which was first of all an object of thought and only thereafter an experiencing subject. Because this "nature" was inaccessible to the descriptive and experimental sciences, "nature" tended to be identified as behavior and person as personality. Theories of behavior or theories of personality replaced the more traditional theory of being (ontology) as a way of answering the question, What is a human person? In philosophical thought, existence as a phenomenon of being replaces essence as a theory of being. While existentialism claims to be more a "humanistic" attempt to define the nature of persons than the naturalistic assumptions of the behavioral sciences, both would agree that it is impossible to speak of human nature as a substance or essence which determines existence and behavior.

The fact that a humanistic philosophy can speak of moral and even reli-

---

4. In discussing the medieval development of the distinction between nature and grace as anthropological components, Hans Urs von Balthasar says: "What theology pondered here in a purely experimental and abstract way was soon, in English free thought and in continental enlightenment, to become the actual model of humanity. It lay in the nature of the case that the Adventlike openness of late medieval philosophical theology could no longer be reestablished, and that now in enlightened anthropology the original doubts about the nature of man became far more acute." *A Theological Anthropology* (New York: Sheed and Ward, 1967), p. 84.

gious values as basic to human experience has given some people reason to hope for a synthesis between the naturalistic assumptions of the behavioral scientists and the more existential assumptions of the philosophers, which will in turn lead to a new Christian anthropology to fill the vacuum left by the demise of more traditional views. This may be a good corrective to the impersonal and non-humanist assumptions science often brings to the study of the human, but it remains to be seen whether or not a "religious anthropology" formed primarily on intrinsic values viewed phenomenologically can properly be called a "theological anthropology." A closer and more critical look must be taken at this possibility.

THE PROBLEMS OF A
NON-THEOLOGICAL ANTHROPOLOGY

The older, more classical anthropology of the church was considered a theological anthropology because of its presupposition that the human person is created and sustained by the Word and grace of God. Our cursory survey of the development of this anthropology has shown how its basic assumptions were undermined in the post-Enlightenment period of modern thought and scientific research. Although not everyone would agree with this generalization, it could hardly be disputed that it is the prevailing mood among both secular and religious scholars today. Before attempting to outline a theological anthropology which can stand against the reductionism of the more contemporary theories, we need to see the particular problems with some so-called non-theological anthropologies.[5]

It is helpful first of all to see that there are various anthropologies which can be placed on a continuum from Myth to Science, with Philosophy located in the middle. All of these approaches to describing the nature of the human person can be said to be phenomenological. That is, they all start from the viewpoint of the human situation. Or, to put it another way, these anthropologies can be said to be Cartesian, because like Descartes they seek to explain the mystery of the human in terms of the human subject.

In mythical anthropology the human subject is contained and defined within the closed cycle of nature. In philosophical anthropology the human person is understood within the categories of self-knowledge. In scientific anthropology humanity as either a social or individual phenomenon is described from the perspective of an observer. Mythical and philosophical anthropology may be grouped generally in the category of "speculative

---

5. I am indebted for the following analysis to the discussion of non-theological anthropology presented by Karl Barth in *Church Dogmatics*, III/2.

anthropology," while scientific anthropology is by its nature not concerned with questions of ultimate truth or of "world view" but seeks an impartial (if only partial) view of the human.

Mythical anthropology is at once the most primitive and most contemporary, because it operates in a non-historical perspective. The element of myth is always present when human existence is linked in a cause-and-effect relationship with the powers and portents in nature. The anthropology of ancient peoples, who understood their daily existence as the outcomes of non-historical events in a world where the natural and supernatural interpenetrated, was mythical. But today's devotees of astrological charts and signs are no less mythical, even if they may be more sophisticated. A sense of history is related to self-consciousness, which differentiates between subjective and objective reality, something that myth does not recognize. When the human person moves out of a mythical anthropology, there is a summons to respond personally and with freedom to laws or principles which are determinative of humanity itself, not merely blind and purposeless movements of nature.

In Genesis 3 Adam and Eve attempt to take refuge in the deeper recesses of nature: they hide from the Lord God among the trees of the garden. At that point they become non-historical. They interpret their lives in terms of events which happen to them, rather than exercise the freedom and accountability which is theirs by nature. But God does not permit them to take refuge in this mythical world. Out of the place where their guilt has merged with their nature, resulting in a destiny that is fatalistic, he summons them into personal accountability and restoration. Their "guilt," which has become a "natural way of life," now becomes differentiated from their nature in terms of sin, and thus a contradiction of their true nature:

Even the classical forms of myth, as highly developed by the ancient Greeks, sought to account for the phenomena of human existence as a more or less fatalistic result of the conflicts, jealousies, and desires of the "gods," who were caught like the humans in the non-historical realm of nature and being. To say that mythical anthropology is non-theological is therefore to say that it has neither a transcendent source nor a revealing and speaking God. It is characterized by what Kornelis Miskotte calls the silence of the gods.[6] Even where supernatural beings are assumed to be the source of human experiences, there is no fundamental differentiation and communication. While mythical anthropology purports to explain to humans why their humanity is necessarily the way it is, this "kerygma" is not the Word of God,[7] and in this sense it is non-theological.

---

6. *When the Gods are Silent* (London: Collins, 1967).
7. For a discussion of myth and kerygma, see Helmut Thielicke, *The Evangelical Faith* (Grand Rapids: Eerdmans, 1974), I, 66-114.

One might ask whether a Freudian theory of psychoanalysis, to the extent that it goes beyond a therapeutic technique and becomes a definitive view of human nature, does not tend to be a mythical anthropology. Indeed, science is particularly vulnerable to the seduction of the mythical because it has no kerygma of its own. Having divorced explanation from understanding, the scientific method, applied to human behavior, will tend to resort to mythical solutions in search of a kerygma. Just as astrology emerged in the fifth century B.C. as the integration, on a naturalistic continuum, of mathematical astronomy into mythical concepts of human experience, one might see the emergence of "cultic psychology" today as a kerygmatic response to the hiatus between explanation and understanding created by the tyranny of "objective" science and technology over the human self. It is not because a non-theological anthropology *lacks* a kerygma that it is non-theological, but because the kerygma by which it purports to give meaning to personal human existence is a pseudo-kerygma. It is a "word" which has been conceived in silence and fabricated out of desperate longings and lonely desperation. Perhaps a mythical anthropology is at the heart of all non-theological anthropologies, precisely because (to use Ernest Becker's phrase) persons in every age have to "tame the terror" of being alive by seeking to relate the self to a larger-than-life identity.[8]

Thus as we move along the continuum to look more closely at philosophical anthropologies, we never leave the mythical completely behind. True, through self-reflection the philosopher can differentiate between subjectivity and objectivity, whereas in the reflection on existence of mythical anthropology, nature itself becomes an extension of subjectivity. Philosophical anthropology introduces into the continuum a discontinuity between nature and the human person. The monism of the mythical world gives way to the dualism of the world as seen and understood by the self as a thinking subject.

Alongside the highly developed mythical view of human existence among the ancient Greeks, a very sophisticated philosophical anthropology also appeared, expressed in terms of the discontinuity between the self as a reality anchored in a non-material, eternal entity, and the material, natural world which is only a shadow of the reality. One form of this philosophical anthropology is the distinction in Platonic thought between the sensual or intelligible world and the numinal or non-material world. While Aristotle argued that the essence (eternal nature) of a thing did not exist apart from the existence of the thing itself as an object of the sensible world, he nevertheless continued to maintain the dichotomy and discontinuity between the essence of a thing and its appearance. Aristotle's insistence that the essence of the human soul

---

8. Becker, *The Denial of Death* (New York: Macmillan, The Free Press, 1973), pp. 150, 283.

is rational correspondence to the eternal quality posited as the *telos* of the human led him to his well-known conclusion that a male infant does not become human until approximately the age of two years — and a female somewhat later! The justification of infanticide in ancient Greece was based on this philosophical anthropology.

Distinctive to philosophical anthropology is the attempt to define the essence of the human self as self-transcendent with regard to the natural world in which it exists. This frees the self from the determinism of nature, which mythical anthropology is unable to do. The problem, of course, is keeping the self in view as an object of thought while at the same time asserting its transcendence over its existence on the continuum of the natural world. Aristotle abandoned the Platonic transcendence of the self based on the concept of "eternal ideas" from which temporal existence is derived, but he maintained the transcendence of the self as the non-material, yet materially embodied, essence of the person. As we saw, this served very well the concerns of the medieval theologians who wished to maintain a distinction between nature and grace.

However, following the thought of René Descartes, the seventeenth-century French philosopher, the discontinuity between the self as the object of divine grace and the self existing in the objective world of experience became an absolute distinction. For Descartes, the source of reality was the human mind, rather than deductions drawn from the natural world of experience. All appearances are fallible, argued Descartes, even the perceptions and experiences of our own senses. Only the mind is real, because in doubting all that is perceived through sense experience, the mind cannot doubt its own existence. *I think, therefore I am.*

The anthropological implications of this were immediate and far-reaching. When the reality of the human person is located entirely in subjective mind, as opposed to the objective world of sense experience, the synthesis between the material and non-material self, fundamental to Christian anthropology as taught by the medieval theologians, broke apart. Metaphysics, which had well served the theologian under the tutelage of Aristotle, now became a source of pure Idealism — with being merging with thought itself (Hegel) — or the cause of agnosticism, in which a theory of being gives way to practical will (Kant). Philosophical anthropology, which posited self-transcendence in reflection on existence as the core of the person as thinking self, found in a post-Kantian age that such a transcendent basis for the self was "unthinkable" and thus without content or meaning. Kant attempted to preserve an anthropological element in his critical philosophy through the categorical ethical imperative as a practical norm for living a human rather than non-human life. But if human nature is only human because one's behavior conforms to an ethical imperative,

and if the transcendent source of that imperative is unspecifiable and con-
tentless, no ontological basis for anthropology remains. Kant conceded this,
though he continued to insist on the meaningfulness of his distinction between
human and non-human based on a concept of an intrinsic ethical nature.

Clearly mythical and philosophical anthropology share a common assumption: both emerge out of what the human self can understand and say
about itself. In the case of mythical anthropology, the kerygma is conceived
in silence; there is no speech or communication between the gods and human
persons. In the case of philosophical anthropology, the kerygma is conceived
out of human thought and words in the absence of the gods. The writers of
the myths humanized their gods by creating speeches for them. These speeches
became the kerygmatic utterances which gave meaning to life. The philosophers took the words out of the mouths of the gods and divinized human
speech, or, failing to make that credible, located kerygma in actions rather
than in speech itself.

Existential philosophy seems to be based primarily on anthropological
concerns. Feeling deeply the estrangement between the self and the natural
world, without the comfort of a mythical worldview in which the self loses its
identity in nature, the existentialist reaches out for transcendence. However,
critical philosophy has established that this transcendence can no longer be
an object of thought and must thus be approached through being itself. The
existentialist endeavors to recover being as authentic personal existence, and
only then and understood in that way does language have content and meaning. But here philosophical anthropology begins to come full circle and lose its
power to differentiate between the self as being and all else as being. Heidegger's attempt to maintain this differentiation by distinguishing between "being"
and "Being" is not at all convincing, particularly when he asserts that silence
rather than language is the pathway to Being.

The point is this. Philosophical and mythical anthropology are both non-
theological, despite their claims to be religious (or at least ethical), precisely
because there is no Word of God through which and by which the human
exists. Even the "theistic anthropology" of Paul Tillich falls short of this. Adopt-
ing the fundamental ontology of Heidegger, by which he is able to say that
God is "Being itself," and the "ground of all being," Tillich argues for a theon-
omous anthropology rather than an autonomous or heteronomous anthropology. We are neither self-determined beings nor beings determined by some
other self; we are beings under the determination of God. However, Tillich's
theistic anthropology can be bracketed with philosophical anthropology to the
extent that the word "God" is itself only a symbol for a nameless and unspecifiable "Being" which emerges from the depth of each individual human being.
I do not mean to diminish Tillich's profound contribution to the integration

of faith and culture through his theistic anthropology. Perhaps no one has asked the question of human existence as profoundly and creatively as Tillich, but a question is still a question, even raised to the level of "ultimate concern."

Though we have placed scientific anthropology on the same continuum of non-theological anthropology as the mythical and philosophical, there is one significant difference. Science ordinarily does not raise the claim to truth. By its very nature it is relative and partial as a mode of inquiry. True science has no kerygma; in fact, it disavows having a kerygma. To this extent, scientific anthropology can just as well build on a theological presupposition as on a non-theological one. To the extent that myth and philosophy presuppose the primacy of the human point of view in developing an anthropology, their kerygma may not be, and usually is not, compatible with the kerygma which issues from God's revelation as determinative of human existence. In this sense compatibility between scientific and theological anthropology ought to be more likely.

But this may be a dubious assertion on at least two counts. First of all, it may not be strictly correct to speak of "scientific anthropology," for science, as a method of discovery or inquiry into the nature of reality, must permit the nature of what it wishes to know to determine the method of inquiry and examination. If a scientific inquiry is carried on and results are determined on the basis of presuppositions which cannot be verified as the nature of that which is to be known reveals itself, science has already compromised its methodology. However — and this is the second reason to question the assertion — in actual practice science, especially behavioral science, operates with some degree of philosophical commitment to the nature of reality as expressed by the subject under investigation. It may well be then that the line between scientific anthropology and philosophical anthropology is blurred, so that the distinction remains only a formal one. The advantage of making this distinction, however, is to assert that a theological anthropology is not inimical to scientific methodology, inasmuch as the scientific method in principle carries no intrinsic commitment to a kerygmatic assertion concerning the meaning and purpose of human existence.

Natural science rightly attempts to place the human person within the cosmos as a distinctive phenomenon and a subject of study. The human person is a creature of time and space with an objectivity accessible to investigation and interpretation. If an anthropology emerges under this kind of observation and experimentation, as it often does, it will be reductionist to the extent that it excludes aspects of the human self which cannot be manipulated or controlled under objectifiable conditions. For example, nineteenth-century scientific objectivism rigorously excluded all subjective phenomena, such as self-consciousness with respect to the study of the human brain. This led to conclusions that the brain as the center of the human self was basically, or nothing but, an organic entity with complex biological, chemical, and electrical activity.

Some recent scientists have begun from the premise that self-consciousness as a phenomenon and activity of the human self must be viewed as a component of the empirical data, along with the material elements of the brain and nervous system.[9] This assertion, of course, is the source of debate among scientists themselves. However, the point being made is that natural science must be an open-ended inquiry into the nature of the human to avoid becoming a non-theological anthropology. It is to be hoped that a theological anthropology will be shown to serve the cause of science by its own kerygma, through which the kerygmatic and often dogmatic assertions of mythical and philosophical anthropology can be qualified and corrected.

The fundamental problem with all non-theological anthropologies is that they proceed from *anthropos* rather than from *theos*. At best, non-theological anthropologies are "symptoms of real humanity, not real humanity itself."[10] To this extent they can genuinely contribute to the knowledge of the human person, but the sum total of them is not the true person. For this reason, says Karl Barth, "in the last resort, there is something tragic in every non-theological anthropology."[11] In the end, it is more tragic for a philosophical or even a theistic anthropology to point to the necessary transcendent source of the human without being able to give content to that source than it is for natural science to conclude that the human self is nothing but a cluster of molecules in search of a name.

In *Look Homeward, Angel,* Thomas Wolfe started out with a quest for that which lies beyond present experience: a place we have never visited but for which we are ever homesick, words we have not heard but can never forget. At the end of that magnificent book, when Eugene has, through his own sensual and spiritual and aesthetic experiences, plunged deeply into all that the human mind and body can know and experience, he meets his dead brother Ben in a vision.

"Fool, why do you look in the streets?", questioned Ben.
Then Eugene said: "I have eaten and drunk the earth, I have been lost and beaten, and I will go no more."
"Fool," said Ben, "what do you want to find?"
"Myself, and an end to hunger, and the happy land," he answered.
"For I believe in harbors at the end. O Ben, brother, and ghost and stranger, you who could never speak, give me an answer now!"

---

9. This is the position taken by John Eccles, *Facing Reality* (London: Heidelberg Science Library, 1970); see also *The Human Mystery* (Berlin, Heidelberg: Springer-Verlag, 1979).
10. Karl Barth, *Church Dogmatics,* III/2, 200.
11. *Ibid.,* 429.

Then as he thought, Ben said: "There is no happy land. There is no end to hunger."

"Where, Ben? Where is the world."

"Nowhere," Ben said. "You are your world."

"I shall save one land unvisited," said Eugene. "*Et ego in Arcadia.*"[12]

This is the highest point to which a non-theological anthropology can reach. But it is at the same time a tragic insight. What is a human person? If once we thought we knew, the answer no longer can be given with confidence or certainty.

THE BEGINNING OF
A THEOLOGICAL ANTHROPOLOGY

We seem to have come full circle. Having begun with Job's lament we have now listened to a more contemporary poet argue for a better end to human existence than his life appears to offer. We must begin again. But where do we start? If all non-theological anthropologies come to grief over the silence of the gods when viewed from below, can one overcome this difficulty by stepping out of our humanity while we search for clues? Unfortunately not. A theological anthropology has no starting point but human existence itself, within this world of time and chance. There are no privileged data, withheld from the eyes of mortals, to which we have access. For we are mortals, and we who are dying must write of life. But (to cite Job again) "who can bring a clean thing out of an unclean?" (Job 14:4).

If we must begin with what is human in order to discover the nature of the human, and if there is no humanity free from distortion, does this not pose almost insurmountable difficulties for a theological anthropology? Precisely. And this is the difficulty which confronts us, says Karl Barth:

> In these circumstances how can we possibly reach a doctrine of man in the sense of a doctrine of his creaturely essence, of his human nature as such? For what we recognize to be human nature is nothing other than the disgrace which covers his nature; his inhumanity, perversion, and corruption. If we try to deny this or to tone it down, we have not yet understood the full import of the truth that for the reconciliation of man with God, nothing more or less was needed than the death of the Son of God, and for the manifestation of this reconciliation, nothing more or less than the resurrection of the Son of Man, Jesus Christ. But if we know man only in the corruption and

---

12. *Look Homeward, Angel* (New York: Random House, 1929), p. 624.

distortion of his being, how can we even begin to answer the question about his creaturely nature?[13]

It is not as though non-theological anthropology errs by starting with humanity in its distortion, and we who wish to write a theological anthropology can avoid this mistake. The problem of a non-theological anthropology, it turns out, is not that the human person is the starting point, but that the human person seeks to have the final word, the decisive judgment, as to the nature of humanity.

While a theological anthropology must begin with humanity itself, it must also take into account that the Word of God has come to that humanity and, in the midst of that humanity, however distorted and perverse it may be, revealed the true form of that which is human. "In this radical depravity," says Barth, "there is necessarily hidden his original form."[14] Of course, the phrase "radical depravity" is already a polemic against any other description of the sickness or disturbance in human nature. But it is precisely by starting with humanity as it comes under the most radical judgment of God and as it experiences the most radical grace of God that the original form of the human is revealed to us.

It is then to the humanity of Jesus Christ, the one crucified and judged for all humanity, who bore in his own humanity the radical judgment of God, that we turn as the starting point for theological anthropology. It is in the crucified form of humanity as seen in Jesus Christ that we discover the original form of our humanity. In him the radical form of the original is present; he reveals the true form of humanity not as one who in his innocence kept a distance from our humanity but as one who took on himself our own humanity.

Three comments may be made to elucidate this basic thesis. First, the form of humanity as revealed through the crucified humanity of Jesus Christ cannot be grasped directly, either by speculative or scientific anthropology. Neither myth nor philosophy nor science can grasp the meaning of the crucifixion as a truth of humanity. In order to penetrate the truth of humanity under judgment, one must himself or herself come under judgment. There is no point of scientific detachment or logical rigor from which to look on the form of the human as it hangs on the cross in the person of Jesus of Nazareth and gain insight into the truth. Yet this truth is accessible at the human level. It is not revealed only to those who know or guess the secret words, as the gnostics in every age like to think. It is rather a truth which destroys privileged assumptions and renders all persons open before God. It is a truth which comes by way of repentance and faith.

13. *Church Dogmatics*, III/2, 27.
14. *Ibid.*, 29.

Non-theological anthropologies can tell us nothing about crucified humanity. They cannot infer the true form of humanity from humanity under judgment. One cannot infer a healthy being from a sick one. One cannot reconstruct order from disorder. The absence of sickness is not yet health. Even if one would dare on strictly moral grounds to call the sickness of humanity sin, one cannot posit grace as the cure for sickness. For in this case the grace, if radical enough in its cure, will destroy the humanity in order to correct the sin. Even more serious, one will not be able to differentiate between human creatureliness and sinful human nature on strictly empirical grounds.

"Who sinned, this man or his parents, that he was born blind?", the disciples asked Jesus. "Neither," replied Jesus, though he went on to warn them against the presumption that anyone is free from judgment (John 9:2-3). There is no direct equation between human creatureliness and sin. But this is only revealed to us through the humanity of Jesus himself. As the incarnate Word of God himself, Jesus took as his own mode of human existence a creaturely form which is common to every other human being (cf. John 1:14; Gal. 4:4-5; Heb. 2:14-18). Sharing fully in human creatureliness and even experiencing the judgment of God against sin in his own death, he was nevertheless personally without sin as an act of defiance and disobedience to God (John 8:46).

This leads to our second comment. The cross reveals the interconnection between the Word of God, sin, and human creatureliness. The cross authenticates sin for what it is, a contradiction of the Word and will of God, expressed in human rebellion against God. In his crucifixion, Jesus brackets both sin and creatureliness in the same moment, but in such a way that the connection between creatureliness (human nature) and sin is broken. There is no necessary relation between them. Because our humanity is creaturely we are not inevitably led to sin. Jesus himself is demonstration of that. And yet, if we are tempted to minimize how radically destructive sin is to our humanity, Jesus demonstrates the absolute judgment on sin demanded by the Word of God. Thus on the cross and in the crucified humanity of Jesus Christ, both sin and human creatureliness are authenticated as under the determination of the Word of God. When he was tempted, Jesus did not sin, but responded, "Man shall not live by bread alone, but by every word that proceeds from the mouth of God" (Matt. 4:4). The deterministic principle of sin is broken, and grace is revealed as the true order of humanity. Later we shall discuss further how sin confuses and distorts our humanity. The point here is that a theological anthropology dares to begin with humanity because it can find in the humanity of Jesus Christ the true order of humanity and the true nature of sin as the source of disorder and destructiveness.

Recent writings in psychology have introduced the concept of sin as something more hopeful than mere sickness. In his book, *The Crisis of Psychiatry and Religion,* O. Hobart Mowrer has a chapter entitled "Sin As the Lesser of Two Evils," in which he argues that considering sin as a condition which produces guilt expressed as psychical distress is more hopeful than merely considering the patient "sick." Sin, writes Mowrer, "opens up to us the radical possibilities of redemption." One might also mention in this connection Karl Menninger's book *Whatever Became of Sin?,* as well as Ernest Becker's treatment of neurosis as sin in *The Denial of Death.* It is difficult to see, however, that an equation of neurosis or psychological guilt with sin can free a person from the tyranny of sin as a phenomenon of creatureliness itself.

In the third place, by beginning with the crucified humanity of Christ, we find the true order of humanity as disclosed through the resurrection of Jesus from the dead. The continuity between Jesus of Nazareth as the crucified one and Christ the Lord as the resurrected one is the indispensable foundation for a theological anthropology. What the cross and death appear to have cancelled out, the resurrection restores and affirms. Jesus' resurrection authenticates humanity as creaturely humanity under the determination of the Word and power of God, fully able to live within the conditions of temporal and earthly existence but not finally subject to the determination of a creaturely nature.

Karl Barth, more than any other theologian of the church, including the Reformers, has developed a comprehensive theological anthropology by beginning with the humanity of Jesus Christ as both crucified and resurrected. We must first go to Christ to learn about humanity, says Barth, and then to Adam. Both Adam and Christ are part of the human story which makes up redemptive history. But even though Adam precedes Christ chronologically, Christ precedes Adam as the true form of humanity, of which Adam — especially Adam the sinner (and do we really know any other Adam?) — is the image and likeness.

This chapter has set the agenda for the rest of the book. We began by discussing what a human person is. Our brief survey of the development of theological anthropology from the early church theologians to the present has shown that the answer is more inconclusive than ever. Our analysis of the problems inherent in non-theological anthropology sought to show why this is so. When the human person is the one who makes the final determination as to what is the nature of the human, both religious and atheistic anthropologies end with a question rather than with an answer. Even though the existentialist is most painfully honest in making a "kerygmatic" utterance out of the question, the intrinsic tragedy of the human cannot be shaken off.

We have attempted in the last few pages to state the basic presupposition of this series of studies in theological anthropology. The knowledge of ourselves as human beings must be determined by and be correlated with our knowledge of God as the one who reveals himself finally and completely through Jesus Christ. A theological anthropology such as we seek to develop, then, will be critically limited and determined by the dogmatic assumption that Jesus Christ is the incarnate Logos of God, the enfleshed Word, fully human and totally divine in the unity of his person. The humanity of Christ, by which he shares our creaturely nature and bears our sin, discloses the radical form of true humanity and how reconciliation leads to wholeness and holiness alike.

The remaining chapters in Part One will examine more precisely and critically the relation of humanity to creatureliness. This is the beginning of a theological anthropology.

CHAPTER TWO

HUMANITY AS
CREATURELINESS

I T MAY COME AS A SURPRISE THAT A THEOLOGICAL ANTHROPOLOGY SHOULD begin its discussion of the human with the phenomenon of creatureliness. After all, one might assume that theology has some access to the original mold from which humanity as we experience it was formed. But whereas the Greeks visualized the human form as a divine and timeless ideal, the Hebrews experienced their God in crude but down-to-earth anthropomorphisms. And the "many-splendoured thing" (to borrow a phrase from Francis Thompson) is more often than not concealed and disclosed to us in the lump of clay which looks suspiciously like our Uncle George.

We begin to delineate the form of the human by giving attention to what actually exists, not what ought to exist or exists ideally in the mind. If existence is human at all, it is creaturely existence. By "creaturely" we refer to the broad continuum of organisms inhabiting the natural world and carrying that indefinable, but absolutely necessary, breath of life. The creaturely is "of creation," bound up in the solidarity of life which is from the earth and dependent on its environment (or one like it) for the relatively brief span of time allotted to it. By "creaturely" we also mean "creature of God," although it remains to be seen whether this means any more than "of creation." In the broadest sense the creaturely is summed up in the poignant epitaph pronounced by the ancient Hebrew sage:

> I said in my heart with regard to the sons of men that God is testing them to show that they are but beasts. For the fate of the sons of men and the fate of beasts is the same. As one dies, so dies the other. They all have the same breath. And man has no advantage over the beasts; for all is vanity. All go to one place; all are from the dust, and all turn to dust again. Who knows whether the spirit of man goes upward and the spirit of the beast goes down to the earth? (Eccl. 3:18-21).

This is not the mere rhetoric of "mid-life crisis." Biblical anthropology supports this lament as a prima facie condition. Animal creatures, as well as humans, possess the same "breath of life." The Hebrew *nephesh,* often translated "soul," is used indiscriminately of both animals and humans.[1] From a purely phenomenological point of view, there is a fundamental ambiguity as to the nature and destiny of human persons when compared to animals. But given this ambiguity, we nevertheless search for what is distinctively human. We have no other place to look but into the "soul" of our creatureliness. In so doing we must recall Nietzsche's warning that "he who stares into an abyss must be careful that the abyss does not stare back into him." In looking into the face of the creature, we must remember that we are looking for that which enlightens the face of the human, not darkens it. But what is the difference?

IF THE SAME,
WHAT IS THE DIFFERENCE?

We are obliged to assume that there is a difference if we are to continue our exploration into the nature of what is human. Certainly human persons rather consistently act as if there were a fundamental differentiation to be made between human and non-human. We may personify our pets, even to the point of creating pet cemeteries as a form of remembrance, but anthropologists tell us that no human society, however primitive, has failed to make this distinction between human and non-human a cultural practice. Our assumption — to be clarified through analysis — is that it is appropriate and meaningful to designate that distinction as the first step in defining what we mean by "human." For now, it means no more or less than what this fundamental distinction entails at the most practical level. Despite the sameness which exists between humans and non-humans at the creaturely level, we will assert that there is a fundamental difference.

We will take an axiomatic approach in order to carry our analysis a step forward. The basic axiom for the discussion in this chapter is that *creatureliness is an undifferentiated field upon which the occasion of the human occurs.*

It is essential to observe in this axiom that creatureliness is not given the power of differentiation. Creatureliness is itself differentiated from the human, but in such a way that the human is no less creaturely. To say that the human is an event which "occurs" on the continuum of creatureliness is to imply that it may or may not be present as an event of creatureliness. Karl Barth makes this point more dramatically:

> Thus the fact that I am born and die, that I eat and drink and sleep,
> that I develop and maintain myself; that beyond this I assert myself

---

1. For a more detailed discussion of soul, particularly as distinguished from body and spirit, see Appendix A.

in face of others, and even physically, propagate my species; that I enjoy and work and play in fashion and possess; that I acquire and have and exercise powers; that I take part in all the work of the race, either accomplished or in process of accomplishment; that in all this, I satisfy religious needs and can realize religious possibilities; and that in it all I fulfill my aptitudes as an understanding and thinking, willing and feeling being — all this as such is not my humanity. In it I can be either human or inhuman. In it all I must first answer the question, whether I will affirm or deny my humanity. It is only the field on which human being either takes place or does not take place as history, as the encounter of I and Thou; the field on which it is revealed or obscured that "I am as Thou art." That I exist on this field, and do so in a particular way, does not of itself mean that I am human.[2]

What Barth calls the field of humanity, on which I may or may not experience "human being," I have called the field of creatureliness. From a phenomenological perspective, this creatureliness exists as a state of being common to all who have been given a *nephesh*, or creaturely soul, by the Creator. All creatures who have this breath of life exist on a continuum, with an indeterminate number of variations, but with a common creaturely existence. If this is so, it will be impossible to establish the uniqueness of human being as one particular form of creatureliness, even as a creature which has "breath of life" as opposed to non-living entities within creation. On the other hand, we can never say less of human being than that it is creaturely being. In Genesis 1, the sixth day of creation is when animals and humans, both of whom have the "breath of life," are brought into existence. Helmut Thielicke calls this the "solidarity of the sixth day," the inescapable bond which we as humans share with all other creatures.

Theologians in particular ought not to be surprised that many of the physical organs belonging to animals can be transplanted into the bodies of human beings; for it is clear from the Genesis account of creation and other biblical statements that humans share a common creatureliness with non-human creatures. This advance in medical science does not appear to violate any intrinsic sanctity of the human person, and any limitations on such practices will be more functional or aesthetic than theological.

The common field of creatureliness which humans share with non-human creatures may not be limited to the physical alone. It would not be surprising if humans shared, at least to some extent, psychical nature with non-human creatures. Because the breath of life constitutes, in a certain sense, the "soul" of living creatures, we might expect that this dimension of creaturely being, too, is part of the broad field.

---

2. *Church Dogmatics*, III/2, 249.

Here one can only suggest such a connection, leaving room for further empirical exploration. But many people have had experiences strongly suggesting such a phenomenon. I can recall just such a sense of psychical communication as a young boy on a family farm with animals raised for slaughter. During the winter, the young steer was kept in the barn and became accustomed to humans entering the stall to clean it or provide food. The animal showed no fear of the implements used for these chores, nor of us who invaded that space. But on the day chosen to put the animal to death it was a different matter. As one entered the stall with the wooden-handled heavy hammer to stun the animal before cutting its throat, the steer would cower in the corner, fear and panic in its eyes. I always suspected that the animal knew in some strange way what its fate was. Now I wonder if what took place may not have been some sort of psychical transference, in which the fear and apprehension of our own souls as we participated in the event of death was communicated to the dumb beast. The momentary demonstration of fear expressed in this intimate and yet terrible event of death may have showed a glimmering of the solidarity of the sixth day.

The point is that there appears to be a continuum of creaturely life which we humans share with non-human creatures. Therefore, what is unique and distinctive to human being is not an absolute physical or even psychical differentiation between humans and animal creatures. The distinction must be found elsewhere. The Genesis creation account, of course, goes beyond the sixth day to the seventh. As far as we know, non-human creatures do not participate in the fellowship and relation with God designated by the seventh day. Perhaps there is a clue here as to what is distinctively human. The human may be differentiated from all that is of the sixth day, even its own creaturely nature, by the Creator's summons to participate in the seventh day.

But this, too, will have to await further development. What we need to say just now is that creatureliness is both a presupposition and possibility for our humanity. We cannot deny creatureliness without denying the possibility of our own humanity. We must come to terms with our creatureliness, with its mortality, with its limitations, with its mute psychical depths, with its mysterious yearnings as well as the sheer fact of it. And yet with the human creature there is a difference more profound than the difference between the living and non-living things of creation. We still hold to this.

IF THERE IS A DIFFERENCE, WHERE DOES IT LIE?

We now return to our basic axiom: creatureliness is an undifferentiated field on which the occasion of the human occurs. By investigating this axiom, we are seeking a critical principle by which to discern and make more visible the fundamental difference between the human and non-human. To do this, we will draw forth three implications from the axiom, and then make a more practical application to test our conclusions.

First, our axiom implies that there is a contingent, or non-necessary, relation between creatureliness and human being. It is a contingent relation because the human is not said to be a differentiation inferred from creatureliness itself. If something is not the necessary result of a basic idea or entity, it may be said to be contingent; that is, it must be upheld by something other than its own existence. The axiom implies that this is the case with the human. It does not exist as a necessary result of creatureliness itself. Rather, that which upholds the human creature is something other than creatureliness itself.

This leads further to the conclusion that creatureliness does not contain the *telos*, or final purpose of the human. Within creatureliness there is no teleological principle which, given the proper conditions, will result in the human. To put it another way, humanity is transcendent to creatureliness, not an immanent constituent of it. Not all creatures are human, nor can it be said that any creature *must* be human by virtue of being creaturely. However, all humans must be creatures, for creatureliness is the field on which the human occurs.

Perhaps we can illustrate this by referring again to the distinction between the sixth and seventh days of creation. If the seventh day means the "last day," as is the case with the biblical term, it can be said that the seventh day is contingent on a determination from beyond or outside the continuum of the first through the sixth days. If you were told to start counting progressively from the number 1 and stop when you reached the "last number," it would be an impossible task. There is no principle intrinsic to an infinite sequence of numbers by which one can determine the "last" one. The seventh day, in the case of biblical revelation, is the "last" day, and the sequence must be started over again, as with the seven-day week. This determination of the seventh day as the last is not a teleological determination, but an eschatological determination. That is, it is a determination made on the basis that the "end" or "last day" is already known (to God) and therefore can be made known to those who are the objects of his revelation.

To apply this analogy to the situation in regard to creatureliness and humanity, then, we would say that creaturely being, as a continuum on which there are infinite variables, has no intrinsic *telos*, no principle by which to differentiate absolutely that which is human from the continuum of creatureliness itself. That there is in fact such an absolute differentiation is only an assumption we are making. Those who do not wish to make such an assumption have to account for the existence of human creatureliness as a relative distinction within creatureliness. Because this latter position does not seem to accord with how human beings in practice think of themselves, and because it is quite clearly not the position taken by Scripture, we will continue to hold to the original assumption. In so doing, however, we are obliged to articulate the distinction and differentiation in a way that upholds the contingent relation of the human to creatureliness without breaking the bond of solidarity uniting all that is creaturely. It remains to be seen, then, what produces the differentiation between creatureliness and the human, but we must say at this point that creatureliness itself cannot determine the human.

That may be, someone might respond; but don't humans reproduce as creatures and consequently produce other human beings? And doesn't reproduction, which is surely a function of creatureliness, then determine — or at least enable — the survival of the human on the field of creatureliness? Apparently so. But only apparently. For describing the relation between the human and the creaturely as contingent is not the same as saying that it is episodic or idiosyncratic. The empirical fact that all offspring of humans produced through creaturely means appear to be human does not disprove our axiom nor the implication of contingency, for the field of creatureliness includes the mechanism of reproduction. Reproduction does not entail differentiation. It is no more a mystery that the creaturely offspring of a human should be human than that the parent is also human! The mystery is not denuded through regularity and even predictability.

We do not ordinarily think that there is great risk of producing an offspring that is non-human, though not all agree at what point humanization occurs after fertilization or when it ceases to exist at the time of dying. Nor are we ever quite sure of ourselves when it comes to identifying a creaturely monstrosity as to its humanity. Is a two-headed child one human or two? Or is it sub-human, or even non-human? At the margins of humanity, the fact that the relation between the human and the creaturely is contingent becomes more visible, though even less explicable. *Normally* — and we must stress the word — we take it for granted that the process by which one human creature gives life to another creature is also a process by which a human person comes to be. This is certainly why, out of respect for human life, a human fetus is valued as "potentially a person" and therefore already more human than non-human.

In asserting a contingent relation between the creaturely and the human, we are not making a distinction between potentiality and actuality, or between a human fetus and a human person. Rather, we are making a distinction between what cannot become human (because it is merely creaturely) and that which is also both human and creaturely, regardless of whether it is either potentially or actually so. This, at least, is a theological point of differentiation. Otherwise, there would be no place for God's special creative act causing the human to come into being, as the Bible clearly sets forth in the Genesis account of creation and reaffirms elsewhere.

Our axiom implies that there is a contingent relation between the human and the creaturely. This contingency is the indispensable point of differentiation. We can say in the second place that the human, as creature, can be known only through the phenomena of creatureliness. And yet the human will never be fully accessible to a phenomenological method of study. The human person must necessarily exist as creature. There is no way to bypass creatureliness in order to apprehend the human more directly. The only direct apprehension of the human is as creature.

There is a methodological problem here. The problematic in the relation between the creaturely and the human is one in which creatureliness can be known by humanity, but not humanity by creatureliness. This is no philosophical paradox to be resolved by "faith," but an inherent structure in the nature of reality, to be discovered and identified in the same way that a physicist discovers and identifies the structure of reality in terms of laws and principles not known before. As an analogy, recall that a physicist who operates with the theoretical structures of reality known as "field theory," developed by Einstein, can nevertheless continue to explain things in accordance with Newtonian physics. But one who operates on the basis of Newtonian physics alone cannot explain or even accept field-theory physics. Such is the case with the structure of that which is human with respect to creaturely reality. Natural science can deduce principles of nature by observing that which is creaturely, but these principles do not lead by logical extension to apprehend that which is uniquely human.

All creatures but the human give up their secrets to the observing scientist. What barriers remain are largely due to ignorance or lack of technique and technology rather than to any ontological resistance to another being. But there is such resistance in the case of human being. Not the kind of resistance which can be accounted for by psychological dynamics, but resistance to the only methodology appropriate for the study of creaturely nature. Using the methodology of natural science, one can learn much about human beings in terms of their creaturely nature. But this "objectifying" process, which extracts information by submitting the object to be studied to critical analysis and experimentation, will not penetrate to the core of being, which is essentially subjective. In this sense, human nature can be said to resist a purely objective methodology.

To take another analogy from physics, N. Bohr held that the interior movements of an atom are inaccessible to direct observation, because the technical means used to penetrate this "inner life" of the atom inevitably distort that life, so that our perception of it is not a true perception. Thus, he concluded, reality may be inaccessible to direct observation and yet verifiable through accurate representational models which correspond to the physical reality itself. The language and even the thought-forms by which this reality is represented must be worked out axiomatically, for the theoretical structure of that reality is part of the physical structure, not simply a prior concept of the mind.

Therefore, positing inaccessibility as a factor in our knowledge of that which is distinctively human does not lead to sheer agnosticism. For the inaccessible aspect of human being is not a fundamental block, but only a methodological limitation. And this limitation can become the creative key to unlock the disclosure of the human. With this disclosure will come the imperative of finding appropriate criteria to identify and verify it. This, too, is more a scientific than a philosophical task, for the means of knowing the human will be determined by actual knowledge of the human, not as a prior application of fixed principles.

The contingency we have posited as the critical point of differentiation between the creaturely and the human thus has an epistemological implication. What we now call the human must be self-authenticating. That is, one must *be* human before being able to discern and recognize that which is human. Yet this knowledge of the human, which is inaccessible to a methodology that does not respect the criteria pointing to the human, cannot be separated from the knowledge of the human as creaturely humanity. There is thus a necessary integration between knowledge of the human *qua* human and knowledge of the human as specifically creaturely humanity.

There is no basis here for a dichotomy between "faith and reason," or between an "objective" and a "nonobjective" kind of knowledge. Theologians do not have privileged access to the nature of human persons which allows them to ignore what medical science knows. The same must be said about the relation between theologians and psychologists. We shall return to this in subsequent chapters, but it is important at this point to show the intrinsic relation between the creaturely and the human in terms both of what can be known and what can be done to help and heal persons. The contingency factor requires a more complex approach to human being, but it does not render such an approach impossible any more than it dictates that the approach should only be taken from one perspective.

We must look at a third implication of our axiom before focusing more specifically on one particular phenomenon of creatureliness. We have asserted that creatureliness is a necessary but not sufficient ground on which to posit the human; we must now add that creatureliness as a condition of human being is not the ultimate ground of being human. As far as we know, there is no other condition under which the being which we call human being can exist except as creaturely being. Whatever the implications of the eschatological teachings concerning the future state of being following a resurrection from the dead, we are sure that we shall always be creatures, and that whatever transformation of our creaturely nature is entailed, we shall not lose our essential identity (cf. 1 Cor. 15).

The point is that creatureliness as a condition of existence is not the last word concerning the nature or purpose of that existence. There is something fundamentally "unconditioned" about human being, even in its creaturely condition. If creatureliness has no immanent teleology which determines the human, we must attribute the *telos* of humanity to some source other than the creaturely condition under which it exists. If the occasion by which the human occurs on the field of creatureliness is contingent to the creaturely itself, it must be supported by something which is from beyond yet actively present.

From this we conclude that the term "human being" is not just another category within the open-ended taxonomy of creaturely beings. For all other creatures, there is no fundamental differentiation, there are only variations. Where the variations are pronounced and identifiable, one creature is marked off from another. For the human, however, no single attribute or group of creaturely attributes constitutes sufficient grounds to define that which is uniquely human. Human beings are not distinguished from other creatures through a set of variables controlled by a "genetic core," but are differentiated from all other creatures on the basis of an independent — or, as we said earlier, transcendent — determination. This of course can be proved only if one grants the original assumption that human being is qualitatively and absolutely differentiated from non-human beings. What we are attempting to show here is that it emerges axiomatically from the contingent relation between creaturely being and human being.

The practical effect of this assertion is to relativize creaturely nature as a determinant of our humanity. To a great extent our creaturely being will certainly determine how far we realize our human potential. Genetic defects at conception or pathological conditions of gestation and birth may cause a human being to enter life grotesquely disfigured and deformed. Yet, because creaturely being is insufficient as a determinator of human being, it is also powerless to deprive a human being of that which is distinctively human. This is true even though creaturely being can be a torment to human being, and in extreme cases, make it virtually impossible for human life to exist.

But we are not thinking only of those extreme cases. Every human being experiences human existence under some limitation and restriction caused by the creaturely nature in which the human necessarily exists. It is helpful to be reminded that creatureliness has the power neither to give nor diminish human being. For those who tend virtually to identify humanity with creaturely existence, both in valuing themselves and in dealing with others, this can be a liberating insight. But theological anthropology will as quickly warn those who despise their creatureliness and treat it with indifference that what is done to impoverish or imperil the creaturely nature of human beings is an offense and indignity to the person. For there is no person other than the one who meets us as a creaturely being.

IF THERE IS ALWAYS SICKNESS, WHAT IS HEALTH?

To test the contribution our analysis of humanity as creatureliness can make to theological anthropology, let us focus on one phenomenon of human existence. We have asserted that abnormality and distortion at the creaturely level limit, but do not absolutely condition, the existence of the human. It is common knowledge that there is a pathological aspect to human existence. The disorders of humanity are, in a strange sort of way, universal indicators of humanity itself. Even as it can be said that the human does not exist except as creatureliness, so it might be said that human being is, to some degree, disturbed being.

I suspect that human beings can survive a greater loss of creaturely function than non-human creatures. The movie title, *They Shoot Horses, Don't They?*, reflects the commonly accepted practice of disposing of animals which have been so severely injured or deformed that they are no longer useful. On the other hand, some have observed that of all offspring born in the creaturely realm, only the human lacks the natural instincts to survive without parental care in the earliest stages of infancy. Thus, it would appear that human beings are both more vulnerable at the creaturely level and yet have more tolerance for creaturely disorder. Certainly it is also true that from the beginning each human being must cope with some degree of disorder and disease at the creaturely level.

This raises the question we asked in the last chapter: Can order be inferred out of disorder? Can health be inferred out of sickness? If all empirical study of human personhood must begin at the creaturely level and with some degree of disorder, by what criteria can we establish the true order of the human as a goal for life, or as an objective in therapy? If something is to be inferred out of disorder, it may only be that the nature of the disorder is such that it points to an order of human existence which lies beyond creaturely possibilities.

"This disease is beyond my practice," said the physician called in to treat Shakespeare's Lady Macbeth.

> Foul whisperings are abroad: unnatural deeds
> Do breed unnatural troubles; infected minds
> To their deaf pillows will discharge their secrets.
> More needs she the divine than the physician.
> God, God forgive us all! (*Macbeth*, V, i).

At the creaturely level alone, the "unnatural deeds" and "unnatural troubles" cannot be taken seriously. For to do so results in a judgment that one is dealing with the bizarre or demonic, not the human. There are no categories within natural creatureliness to deal with unnatural behavior in a positive sense. Thus, a "natural" psychology tends to reduce the disorder to impersonal phenomena, to treat the unnatural as disease or dysfunction, rather than to take it radically and seriously as an ontological aspect of personhood.

At precisely this point an anthropology informed by divine revelation exhibits courage and resourcefulness. Just where the riddle of humanity seems impenetrable, where human nature itself is covered with disgrace and exists in disorder, there the divine Word reveals the nature of the contradiction to be personal sin, not impersonal and dysfunctional creatureliness. "In the radical depravity of man there is necessarily hidden his true nature," says Karl Barth, "in his total degeneracy his original form."[3] As we saw in Chapter One, this forces us to look to the humanity of Jesus Christ as crucified and resurrected humanity in order to see humanity in its original form. In the personal humanity of Jesus Christ, not only in the atoning death on the cross, we find the source of liberation from the determinism which clings to the formulation "we sin because we are sinful in (human) nature." Here we see again the positive value of the critical differentiation between humanity and creatureliness. Here we can avoid the deterministic error of equating physical or psychical dysfunction with sin, and yet deal with sin radically and thus redemptively without fear of destroying or offending that which is truly human.

But let us focus more specifically on what is "normal" or "healthy" humanity. In discussions between psychologists and theologians this issue is often framed in terms of "wholeness and holiness." Does normal, healthy human personhood result from or depend upon a "wholistic" integration of the self as a functioning person, or can one be "sanctified" by the Spirit of God and achieve a spiritual and therefore personal health short of wholeness as a therapeutic goal?

Certainly, establishing psychological wholeness as a goal of therapy is a valuable gain for the person. One could consider this wholeness as creature comfort vital to the human who must also exist as creature. Would one not say the same about medical health? Undoubtedly a person sanctified by God's

---

3. *Ibid.*, 29.

Spirit inwardly has no less need or right to be physically whole if at all possible. But emotional health is more difficult to define than physical health as an objective in therapy. A broken leg or a blinded eye is less likely to be interpreted as a sign of spiritual immaturity than, say, the bitter complaint of a Jeremiah or the vindictive spirit of a David. Not a few of the Bible's "spiritually great" figures manifested traits of temperament which most psychiatrists would label unhealthy.

And are we really sure that love, as the most valued evidence of spiritual maturity in the New Testament, excludes temperamental traits which inhibit good human relationships and which may clearly be seen as neurotic? Probably not. One could well paraphrase the argument of James 2:18: "Show me your Christian love apart from your psychological self, and I will show you my love by my psychological wholeness."

The distinction and suggested tension between wholeness and holiness may not be a very helpful way of putting the question, but the issue is a critical one. To what extent does the quality of human personhood as that which God wills as normal and healthy depend on the health of the person at the creaturely level? Here again we have a kind of irreversible relation. The health of the human person as willed and determined by God includes the health and well-being of creaturely humanity as well. It would be intolerable to think that God is less concerned for the creaturely aspect of our existence than for the human, for under his determination they are experienced as a unity of being. However, because of the contingent relation between the human and the creaturely, one cannot produce a human person by perfecting the creature, nor can one destroy the human (in the sense of invalidating what God has given) by afflicting the creature.

To the extent that wholeness and holiness reflect these two concerns, the view of human personhood we are advancing reverses the causality which tends to exist between these two. While wholeness is not a presupposition of holiness — as though good creaturely health could insure good personal or spiritual health — holiness anticipates and seeks wholeness. To the extent that psychological health, measured in terms of the integration of psychical strivings for the sake of realizing the goals and objectives of personal life, can be viewed as a creature comfort, it is a "relative" necessity. One cannot say that it is unnecessary to have two good legs in order to be human, if one means thereby that there is no obligation to heal or correct a deformity in one leg. Likewise, one would not want to say that it is unnecessary to receive help to overcome neurotic hindrances in order to enhance one's motives of love.

If one is informed by a theological anthropology in seeking to help others, one is freed from the tyranny of perfectionism and the obsessions about physical and psychological concerns which it produces. Perfectionism is essentially bondage to a deterministic principle, whether the principle is grounded in natural or supernatural causes. Perfectionism holds out the carrot of "security because of good health" or "favor with God" at the end of a stick labeled "correct behavior" or "conformity to the right rules." Theologically speaking, it is more important to be a liberated person than a "healthy" or "good" person, if liberation is understood as human creatureliness set free to realize its destiny in God, while goodness or health is merely the perfection of the creaturely for its own sake. In salvation history, holiness produces liberation as actuality and then sets forth wholeness as possibility. Thereby, theology can preserve both religion and psychology from methodological perfectionism. This is its critical task.

> Thus man, healed and made whole in the salvation of God, and thus in this simple basic sense holy, rests in a mysterious suspension he does not himself understand and which on that very account is strangely exhilarating. He is clearly aware of earthly imperfectibility, which does not become for him the oppressive prison. The thought of having to perfect himself at any cost does not become an obsession. Knowing of the house built up in grace for him with God, he can cheerfully inhabit his tumbledown hut and free himself through time.[4]

In this chapter we have sought to show how the abstract concepts of contingency and differentiation apply to the practical side of human existence. We posited the axiom that creatureliness is an undifferentiated field upon which the occasion of the human occurs. From this we developed the critical principle of contingency as the point where differentiation between the human and non-human can be located. This led to the assertion that humanity *per se*, while necessarily experienced through creaturely existence, is neither accessible to nor finally determined by creatureliness, either methodologically or existentially. The true order of humanity has its locus in a transcendent source, which gives ontological stability to personhood at the creaturely level, despite its contingent status. If these implications are applied to the problem of human disorder and sickness, there are positive gains in overcoming the effects of determinism and perfectionism.

What remains to be established is the nature of the transcendent source claimed as the ontological determinant of human personhood. In particular, we must analyze how the continuity and therefore predictability of the human at the creaturely level can be understood in view of the assertion that humanity is always contingent to creatureliness.

---

4. Hans Urs von Balthasar, *A Theological Anthropology*, p. 101.

CHAPTER THREE

HUMANITY AS DETERMINED BY THE WORD OF GOD

HUMAN BEINGS ARE CREATURELY BEINGS. OF THAT THERE CAN BE LITTLE doubt. What is debatable is the assertion that *being* human is the result of more than that which creaturely existence can produce and sustain. Nevertheless, this is fundamental to our discussion of humanity. If there is any differentiation at all between the human and non-human on the broad field of creatureliness, we have argued, that difference must be absolute. Therefore, the ontological status of humanity transcends creatureliness. This does not mean that human beings have arrived from some other planet or are supernatural beings, but that the source of the particular life we designate as human life is a power which is neither a potential nor a possibility of creaturely being itself. Yet, human being is at the same time creaturely being in every sense of the word.

Earlier we quoted Barth's provocative statement concerning the field on which humanity may or may not occur. After speaking eloquently of all the rich possibilities of the creaturely, including the artistic and the religious, he concluded, "all this, as such, is not my humanity."[1] This is a very radical statement. What Barth ascribes to the creaturely realm of being many people would identify as that which is distinctive to humans alone — artistic ability and religious practice. What Barth wishes to make very clear is that there may well be potential for both within the realm of the creature, but the development of these creaturely possibilities can never become the basis on which the human is posited. If it were, there would be no need for a doctrine of creation nor a place for a Creator as the one who originates and sustains life.

Of course, one might propose a doctrine of creation which includes the possibilities for the human, but this would make differentiation between the human and the creaturely impossible. In that case, there would be only a naturalistic determinism, to which even the highest possibilities of creaturely life would be subjected. Nature then becomes destiny, and there is no seventh day. The author of Ecclesiastes has already pronounced the verdict on such an

---

1. *Church Dogmatics*, III/2, 249.

existence: "Vanity!" We will continue to argue for a differentiation between the creaturely and the human, and for the existence of that transcendent source of human life.

DIFFERENTIATION
THROUGH THE WORD OF GOD

The Psalmist sang: "By the Word of the Lord the heavens were made, and all their host by the breath of his mouth" (Ps. 33:6). The Genesis creation account is built on the semantic structure: "And God said. . . ." Within the creation of the man and woman, there is also the speech of God directed to the creature: "And God said to them . . ." (Gen. 1:28). God's address to his human creatures marks the distinction between a state of being and a history of being. The fact that human being is also creaturely being does not give it a history of being. The concept of history in its anthropological sense, as distinct from a state of being,

> is introduced and achieved when something happens to a being in a certain state, i.e., when something new and other than its own nature befalls it. History, therefore, does not occur when the being is involved in changes or different modes of behavior intrinsic to itself, but when something takes place upon and to the being as it is. The history of a being begins, continues and is completed when something other than itself and transcending its own nature encounters it, approaches it and determines its being in the nature proper to it, so that it is compelled and enabled to transcend itself in response and in relation to this new factor.[2]

Alteration of behavior can be produced at the creaturely level, but this does not result in what Barth calls "history of being." In this sense, there is no "history" which results from God's creation of the non-human creatures. While God said "let there be," as the creative act of his Word, in his address to the animal creatures his Word did not encounter them and enable them to transcend their own nature so as to respond to him. Nor do animals have a history among themselves, because they do not have this particular endowment of "word," though they may have a creaturely mechanism for communication. God has differentiated between the creatures and himself through his Word. However, the creatures themselves have no power of differentiation because the Word has not come to them in such a way that their creaturely nature becomes a vehicle for expressing that Word. "Human speech can never 'develop' from animal noises," says Hans Urs von Balthasar. He goes on to suggest that

---

2. *Ibid.,* 158.

the human person is not awakened to speech except by being addressed by the absolute Word.[3]

For the man and the woman, however, the creatures who are the object of God's Word of address, there is a differentiation between the human and the creaturely, manifested as a history in which God himself participates. Not only is the Word the divine activity by which he expresses himself in creation (Heb. 11:3; 1 Pet. 3:5, 7), but that which the Word creates exists in its own right according to the purpose and nature God has for it. In the activity of the divine Word, God differentiates between himself and that which the Word brings forth, so that he exists as the transcendent source of creation. In this way, creation itself is contingent on the Word by which it exists and is sustained. Creation cannot sustain itself indefinitely. It has no power to differentiate itself in such a way that transcendence will emerge as a new order of being.

Theologically, the doctrine of creation *ex nihilo* protects creation from both determinism and perfectionism. The possibilities of creation are not a necessary extension of its own nature, but it can become a "new creation" through the power of the Word of God. This "perfecting" of creation is thus a promise to creation, rather than a judgment on that which is yet imperfect. The creation is "good" even before it is a new creation. Thus, the creaturely aspect of human being does not demand the realization of some "potential" good or perfection before it can be affirmed as good for the human in its present state. The doctrine of creation *ex nihilo* also preserves the differentiation between Creator and creature, which makes a genuine relation between God and his creature possible, something that pantheism is never able to assert.

Therefore, to assert that the human creature is determined by the Word of God preserves both the true creatureliness of human nature and the differentiation of the human from all else that is creaturely. For to assert that the human is determined by the Word of God is to assert that creatureliness is the appropriate condition determined for human existence.

DIFFERENTIATION
AS RESPONSE-ABILITY

To assist in analyzing what it means that the human is determined by the Word of God, let me state the argument in the form of a thesis to be explicated: *that which we call human being is differentiated creatureliness, experienced as response to the creative divine Word.*

---

3. *A Theological Anthropology*, p. 85.

We have chosen the technical term differentiation to express the absolute distinction which can be made between the human and the non-human. Though it has the capacity for reproduction, the creaturely itself has no power to make this kind of differentiation. Thus, sexuality at the creaturely level alone does not differentiate, either as an experience or in the progeny which results. At the creaturely level, human sexuality and non-human sexuality serve as a reproductive mechanism: the distinctiveness of human nature does not depend on the means of reproduction, for reproduction itself, as a creaturely function, has no power of differentiation.

So far we have used the term "differentiation" in reference to the theoretical or formal point of distinguishing the human from the non-human. But as the critical point at which we make this distinction, differentiation has more than this formal characteristic. There is what we might call a material, or historical, dimension to that which differentiates. The differentiation which constitutes the boundary between human and non-human also constitutes the content of life which the human experiences at the creaturely level. As the source and the power which determines the human, the creative Word of God not only establishes the formal distinction between the human and non-human creature, but also gives content to that differentiation, expressed biblically as the "image and likeness of God" (Gen. 1:26-27). Even as God exists as differentiated from his creation, he also exists as a differentiated being. According to the Christian doctrine of the Trinity, God exists as three in one. As Father, God is differentiated from the Son, and both Father and Son are differentiated from God as Spirit. This is revealed through the incarnation, which shows God to be "on both sides" of the relation between himself and his people. Our purpose here is not to elaborate on the doctrine of the Trinity, but merely to point out that differentiation as we now are considering it denotes how God as being experiences himself, and thus by analogy how human beings experience themselves.

What is meant by differentiation in this sense can be seen more clearly in the second creation account (Gen. 2). As the solitary male Adam is presented as creaturely, yet differentiated in his creatureliness from all other creatures. We spoke of this as the formal differentiation marking the boundary between the human and the non-human. God says that it is not good for the man to be in this state of singularity (Gen. 2:18), and he creates other creatures to see what Adam will call them. When Adam "names" the animals one by one, the formal differentiation is confirmed. The man continues to experience himself as different from the animals. Yet God observes that there is still a lack in the solitary male. This lack we have called the material aspect of differentiation. In order to be completely human, one must experience differentiation as the content of one's own life. In naming the animals, there was apparently no "response"; there was no correspondence between the being of Adam and the being of the other creatures, even though both share a common creaturely nature.

From this we conclude that there are no possibilities within creatureliness itself by which differentiation can be developed and experienced as a specifically human life. God then puts Adam to sleep and "differentiates" his state of singleness by creating two where there was only one. This is instructive, for it demonstrates that the material content of differentiation, while experienced as a creaturely reality — "this at last is bone of my bones and flesh of my flesh" (Gen. 2:23) — has no source in the formal differentiation itself. The differentiation which constitutes human being as "co-humanity" is the primary differentiation, from which the formal differentiation of human/non-human is derived. It would appear that the purpose of Genesis 2 is to teach that very truth. The original statement regarding the creation of the human in the likeness of God expresses first of all the material differentiation: "Male and female he created them" (Gen. 1:27). Only thereafter is the formal differentiation between the human and non-human made clear.

The differentiation which constitutes the true order of humanity can thus be said to be "response-ability." The creature to whom God speaks is thereby enabled to respond to him. This response is experienced not only as that of a single being but as co-humanity, the one responding with the other. The extent to which this co-humanity is also determinative for true humanity will be explored in the following chapter. It is enough here to call attention to it as the effect the Word of God produces in determining that humanity exists as divine likeness.

THE RESPONSE OF THE SOUL

Human being, our thesis states, is differentiated creatureliness, experienced as response to the creative divine Word. We have shown that differentiation is produced as co-humanity, which is how humanity is concretely experienced. Now we must analyze what it means to say that differentiation is essentially response to the divine Word. Remembering that humanity cannot be established on non-creaturely terms — though it necessarily exists as creaturely if it exists at all — we should be able to detect certain marks of differentiation at the creaturely level, even though we cannot explicate these marks in creaturely terms alone.

Theologically, we can say that true humanity is determined as existence in covenant relation with God. "Real man," says Barth, "is the being determined by God for life with God and existing in the history of the covenant which

God has established with him."[4] The covenant, as a presupposition for human existence, accounts for the ability of the human creature to be aware of God and to be approached by God. This perception of God as the one who exists for the human creature constitutes an *awareness* of both God and the other which is itself prior to and constitutive of what we call relation. Differentiation is therefore experienced as a creaturely awareness of the Creator as a covenant-partner, and consequently of the self as a being who exists only in this relation. The creaturely "soul," which is ambiguously neutral at the creaturely level (witness the indiscriminate use of *nephesh* for both human and non-human), becomes differentiated in the human and thus capable of experiencing itself as "spirit." Spirit is not a third component of the self along with the soul and body; rather, it is the experience of the self as ensouled body and embodied soul in relation to God. The creaturely soul of human beings is constituted a spiritual soul as against a nonspiritual soul. Common to human and non-human at the creaturely level, the soul becomes differentiated in the human by spirit. The sign or mark of this differentiation is "awareness" of God as the one who is the source and goal of one's own life.[5]

I am using "soul" in a nontechnical sense here to denote that awareness or openness to God which is distinctive to the human and impossible for the non-human, the basic spiritual dimension of a human person's animated existence (*nephesh*). Because the soul in this sense is itself a mark of differentiation as response of the creature to God, it is more essentially human than "mind," another word understood popularly to signify intellectual capacity or thought. No antipathy between soul and mind is intended here; the point is simply that "mind" is more or less accessible to a methodology based on creaturely functions while "soul" is not. Observation and experimentation give some evidence that non-human creatures may have some mental life or even some intellectual capacity. However, it is assumed that the "spiritual soul" which we attribute to human beings is absolutely unique to humans and is not subject to the same methodological analysis. If it is present, it is self-authenticating as an openness or awareness of God. There is no way of accounting for its presence other than that God has "approached" the human creature and endowed it with this response-ability. The soul which is aware of God will also have God as an object of thought and reflection. But the human self must have awareness, and not mere thought, in order to be essentially human. For this awareness is itself a mark of differentiation, and thus presupposes and creates the possibility of relation and reflection on that relation. Whereas thought tends to abstract from relation and to focus on the

---

4. *Church Dogmatics*, III/2, 204.
5. For a more technical discussion of soul, body, and spirit, see Appendix A.

formal and critical principle of differentiation (distinction between human and non-human), the soul, in its awareness of God and the other person, makes differentiation as a concrete and creaturely reality manifest.

In child development, for example, an infant's earliest responses are not primarily mental but affective. The child develops a sense of the self through the differentiation that takes place in relationships between itself and the parents. The fact that love expressed toward a human infant brings a response different from that elicited by love expressed toward a non-human creature manifests the "spiritual soul" of the child. (Obviously, many other factors enter into this process as well.)

The phenomenon of self-consciousness is problematical for a methodology based on strict empiricism, that is, of a creaturely sort. For self-consciousness has its origin in the soul; in "sensing" the other one also learns to "sense" oneself. A theological perspective on self-consciousness, then, as a phenomenon of the human, views it as a mark of differentiation, and a tangible sign of the divine determination which establishes the self as a covenant-partner of God. It is in this sense that approachableness is an indication of authentic humanity and is a mark of the soul.

The existence of a human person in an historical sense — that is, as part of a social context — depends on this "spiritual" capacity. Insanity can thus be understood theologically as an eclipse of the soul, a slip into sheer unhistorical creatureliness. It is understandable that this can often happen to persons who have particularly brilliant minds, for the soul, as the differentiation produced by awareness of God, is the essence of rationality; and it only exists as a differentiated response to or awareness of the divine Word. Thus, the perverse hardening of the heart and deliberate closing of one's soul to God (and consequently to the brother or sister) is considered in the Bible to be at best foolishness and at worst madness, or even demonic.

Self-consciousness as an empirical phenomenon may be the object of study in the psychology of religion; but there will be methodological limitations on such a study, for unless one assumes that this self-conscious life is itself response to a divine summons to be human, it will be interpreted as a variety of creaturely experience. Theological anthropology, on the other hand, expects self-consciousness to know more than it can tell. For self-consciousness is more than an attribute of the personality; it is a mark of differentiation which places us in direct contact with the very soul of the person. In coming into contact with the soul of a person, therefore, we are apprehending that which differentiates the soul — the reality of the divine creative Word of God.[6]

---

6. Cf. Barth, *Church Dogmatics*, III/2, 402-406.

THE RESPONSE OF THE PERSON

Not only does the Word of God determine that as a creaturely phenomenon humanity occurs as a covenant-partner, bearing the mark of awareness, but also as a freedom-bearing and responsibly acting person. Thus, a second mark of differentiation may be identified as freedom, spontaneity of action in response to the approach of the other. We have spoken of history as that which results when one's being is encountered and acted on by the being of another. While creaturely nature determines our behavior (which might be called a response of a sort), our humanity frees us to respond. In this sense the dialectic between freedom and determinism is broken by the power of God, which determines that we should have freedom. This "spiritual determinism" enables the human creature to do what no other creature can do — freely respond to another being out of one's own self. This freedom to respond as a person to another person results in the "meeting" of one being with another. In this meeting there is recognition based upon mutual awareness and communication of the self manifested in actions which evince a will to commitment.

In Genesis 2 Adam experiences the material reality of differentiation at the point when the woman is brought to him. His awareness of her and his self-conscious response is the first mark of differentiation. No encounter with other creatures had brought about this response. Although the response of the woman is not recorded, one may at least hope she felt the same way![7] In any event, response is not only awareness, but also the enacting of that awareness and recognition in a freedom of the self which is expressed as pledge, word, or even vow. In his own freedom of being, God enters into covenant with the human creature, pledging his Word and enacting his own awareness of his creature with irrevocable signs and vows. The fact that human beings "create" this response in each other by acts which reveal openness and awareness of being is itself a mark of this freedom which has its source in the differentiation produced by the Word of God.

"To be a man is to respond to what is said to man," writes Barth, adding that

> if his rationality and responsibility are related to the fact that they
> constitute the freedom of a human subject, his capacity to have ex-
> periences of his own to hear the word addressed to him and to fulfill
> his own responsibility in answer to it, then by this freedom we may
> understand what is usually rather obscurely called the personality of
> man.[8]

---

7. Barth suggests that the statement of the woman in Song of Solomon 8:6, "Set me as a seal upon your heart, as a seal upon your arm," may be intended to break this silence and provide Eve's response to Adam. *Ibid.*, p. 294.

8. Ibid., p. 126.

Personality, like self-consciousness, tends to emerge as a phenomenological attribute of humanity as observed by a behavioral scientist. While self-consciousness may be ambiguous when described as a creaturely phenomenon, we have asserted that it is actually a window of the soul, and as such is a mark of differentiation and thus of true humanity. In the same way, personality as a creaturely expression of being can be viewed as uniquely human, and thus a mark of differentiation. Not that empirical study of either self-consciousness or personality can establish the reality of the "soul" or even of the divine Word which differentiates the soul: remember that the human is not accessible through a methodology developed on the basis of creatureliness alone. However, to say that certain creatures are "human" and that others are "non-human" obviously calls for both theoretical and practical criteria. Differentiation provides both the theoretical and the practical criteria by which one can say that human is a determined state of being, not merely an altered state of being. Determination is then shown to consist of differentiation, by which creatureliness itself as a state of being experiences both self-consciousness and personality — or, to put it more theologically, awareness of God's approach and freedom to approach God.

We shall not discuss personality theories in this context. As a cluster of behavioral tendencies and practices, personality is a serviceable concept around which to organize these phenomena. Personality, however, does not appear to be a very reliable indicator of personhood. Non-human creatures may exhibit almost identical personality patterns. As a mark of differentiation, however, the human personality is an indicator of a freedom of person which goes much deeper than mere behavior as a predictable pattern.

A more philosophical approach would probably prefer to speak of self-transcendence as the mark of that which is uniquely human. Both self-consciousness and personality as phenomena would be interpreted as signals of self-transcendence, by which the human self is manifested. Theologically, we prefer to speak of transcendence as the approach of the Word of God which creates and determines response. The response may also be in fact a form of self-transcendence. This is not, however, the originating act of personhood, but a sign of personhood as a result of determination by another. In the broad sense in which we originally defined it, the concept of "soul" continues to serve very well as the fundamental differentiation of the human which has various expressions.

The concept of soul also serves to identify in a non-technical sense the point at which continuity is established for the occurrence of the human, and by which one can meaningfully speak of a "human race." The fact that the soul is itself a differentiated reality of human being makes it contingent to creatureliness as such; for creatureliness, as we saw, has no power of differentiation. Although creatureliness provides the state in which the human race exists, however, it cannot provide the basis for the continuity and preservation of the soul. If the soul as the essence of humanity exists at all, it actually exists, rather than being a potentially of creatureliness. Though many potentialities (mental, emotional, and physical) for creaturely behavior on the part of humans may be discovered in creaturely nature itself, these are not potentials of humanity, but only the state in which humanity exists as divinely determined.

What then insures that the offspring of human beings have "souls" in this sense? If reproduction itself does not differentiate, what prevents a lapse back into sheer creatureliness? Why is there such a strong degree of predictability which appears to guarantee the preservation of the human race?

Medieval theologians alternated between two views on this question. "Traducianists" held that the soul originates in the act of conception. A "soul-seed" (in contrast to a "body-seed") detached from the soul of the parents becomes the independent soul of the child. This view was advocated by Luther and has generally been taught in Lutheran theology. "Creationists," on the other hand, held that the soul was implanted at the moment of conception by a divine act, an immediate creation *ex nihilo*. Through the sexual act the parents create the proper physiological conditions for the existence of a human being, but they are only secondary agents in the process. This has been traditionally the view of the Roman Catholic Church and of the Reformed churches.[9]

Earlier we asserted that there is no greater mystery to the fact that the offspring of humans turn out to be human than to the fact that the parents are human. The unsolved problem of how to account for the so-called "transmission" of the soul from parent to child is not the fundamental problem. On empirical grounds we cannot account for a creature's possessing what we call a spiritual soul at all. Biblical revelation claims that the uniqueness of the human soul is that it bears the "image and likeness of God." If we accept this as a theological answer to the question of what a human being is, we are still left with the mystery of *how* this can be. The most we can say is that a human person begins as any other creature, as a biological event which entails fertilization and cell-division. However, in that process the resulting life-form carries the form of the human, even in its prenatal stage. We are bound theologically to affirm both statements as true. In its creaturely origin, a human being is nothing more than a biological phenomenon, but in its actual life-form it is from the very beginning nothing less than human. The existence of the human

---

9. Concerning this rather bizarre debate, Barth says, "none of the various attempted solutions, each of which outdoes the other in abstruseness, leads us even the slightest step forward." *Ibid.*, p. 573.

being as a life-form cannot be reduced to biological necessity. No theological anthropology based on Scripture as divine revelation can accept the idea that humanity emerges out of the continuum of creaturely being through natural determinism.

This leaves us with no alternative but to posit the sovereignty of God as the "binding element" linking human being to creaturely being as a single reality. We are not permitted to think of humans in a dualistic sense, as though there exists a biological person alongside of a human person. Nor may we follow the Greeks and posit the human self as an immortal soul temporarily encased in a mortal body. The Hebrews were not permitted to make this distinction between the soul and the body. The human person is a unity of personal life, with both soul and body fully participating in that personal unity of being. In the New Testament, the resurrection of the body affirms the same anthropological truth. A disembodied soul is a concept which strikes the apostle Paul with apprehension and anxiety (2 Cor. 5:1-5). Prior to his ascension Jesus Christ is never experienced apart from his body, even after his death.

The sovereignty of God as a final answer to the problem is not a cop-out; rather, it is an expression of the fundamental contingency of human existence itself. To be upheld in one's personal existence by the reality of God's power through the presence of his Spirit is no abstract theory, but a constant and ever-present reality. This is why the Psalmist can sing: "Let everything that breathes praise the Lord" (Ps. 150:6).

Our discussion in this chapter has centered on the basic thesis that what we call human being is differentiated creatureliness, experienced as response to the creative divine Word. Differentiation, we have argued, constitues both the theoretical and practical basis for understanding what we mean when we attribute humanity to some creatures but not to others. Our point of contact with this differentiation at the concrete level of human existence is self-consciousness and personality (in a non-technical sense). Theologically, we spoke of these phenomena as marks of differentiation in terms of awareness and freedom. As creaturely phenomena they provide direct contact with the differentiated reality of human being itself, which we termed the soul. This accounts for both the contingency and the continuity of human being, with respect to a state of creatureliness.

The material content of differentiation, however, has been identified as co-humanity, existence with the other in the divine image and likeness. Before we can judge whether or not the concept of differentiation is helpful for exploring what it is to be human, we must look further at the concept of co-humanity.

CHAPTER FOUR

HUMANITY AS DETERMINED
BY THE OTHER

T O SOME THE CONCEPT OF DIFFERENTIATION AS THE BASIC FORM OF THE
 human may seem unnecessarily abstract or far-fetched. Yet we have per-
sisted in using this as an analytical device to expose the subtle but profound
line at the creaturely level between the human and the non-human. It is
assumed that the distinction between human and non-human is one that
ought to be made; the task before us is to explicate that distinction from the
perspective of a theological anthropology.

In the first place, we asserted that the human is differentiated from the
creaturely in such a way that we may attribute a qualitatively different sort of
being to the human creature, though not in such a way that the human is any
less creaturely. This was accounted for by locating the source of differentiation
in the determination of the creative divine Word, and not in the determinism
of creaturely nature itself.

As a further step, it was posited that the differentiation fundamentally is
a determination *of* the very structure of human being itself as creaturely being,
not just a formal principle which distinguishes human being from non-human
being. This differentiation as a structure of the human we called co-humanity,
and we termed it the material content of the principle of differentiation. That
is, differentiation actually occurs as a state of human existence in which humanity is experienced as co-existence. This co-existence can be viewed as the
radical structure of humanity itself. In other words, existence as a human
being is fundamentally existence with regard to the other.

It is well to point out here that biblical theology proceeds from the premise
that actual being precedes and becomes the basis for the determination of
being as a theoretical principle. We stressed earlier that the material content
of differentiation expressed as co-humanity is the original differentiation of
the human. Only subsequent to this is the formal principle of differentiation
between the human and non-human given. This is the sequence of the creation
narrative in Genesis 1. Following the statement that God created them in his
own image and likeness comes the specific command which differentiates the
human from the non-human creatures, the so-called cultural mandate: "Have

dominion over. . . ." In verse 27, following the restatement of the image and likeness as "male and female," the mandate of dominion over the rest of creation is repeated. Furthermore, the Word of God itself as an event of revelation is always given as a concrete and historical event from which the principles on which theology is constructed emerge. We emphasize this here to reinforce the point that a theological anthropology, while proceeding analytically and abstractly, must always remember that humanity as actuality precedes and determines humanity as possibility. The basic assumption, then, on which this discussion proceeds is that the actual form of humanity in its original form is co-humanity, from which all of our knowledge of the human is derived.

WHAT IS AN INDIVIDUAL PERSON?

Barth outlines the structure of co-humanity in the form of a threefold statement: humanity is a determination of the Word of God, a determination of being with others, and the determination of one person with the other.[1] The determination of humanity in general as being with others does not dissolve individual being into corporate being, but results in a determination of humanity in its *singularity* as well as its plurality. This singularity, however, is experienced as a reciprocity of being, that is, a being of one *with* the other and also, to an extent, *for* the other.

Here we are concerned with what it means to say that my own particular human existence is determined by the other, as the material content of differentiation. Does this imply that the other so conditions and determines my own "individuality" that I can really never "know myself?" Does the form of co-humanity safeguard against an unwarranted individualism by depriving my own being in its particular singularity of any meaning for me?

These are legitimate concerns. Hence we shall focus in this chapter on the following thesis: the singularity of my humanity is determined by the other. By using the concept of singularity, we intend to preserve the notion of discrete individuality in this structure of determination. The basic form of the human must at least include the "I," even though a certain radical priority is given to the "we."

Barth states the situation this way:

> The declaration "I" in what I say is the declaration of my expectation that the other being to which I declare myself in this way will respond and treat and describe and distinguish me as something like himself. When he accepts my "I" — and in turning to him I count on it that he is able to do so — he cannot possibly regard me as an it or a mere He

---

1. *Church Dogmatics*, III/2, 243.

or She, but I am distinguished from all other objects for him as he is for me, and distinguished from and connected to me as I am from and to him. . . . Thus the word "Thou," although it is a very different word, is immanent to "I." It is not a word which is radically alien, but one which belongs to it. The word "I" with which I think and declare my humanity implies as such humanity with and not without the fellowman.[2]

It is also true, one might add, that the "I" is immanent in the "Thou" which is addressed to the other. This is the basis of the singularity of human being. It is established and determined by the other in the "Thou" by which I recognize and address the other. There is no way in which the "I" can be self-determined, for determination is fundamentally an act of differentiation. And in the case of humanity as co-humanity, this differentiation requires reciprocity of being.

Barth's language here echoes what Martin Buber says about the two levels of being in his classic work, *I and Thou*. At the one level we relate to the "it" world, which is impersonal and cannot lead to the personal. But in the "I-Thou" world, persons encounter their own being in the other. Only in speaking the "I-Thou" word, says Buber, does one's own being come into full existence.

The You encounters me by grace — it cannot be found by seeking. But that I speak the basic word to it is a deed of my whole being, is my essential deed. . . . The basic word I-You can be spoken only with one's whole being. The concentration and fusion into a whole being can never be accomplished by me, can never be accomplished without me. I require a You to become; becoming I, I say you.[3]

An individual person must first of all be differentiated as person in contrast to the world of impersonal being. This can only take place in a reciprocal act by which the other recognizes and affirms the singularity of one's own particular existence. One can only be an individual "to or for another" in this sense. But this requires further elaboration.

WE ARE TWO BEFORE WE CAN BE ONE

We commonly think of an individual person as a psychological expression of selfhood, manifesting particular characteristics of feelings, reactions, moods, and behavior. What we call singularity of being may be said to be social before it is psychological. Or, to put it another way, individuality as a form of human being is a result of differentiation through relation with another. The differentiation which constitutes the determination of humanity as a singular ex-

---

2. *Ibid.*, 245.
3. *I and Thou*, tr. by Walter Kaufman (Edinburgh: T. & T. Clark, 1979), p. 62.

perience is a *history* of the self in encounter — this is the radical social nature of humanity. "To say man," writes Barth, "is to say history, and this is to speak of the encounter between I and Thou."[4] We introduced this concept of history in the preceding chapter. Here we want to give it a more personal connotation by thinking of it as that which results from the basic social structure of humanity itself.

The original differentiation which produces humanity as one form of creaturely existence as against all other forms creates a boundary between existence as social encounter and existence as impersonal event in which there is no continuity of personal being. Creatureliness itself does not constitute historical existence — though natural existence is a condition of historical existence. In a certain qualified sense, one might say that human existence as historical existence is "supra-natural" existence, for it is existence which takes place as a state of creaturely nature but is determined by a source transcendent to nature.

However, as Hans Urs von Balthasar warns, "The encounter of human beings in love and knowledge is above nature, but not supernatural."[5] Human existence is not contrary to nature or totally above nature — as the term "supernatural" might seem to denote — but it is an existence of a creaturely sort which takes place on a different plane from that of "nature" itself as sheer creatureliness. This is why we said earlier that there is a methodological limitation in seeking to define or to explain the human on the basis of "natural science" alone. There is something inaccessible to such an approach, even though human existence takes place in the same world as nature itself exists.

Such a "supra-natural" dimension of human personhood probably lies behind the medieval philosophical distinction between nature and grace. While maintaining the fundamental distinction between "natural creatureliness" and "human creatureliness," we do not accept the idea that the human person is a form of natural existence perfected through the operation of divine grace. Rather, we would hold that the original nature of the human was constituted and determined by grace as co-humanity, and that this was an originally social structure of being from which and by which each person discovered and knew her or his own singular being.

Singularity as fundamental to human existence is thus a consequence of historical and social existence, not the cause of it. Creatureliness provides instances of discrete individuation, but not of singularity. This is how one can understand the remarkable story in Genesis 2, where Adam as the solitary male is put within creation as an incomplete being. He is an individuated

---

4. *Church Dogmatics*, III/2, 248.
5. *A Theological Anthropology*, p. 85.

being, but does not experience singularity of being. The animals result from a process of individuation in which they are presented to Adam to see "what he would call them." But the final verdict was that there was not found for him a "helpmeet" (or counterpart, to use a more modern phrase). Whatever Adam thought he was seeking in naming the animals, he did not find it. Concerning this, Hans Urs von Balthasar says:

> It is strange that human nature, obviously quite different from the animals which were already created two by two, has to long for the other. The other is not simply there, but is brought to him by God, as a grace, which harms him as well as fulfills him. For Eve was taken from his side — he has her within him, and yet she is more than he is and cannot be arrived at from him — in sleep, in defenseless *ek-stasis*, which, according to the old theologians, foreshadowed the cross. Why should not Adam's dialogue relationship to God, in which he received through grace a share in the nature of God, have just as much and even more — beyond his natural capacities — awakened him to and given him the power to attain that for which he had always been intended by God?[6]

The answer seems to be found in the basic form of the human as co-humanity. Adam is not a "completed human" by virtue of being an example or instance of individuated humanity, even in relation to God. Rather, being related to God and being determined by God, Adam cannot be complete without encountering himself in the other as one who is "bone of his bone and flesh of his flesh." There is a differentiation of creatureliness itself which is constitutive of the human, not merely differentiation between the human and the non-human, or even differentiation between the human and God.

Thus the woman emerges as the counterpart to the man out of the act of differentiation, not merely as another instance of individuation. God might have individuated another instance of humanity and brought it to Adam to "see what he would call it"; it is significant that he did not. And while one can only make a suggestion here, where there is no instruction from Scripture, it may be that God's intention was precisely to show conclusively that the form of the human is not individuated nature but rather differentiated nature constituted as reciprocity of social response and existence.

It ought not to surprise or threaten us that the distinction between the human and non-human at the purely creaturely level is blurred on what appears to be a continuum of evolutionary development. What is fundamental to the biblical account of the form of the human is that within creaturely nature itself there is no possibility which can give rise to the human, either

---

6. *Ibid.*, p. 85.

by evolution or by technologically assisted mutation. Individuation can never lead to individuality. Only when the human is experienced as reciprocity of being as an immediate and spontaneous recognition is the freedom of being made manifest. This is what we mean by social being or historical being. In that reciprocity, the one releases the other from sheer determinism at the creaturely level. Blind and mute dependence on a state of existence is overcome through a relation of interdependence. This paradigm of human existence as a social unity gives us a clue as to the source of the true history of the self.

Again, Hans Urs von Balthasar provides a helpful insight: "Through the interdependence of the generations, the social element embraces the individual and influences him."[7] But he also makes it clear that the social element is not simply a description of behavior, such as a sociologist might conclude, but is the original and creative act of love, which by analogy reflects the differentiation of God's own being:

> The essential thing is that the child, awakened thus to love, and already endowed by another's power of love, awakens also to himself and to his true freedom, which is in fact the freedom of loving transcendence of his narrow individuality. No man reaches the core and ground of his own being, becoming free to himself and to all beings, unless love shines on him.[8]

This "narrow individuality" is what we refer to as the "psychological self." It is the self viewed as a discrete entity, individuated within the species as an object of study or of self-reflection. It is instructive to note at this point that the familiar clinical expression "case history" can be misleading. For example, annotating a client's sexual history as a diagnostic technique in therapy is more an inventory of discrete behavior than a window into the self as an historical person. This could be one application of our earlier assertion that the determination which establishes singularity is social before it is psychological.

This distinction between social and psychological is intended only as a logical distinction appropriate to the true form of humanity. If existence with the other, or social existence, is determinative of existence as a singular being, then discrete individuality in abstraction from the other is already a symptom of disordered humanity, not the beginning of a cure. To some extent, deprivation of social encounter constitutes privation of humanity, with at least psychological consequences. Psychotherapy, then, can be construed as a systematic limitation of attention necessitated by the sociopathic condition.

If this is so, what does it say about the extent to which reconstructing the psyche can lead to recovering authentic human existence? Can the "I" be

---

7. *Ibid.*, p. 89.
8. *Ibid.*, p. 87.

healed when there is no significant "Thou?" And if the singularity of my humanity is determined by the other as a social construct of being, is not my health also determined by the other? Could not one suggest that sociotherapy is the larger context in which psychotherapy ought to be practiced?

Might one not also suggest that psychical reconstruction in its most clinical sense is a "pre-human" therapy, sometimes necessary as preparation for encounter but not itself the reorienting of the self in its true humanity? In this sense, behavior modification as a therapeutic technique could be seen as "sub-human," as a clinical model of treatment suggested by certain symptomatic behavior patterns, corresponding to brain surgery as a medical treatment for restoring human consciousness. It would seem appropriate that the "limitation of attention" on the part of a psychotherapist or a brain surgeon in order to correct an organic or psychical disorder serves the overall objective of restoring social being. What is essential, I believe, is that the objective of the therapist is informed by an understanding of the true order of humanity.

This, then, could be one rationale for a Christian perspective in the practice of psychotherapy. The therapist has as an objective the enhancement of true personhood through restoring healthy social relationships for her client, but she has more at stake than the certification of a purely clinical skill. Her own singularity, like that of Adam, might also be in search of completion. For if what we said about the basic form of humanity is correct, there is a search for and a confirmation of the original structure of co-humanity in every encounter of the human.

MALE AND FEMALE
HE CREATED THEM

Singularity of personal being is what we mean when we speak of being an individual. We have explored this in the form of the thesis that singularity is determined by the other. One implication of this has been considered by viewing the social structure of humanity (co-humanity) as the original form and therefore that from which our psychological personhood emerges. Now we must look more closely at what is entailed in positing the concrete, social encounter of the other as the basic form of the human. Singularity is also particularity. That is, one is not a singular person as part of a social structure of human being without also being particularly male or female. To say that humanity is co-humanity is not only to express a fundamental differentiation of a social nature, but also to assert that humanity is determined in its social differentiation as male and female.

The basic text on which a theological anthropology must reflect is Genesis 1:27: "In the image of God he created them; male and female he created

50

them." This leads us to elaborate on our explication of co-humanity as basically social and only subsequently psychological, by saying that the singularity which constitutes the human is originally sexual and only consequentially social. "We cannot say man without saying male or female, and also male and female," says Barth.[9] Barth refuses to discuss the order of humanity in abstract or general terms. For him, to be human is to have concrete, creaturely existence, and that entails either male or female existence:

> In the whole reach of human life there is no abstractly human but only concretely masculine or feminine being, feeling, willing, thinking, speaking, conduct and action, and only concretely masculine and feminine coexistence and co-operation in all these things. There is conflict and fellowship, there is encounter between men and therefore human being, only on the presupposition and under the sign and conditions of this one and distinctive differentiation.[10]

Barth denies the validity of typical stereotypes of masculinity and femininity as personality traits, but he still argues that sexual differentiation is human differentiation. Or, one should say, the fundamental human differentiation which constitutes the true order of humanity is necessarily experienced as sexual differentiation, and this is a *determination* of humanity, not an accidental or incidental manifestation of humanity. There is no human being above the being of humanity as either male or female.[11]

In this we see the distinction between Barth's theological anthropology and the philosophical anthropology of Buber, who also advocated the I-Thou relation as fundamental humanity. Since Buber ignores the sexual identity of the "I" and the "Thou," his concept of the human has a somewhat mystical dimension to it. Barth, on the other hand, cannot ignore what biblical revelation places as foundational in developing any theological anthropology: humanity is always particular, creaturely humanity before it is general humanity. And the particular form of humanity in the image and likeness of God in its creatureliness is male and female, male or female.

To be sure, human existence is profoundly experienced in a multitude of social relations. Brother, sister, parent, child, husband, wife, friend — all these are forms of co-existence and thus manifestations of true humanity. But these are all secondary, not an intrinsic order of humanity. One does not have to be a brother or sister, husband or wife, in order to be human. But one does, according to our understanding of co-humanity, have to be either male or female. The biblical text quite clearly links this with the image and likeness

---

9. *Church Dogmatics*, III/2, 286.
10. *Ibid.*
11. *Ibid.*, p. 289.

of God. All other social differentiations are included within the original determination in which human being is differentiated as male or female, male and
female. The family unit — husband/wife, parent/child — is the basic social unit
of humanity, but these social structures and relationships do not constitute
the original form of humanity, nor therefore the true order of humanity.

While human sexuality is indeed oriented to marriage as a social unit
(Gen. 2:24), this is because it is intrinsically oriented to a covenantal relationship.
By covenantal relationship we mean the original form of the differentiation,
in terms of the I-Thou relation which expresses the polarity of being in the
divine image and likeness. Singularity is a determination of the other. For
theological anthropology, therefore, marriage and family is a *secondary* order,
made possible by the primary order of differentiation as male or female. This
certainly has implications for determining the function of marriage and the
family unit in establishing goals for the fulfilment of human existence.

The church's proper concern for the stability and integrity of marriage and
family life, especially in contemporary society, where disorder and disintegration of these structures prevail, must never mistake these social orders for the
fundamental order of true humanity itself. It is easy to idealize marriage and
family as institutional values, but as a matter of fact they have no ontological
status as such. Rather, they serve as secondary orders to fulfil certain extrinsic
values which belong to the primary order of human being — existence in the
singularity of determination by the other.

The plight of the single person in the social structure of the church today
attests to confusion on this score. It is noteworthy that while the New Testament presupposes a high value on marriage and family as an extrinsic social
structure of the covenant community, it relativizes these social institutions to
the true order of humanity as distinguished by covenantal love, communal life,
and existence as singular components in the Body of Christ. Jesus demon-
strated the highest regard and utmost respect for marriage and family, but in
his own life he set forth a model of discipleship which is consequently made
an imperative for all disciples, that they should live with singular distinction
as those who are determined by others in a community of love (John 13:34-35).

A full-scale discussion of human sexuality will be taken up in Chapter
Eight. Here our purpose is to set forth the basic form of the human. In elaborating differentiation as the basis for the singularity distinctive to human
personhood, we saw that the encounter with the other in a social relation is
fundamental to the identity of the self. Now we have discovered that there is
no such thing as a purely "social" or "relational" humanity which is not also
concretely and particularly either male or female humanity. We have shown
the biblical and theological basis for this claim. But this immediately raises the
question of what is meant by "sexual" differentiation.

As we are using the term, "sexual" means at least — but necessarily more than — biological sexuality. Because human being is creaturely being, the creaturely aspect of sexual differentiation is always present in discussing what it means to be human, and creaturely differentiation at the sexual level is primarily biological and only secondarily social. In fact, this is only a biological distinction at the creaturely level; it is not differentiation of creaturely being experienced as a history of human being. In a certain sense, animals participate in sexual distinctiveness only as part of their creaturely nature: we speak of animals "mating" but not "meeting," in the sense of the meeting of persons in which differentiation produces singularity of being.

For human creatures, meeting is a mark of differentiation. While it may or may not involve mating, it is always a human event which is intrinsically sexual. That is, one is oriented to the other either as male or female. Thus, Barth says, for humans, sexual determination as male or female is the only differentiation.[12] Only as we experience ourselves as the concrete and significant "other" for another person are we differentiated; but this intensifies and enhances the singularity of our being, which is intrinsically either male or female.

Remember that we are not trying to account for all the phenomenological variations in human experience which one might encounter. Genetics and psychological and sociological determinants are also factors in the formation of gender identity. At the creaturely level, gender identity is not always distinct. The boundary line between male and female is determined by a fundamental orientation, which involves both gender identity and biological sexual characteristics at both the primary and secondary level. Where there is sufficient coalescence of factors to produce this orientation (which appears to occur more often than not), male and female differentiation becomes relatively distinct. Theological anthropology argues that this is the true order of humanity, and that the variations experienced at the phenomenological level do not alter this.

Because the determination which is the true differentiation of the human is contingently related to the creaturely, there is room for ambiguity in the actual form in which this differentiation occurs. What seems to hold true for the beginning and ending of human experience at the temporal, creaturely level also seems to hold true for the differentiation of sexual being on the broad field of creaturely sexuality. That is, the assertion that a particular creaturely form of existence is human is a *de facto* determination. At a certain point beyond fertilization, we can say with some degree of certainty that a fetus is human. At a certain point beyond visible life-support functions, we

---

12. *Ibid.*, III/1, 136.

say with some degree of certainty that the "person" is no longer existing and we have only a corpse. But this ambiguity at the boundaries in no way disqualifies us from asserting quite emphatically that a determination of the human is possible and necessary. In the same way, male and female is not a "boundary concept" dependent on precise definitions or descriptions, but it is an order of existence which makes boundary decisions meaningful, though these decisions must always be made in the face of certain ambiguities.

The sexual differentiation of humanity as male or female, male and female, is logically prior to the social structures in which that differentiation occurs. This understanding of the true order of humanity can assist psychotherapy and Christian ethics to determine authentic goals and methods in seeking to orient people to health and fulfilment. (The many implications of this position cannot be discussed at length here, and the reader is again referred to the longer discussion of human sexuality in Chapter Eight.)

Humanity as co-humanity means that the singularity of being a human person is determined by significant encounter with another human person. Thus, we argued, the social structure of co-humanity precedes and determines individuality, expressed as singularity. However, the intrinsic order of co-humanity is manifested in and through creaturely sexuality, so that singularity is experienced as either male or female existence.

To bypass the social structure of humanity is to idealize the psychological structure of the self and consequently to break it off from concrete existence. Treatment undertaken from such a fragmented perspective will be determined by symptomatic conceptualization and thus tend to overly "clinicize" the person. On the other hand, the failure to recognize that the social structure of concrete humanity itself depends on an intrinsic differentiation of humanity as a profound singularity rooted in the sexual order of male and female will idealize humanity in terms of institutions. The consequent treatment methodologies tend to look on behavior modification as an engineering of human potential. Our hope is that the form of the human understood as co-humanity can make all forms of "treatment" legitimate as a "limitation of attention" for the sake of enabling singularity of personhood to be affirmed through healthy social relations.

Singularity is also a responsibility of the self, however, and thus there is finally an element of self-determination in being truly human. To this we now turn as the logically concluding step in depicting the form of the human.

CHAPTER FIVE

HUMANITY AS SELF-DETERMINED

S O FAR THERE HAS BEEN A CERTAIN RESTRAINT IN OUR APPROACH, stemming from the need to hold in check the impulse to begin with what seems most obvious — self-consciousness, or subjectivity, as the essence of humanity. I experience my own humanity as a subjective reality. I am a center of feelings, reactions, hopes, fears, opinions, motivations, and desires. Other persons exist for me. That is, they are within range of my own perception of reality, either as other subjects, whose feelings, motivations, and desires interest or threaten me, or as objects along with other phenomena in the objective world. However, humanity as such does not exist in the abstract, but only in concrete instances. If I know myself more intimately than others, would self-consciousness or subjectivity not be the most fruitful source of information for beginning a study of humanity?

This is in fact the point from which existential philosophy begins to develop an anthropology. Self-transcendence as a phenomenon of subjectivity is taken to be the actuality of human existence and the qualitative distinction between the human and non-human. In his noteworthy book *The Denial of Death*, Ernest Becker views self-transcendence as the ontological nerve which accounts for both neurotic and psychopathic disorder. In this view, disorder is not a disease to be cured but a phenomenon which points to self-transcendence as the synthesis of consciousness itself (spirit) and creaturely existence (flesh) which constitutes the human. For Becker human being is essentially human existence, and existence is a fragile and fearful projection of the self into the unknown with the hope that abandoning the self to the eternal is ultimately meaningful. It can be said, in support of Becker, that he has grasped the reality of subjectivity and self-determination as essential to true humanity. However, what remains obscure in an anthropology based on existential philosophy is the nature of the reality which is the object or goal of this self-transcendence as a projection into the infinite.

It is clear that the reality of God as the object of self-transcendence is dispensable. Many concepts of transcendent reality can provide a goal for self-transcendence as a subjective reality. Camus and Sartre developed a keen sense of self-transcendence, but it was an act which justified the existence of the human person as an existential movement itself. The only meaningful act of existence was to raise meaninglessness to its highest power and then defy it as an act of the self. The "frontier situations" in life, as extreme points at the margins of creaturely existence, may serve to produce the phenomenon of self-transcendence, and even to sharpen the perception of existence itself. In moments where death seems imminent or where there is some threat to existence itself, one's perception of the self is certainly raised to a critical and profoundly important level. But these situations cannot provide content to what is only vaguely identified as the "eternal" or the "infinite." For this reason, existential philosophy as an anthropological model is basically non-theological, even when it uses the categories of religious phenomena to explore the concept of the self. This approach to subjectivity is not a hopeful one.

SUBJECTIVITY AS RESPONSE

Theological anthropology does not despise subjectivity and self-consciousness, nor even self-determination. However, it reaches this as a conclusion rather than beginning here. "If we are to say man," says Karl Barth, "we must unquestionably say subject."[1] This is because God has addressed and continues to address the human creature. Subjectivity is thus posited as a response to the determination of the creative Word. The consequence of this determination expressed in the form of address is the response of the creature. Subjectivity posits subjectivity in the form of divine Word and human word.

Because the phenomenon of the human occurs on the broad field of creaturely being solely because of the differentiating power of the divine Word, we know the object of self-consciousness as complementary to knowing ourselves. We do not first of all know ourselves, and then search for a divine, transcendent Word to know and grasp. We are first of all grasped and known; then follows knowledge of ourselves. Paul expresses this in his hymn of love: "Now I know in part; then I shall understand fully, even as I have been fully understood" (1 Cor. 13:12). Thus, human and personal subjectivity is both a consequence of determination by the other and the source of our knowledge of this determination. For to be human, after all, is to posit one's own being in the differential mode of existence that is peculiar to human being. This is determination as response.

But this "positing of oneself" as self-determination is a response-ability. It is experienced as an answering, not only or essentially as a seeking. Though self-consciousness may appear first of all as a searching, it is an existential seeking of what has already been said and revealed. We might borrow again

---

1. *Church Dogmatics*, III/2, 195.

from Thomas Wolfe: "Which of us has known his brother? Which of us has looked into his father's heart? . . . Remembering speechlessly we seek the great forgotten language, the lost lane-end into heaven, a stone, a leaf, an unfound door. Where? When?"[2] Theologically, this seeking is accounted for by reference to the original Word which has been spoken and which has summoned spirit into response, into response-ability, into answering.

Behind all poetry, the Jewish theologian Franz Rosenzweig reminds us, is the original spoken word:

> Before and beyond it there was prose, and it was nonpoetry; it was nonrhythmical, unbound but not disengaged speech, unmeasured but not extravagantly fulsome (*masslos übermässiges*) word. All poetry which has since come into being within the circle of its light is inspired by its prose spirit. *Since that time* in the dark silence that surrounded the beginning of mankind the door which separates each from the other and all from the Outside and the Beyond *has been broken* and never again will it be altogether closed; the door of the Word.[3]

Theological anthropology does not allow poetry to fade into silence, as Heidegger would like, but behind the poetic expression of self-transcendence is the original Word which has summoned the self into its own use of the word to respond.

This answering, however, takes place as the being of one who enacts being through decision. "Being in the sense of human beings is a process of self enactment," says Barth.[4] The self must be enacted through a response which can be perceived by the other. In the reciprocal relation of word-response, the freedom of action is posited. As the determinative Word which summons forth existence, God is one who enacts his being in his Word. Word and act occur simultaneously with him: he is what he does and he does what he is. We know this through the Word which has become flesh. For Jesus, subjectivity is self-enactment, so that it may be said of him, "he does the truth." To experience discrepancy between self-consciousness and one's own historical existence is to be in a state of "double-mindedness," as James put it. "A double-minded man, unstable in all his ways," will not receive anything from the Lord (James 1:8). Indecision is a suspension of being, and prolonged, it produces a state of non-historical existence. In order to be truly human, self-consciousness must be experienced as self-enactment, and this requires a form of psychical energy not found in self-consciousness as a mere phenomenon. In this

---

2. Thomas Wolfe, *Look Homeward, Angel,* from the frontispiece.
3. "Die Schrift und das Wort," *Kleinere Schriften* (1937), pp. 134ff; cited by Miskotte, *When the Gods are Silent,* p. 204.
4. *Church Dogmatics,* III/2, 127.

sense healthy, vigorous subjectivity is a result of a good relationship, not the cause of it.

SUBJECTIVITY AS DISCRIMINATION

Subjectivity as response emerges as self-enactment. In self-enactment, one is constantly re-positing oneself. In the field of possibilities surrounding the self one must "seize one's own possibility" of human existence. But this subjective act is one of discriminating which possibility is "mine" and which is not. Subjectivity, we can now say, is the discrimination of my own being in a process of differentiation. Here the subjective aspect of differentiation comes into view. Up to this point, we have considered differentiation to be the result of the action of the other — originally of God and subsequently of the significantly human other. But here we see that differentiation is a subjective responsibility expressed as self-enactment through a process of discrimination in which what is actualized from all possibilities becomes my personal existence.

The essence of self-determination is discriminating one's own being *as it occurs*. Not that personal existence is indiscriminate or that we can be anything we wish. There is a form of indiscriminate self-determination, but we do not recognize it as a virtue. Self-actualization without regard to what is appropriate to the nature of the self as human is at best unruly and at worst destructive, often to the self as well. The capacity of discrimination is more than the capacity of will, or even of obedience. Yielding to indiscriminate impulses or desperately willing what is not attainable constitutes a loss of subjectivity. Wilful disobedience to that which is determined for our good is no better than indiscriminate obedience to that which is ultimately designed for our harm. Discrimination is recognition and identification of what is appropriate, or fitting.

This of course cries out for an answer to the question of *how* one determines what is appropriate! By what criteria can such discrimination be made? What does "appropriate" or "fitting" mean? How can one choose between possibilities without an objective criterion by which to define the good as against the bad? And it is precisely these questions which philosophers of a more rational orientation have put to the existentialists. According to this line of reasoning, the nature of being must essentially be known before one can know how to act in an existential moment.

But we have to be cautious at this point. It is the creative divine Word which is the ultimate determinator of human being. This Word is the source of all that is appropriate and fitting for the human, for it summons the human into being and into response-ability. Now we must put the question the other way. Are there criteria originally existing in the human mind or accessible to

58

it by which a judgment can be made as to what is the divine Word? Is the divine Word authenticated on the basis of some "objective" criteria prior to the enactment of response to that Word, or does the Word authenticate itself and thus provide a basis for a discriminate response?

Theologically, there can only be one answer to these questions. The Word of God is self-authenticating and is therefore the "objective" basis for the human subjective response. Here we are confronted with a situation quite distinct from that of either the existentialist or the rationalist. The existentialist would want to say that *any* possibility is appropriate if it can be chosen and enacted in such a way that it leads to authentic existence of the self. There can be no prior act of being which discriminates between the good and the bad, for being does not precede existence but results from it. On the other hand, the rationalist would want to say that being does precede existence, and as an objectifiable criterion of truth, gives each person a critical rather than an uncritical basis for determining response.

Our response to this dichotomy between essence and existence is to point to the unity of essence and existence in the divine Word as the source of both truthful and meaningful subjective human response. We are also reminded that the temptation which led to the original fall was a question about the criteria for discriminating between the divine Word and that which is for the "good" of the human. "Did God say?" was the question the serpent put to the woman (Gen. 3:1). Bonhoeffer calls this the "religious question," because it suggested basing one's discrimination of the divine command — and thus of one's own response to it — on criteria more metaphysical and abstract than the command itself.[5]

Prior to a "knowledge of good and evil" as a metaphysical knowledge, the original man and woman had a knowledge of the command of God which was both limiting and liberating. They were free to eat of any fruit of the garden, but not of the tree of the knowledge of good and evil. The question as to which fruit could be eaten in such a way as to authenticate and complete the personal life of each could only be answered in this way: any fruit that God has set before you as a possibility. In this case self-enactment was completed by choosing and eating, not by questioning and reflecting.!

Obviously, a limitation and boundary is established and must be "known" as such, but our point is just this: the divine command discriminates boundaries and limits, but not specific actions or choices, for human being. The freedom and responsibility to exercise discrimination as a single choice and action amid a multitude of possible choices is the basis for our own subjectivity. The existentialist tends to say that all possibilities are equally determinative

---

5. *Creation and Fall* (London: SCM Press, 1959), p. 66.

of our being, if we choose any of them "with all our being." The rationalist tends to say that each possibility is a question of the "good, the true, and the beautiful," which can be answered before it can be experienced. Theological anthropology says, in response to these alternatives, that the practical life of each person takes place in a world created and affirmed by the divine Word in such a way that the highest wisdom is to receive one's life in the actual living of it, "with thanksgiving" (1 Tim. 4:4). That is, we are subjectively free as well as subjectively responsible to discriminate our own being *as it occurs* within the order of God's creation. There is of course the problem of sin and its subjective effects (which we will have to discuss in due time), but that is not what is at stake here. Our argument is that authentic human existence is also a "becoming" through self-enactment precisely because this is determined for us by God.

Many people are frustrated and anxiety-ridden because they fail to grasp this basic theological truth. Life is composed of a never-ending series of choices among many possibilities, each of which appears to be indiscriminate. This is true of our most significant choices (whom to marry, where to live, what career to prepare for) and of the most trivial ones (what to wear, which dress to buy, where to go on vacation). Earlier we asked how we can determine within any of these possibilities what is appropriate or fitting? If we set aside the question of limits and boundaries (the "tree of the knowledge of good and evil"), what remains occupies the greater part of our time and energy; and it is in this area that our being is linked with our becoming. Precisely here, I suggest, subjectivity emerges as the "seizing of possibility" as my own.

Seen thus, self-determination is not so much a theoretical or ethical question as a very practical one. Such self-determination is not based on criteria which exist in abstraction from the event of existence itself. The divine Word which summons the human into existence confronts the human self with the responsibility of recognizing and choosing one's own being as a reality of existence. In the face of many possibilities which impinge on any given moment we are to seize the possibility which is truly *our* possibility, for it is that which makes possible the enactment of our own personhood at the deepest level. To try to survey all the possibilities in the hope of choosing the "right" one is to court paralysis: one ends up suspending self-enactment for fear of making a mistake. One is reminded here of Jesus' parable of the talents (Matt. 25:14-30), in which the servant who hid his talent for fear of losing it finally had it taken away for failure to invest it.

Consider, for example, the dilemma many people face in the decision of finding the right marriage partner. Because marriage is defined as an irrevocable commitment of the self, and because the possibilities are ordinarily in some kind of mathematical relation to the number of persons of the opposite sex with whom one comes into contact, the determination as to which choice is the "right" one often produces a high level of anxiety. In this situation, to appeal to abstract criteria is just about as useless as asking for advice! For the fact is that there is probably no "perfect mate." Again, given certain borderline limitations, possibilities remain at the center of one's life which do not come labeled as to which is right for us. Someone has facetiously remarked that there are no right choices, only wrong ones!

Applying our thesis to this example, we would say that ordinarily at some point we "seize" a particular opportunity as our own. We thus discriminate between all other possible marriage partners and the one we choose on the basis that this one is "mine" and the others are not. The discrimination of "what is mine," or what completes my own being, is not premeditated. It takes place "as it occurs" in the course of our life. That it does occur is evidenced, not by its matching some abstract criteria, but because our being answers at the deepest level to the being of another. This "knowledge" is inaccessible on a more abstract, conceptual level; witness the often-heard statement: "I don't see what she sees in him!"

The process of making this discrimination is often somewhat tentative at first, but the decision is easier for one who has developed a degree of confidence in his or her discriminations. Subjectivity is a process of growing in the competence to make discriminations which enhance life rather than narrow and impoverish it. The greater one's own sense of self-identity — which is the result of discriminations made at all levels, many quite routine or even insignificant — the more confidence one will have in making discriminations (choices) at the major points of life. Self-confidence, viewed from this perspective, is akin to the concept of "wisdom" in the Old Testament. It is the integrity which exists between the practical or everyday living of life and the inner life of the person. Wisdom thus is happiness, and happiness is the recognition of one's own being as reflected in that in which one has invested his or her life.

From this it is clear that, to some extent at least, the occurrence of one's own being lies within the range and reach of everyone. It is a human possibility and a tangible one. In a sense, my own being is determined for me by the circumstances which narrow down my possibilities to particular places and points in time. But this does not narrow down my range of possibility for determining my own being. For this determination does not rest on the extent of possibilities — some of which may offer something better than others — but on seizing *some* possibility as it occurs. Adam did not wait to see what other females might offer him by way of possibility when God presented him with Eve, but seized that possibility as his own. For in that event he experienced the answer to his own being in her. Someone may ask, Did he love her? Here too it must also be understood that love is the result of a good relationship, not the cause of it.

The determination of my own being in the context of other beings is what results in subjectivity. This is the difficult movement which each infant must make — from undifferentiated and indiscriminate being to discriminate being, from being in general to *my* being. The reinforcement of early discriminations through the differential relations which constitute family and community existence develops the subjectivity of the growing person and trains the person in the act of self-determination which is essential to responsible adulthood (cf. Heb. 5:14). To substitute ethical, aesthetic, or even religious criteria as the basis for the discrimination of the self leads to negative reinforcement, rather than positive. Oriented toward avoiding failure, punishment, or guilt, the self may develop acceptable behavior as far as the mores of society are concerned, but increasingly it will lack a sense of what is appropriate to its own being. The result is either a severe identity crisis or slavish conformity to what Kierkegaard calls the Philistine life. And, he adds, it is a sickness unto death which produces triviality.[6]

SUBJECTIVITY AS "OUTWARDNESS"

We have been speaking of subjectivity as the act by which one seizes one's own possibility of existence as it occurs, and accepts confirmation of it by the significant other. This is the ontological basis for personality.[7] But we must add that subjectivity is the process by which one re-posits oneself in responsible decisions and actions. Self-determination does not mean that we can do anything we wish. Personal life as history of being is the result not of indiscriminate impulses but of discriminating decisions which re-posit the self as an *extrinsic* reality. Or, one could say, subjectivity is as much a public existence as it is a private one. Subjectivity is thus more than mere inwardness; it is "outwardness." The person who retreats from extrinsic subjectivity into the secrecy of inner life actually moves away from true subjectivity and tends to become impersonal and "mere" object. Perhaps in the schizoid personality one could say that subjectivity has been surrendered to indiscriminate inner life which bears no relation to the public life one shares with others.

Here is a guide to true spirituality as a quality of Christian life. Spirituality is not the interiorization of abstract truths, nor even of an impersonal "spirit," but the *externalization* of Spirit in the form of actions. Paul calls this activity of the Spirit "edification" (cf. 1 Cor. 12). The indiscriminate use of spiritual

---

6. *Sickness Unto Death* (Princeton: Princeton U. P., 1954, 1969), pp. 174f.
7. Cf. Barth, *Church Dogmatics*, III/2, 93ff.

"gifts" for one's private life is qualified by the discriminating exercise of gifts which enhance the community. The church has tended to call the interiorization of Spirit a subjectivizing of the Spirit which produces confusion and disorder in the community. However, we would prefer to call such interiorizing and internalizing of Spirit a loss of subjectivity in the true sense. Along with it goes the loss of a corresponding humanity and personal fellowship.

Because the life of the person is structured in co-humanity and is conditioned and determined by the other, there can be no authentic subjectivity without participation in the outward, historical life of co-humanity. The self as a subject exists in and through actions which reveal it to the other. God's subjectivity would be hidden from us if he did not reveal himself through his Word, which is his act. Theologians may struggle with the question of God's existence "in himself" versus his existence "for us." But to introduce a dichotomy between God as pure subjective being and God in his outward actions is to lose touch with the very being of God. The God who acts in creation and redemption *is* the subjective life of God. To know God in his actions is thus to know him in his own life and being. In the same sense, we would say that true subjectivity of human being is expressed in the reciprocal relations which constitute human community. But this must be a continual act of self-determination. Otherwise, the self disappears behind the total objectivity of tradition and role-playing, and is lost to the community.

The self as personal being must continually be re-posited, so that the basis of discrimination between personal and impersonal existence can exist externally to self-consciousness itself. Unhinged from meaningful public or communal existence self-consciousness leads to irrationality and loss of humanity. Likewise, actions disconnected from true orientation in self-consciousness are impersonal and inhuman. The self cannot be posited except through meaningful interaction with an external order of humanity—co-humanity. Where the self is not re-posited in the series of interactions which necessarily make up existence in relation, subjectivity disappears and only impersonal and indiscriminate actions remain.

The essence of human relations is love. Other factors can constitute an aggregation or collection of persons, but without love the human dimension of the social unit is diminished. If it is diminished sufficiently, the social unit actually becomes inhuman. Thus, in close friendships or marriage, it is not enough that certain actions take place which maintain the continuity of the relation. In these actions there must be a re-positing of the self in such a way that the actions are discriminate rather than indiscriminate. The act of reaching out and touching another person merely out of instinct, habit, or by compulsion, is an indiscriminate act, even though it is an act peculiar or habitual to that relation. For discrimination is not achieved by habit, but through an appropriate congruence between act and being.

Love dies, not through lack of actions, but through lack of discrimination. That is, love is maintained as a positive quality in a relation by the re-positing of the self in such a way that encounter of being takes place. Many have testified to the tragedy that marriage can destroy a good relationship! What does the damage in such cases is not the exclusivity of the marriage vow which in some way usurps the freedom of the relation, but a loss of subjectivity which substitutes impersonal routine actions for discriminating personal ones. There is nothing so indiscriminate as familiarity.

Intimacy, on the other hand, is the essence of subjectivity in relation. We are all aware of being offended by someone who touches us in a familiar way, without the right to claim intimacy. For intimacy is earned through the sense of discrimination which is present in the relation. The greater the sense of discrimination, the greater the level of intimacy. And again, by discrimination, we mean the presence of being in the act, so that in the act of discrimination one is both vulnerable and also absolutely secure. The creation narrative tells us that before the fall the man and woman were "both naked, and were not ashamed" (Gen. 2:25). This is the power of subjectivity expressed as co-humanity. The vulnerability is in the defenselessness each has in the presence of the other. When that intimacy is violated by an act of self-determination which betrays the other, there is less vulnerability, because each is now "covered" in the presence of the other. A loss of subjectivity as "outwardness" occurs and consequently true humanity is lost.

When two people seek public recognition of their marriage vow, they also are seeking the conventionality and convenience which such public affirmation gives. They now can be together without fear of violating the conventions of the community. Their relationship has become objectively affirmed by the community. It also becomes more convenient. There is no need for the negotiation of the "meeting" between the two each day, or several times a day. So convention and convenience become routinely accepted. However, the objective security and pragmatic convenience of living together as husband and wife in the institution of marriage is also a potential loss of subjectivity. Routine actions and role relations can become totally indiscriminate, and thus inhuman. The necessary actions continue to take place, insuring the continuity of the marriage, but the necessary subjectivity expressed as outwardness may diminish or be lost altogether. Thus love dies, not through lack of action, but through lack of discrimination, by which outward acts re-posit the self for the other.

We can now see that self-determination, as the existential component of human personhood, is itself a function of co-humanity. Subjectivity is not inwardness but the reality of the self expressed and experienced as a social structure of humanity. The responsibility and freedom of being a human person is itself a response. Therefore, we are persons actually before we are confronted with the possibilities of personal existence. But this rests on the creative Word of God, which summons the human creature into personal existence.

This is the beginning of a theological anthropology. The implications of what we have set forth in these chapters are far-reaching. What we have done in the chapters of Part One has been to outline the critical dimensions of human personhood as differentiated from the non-human by the Word of God. Perhaps the most critical insight is that of the contingent relation between humanity expressed as personal being and creaturely being. This is the boundary line between a theological and non-theological anthropology. Now we shall use this fundamental differentiation at the creaturely level between the human and non-human in evaluating the content of such biblical doctrines as creation in the image and likeness of God, the nature of sin and salvation in terms of personhood, and human sexuality. In addition, we will draw on these insights in taking up such contemporary concerns as responsibility toward the dying, the right to life, and the right to die.

We have expressed the form of the human in analytical and conceptual language. Being human is a more down-to-earth subject, but it requires equal rigor of thought and perception. To that task we now turn in Part Two.

PART TWO

BEING HUMAN

CHAPTER SIX

BEING HUMAN —
IN THE IMAGE OF GOD

1. The Importance of the *Imago Dei* Concept for Theological Anthropology

GOD DID NOT CREATE HUMAN BEINGS BECAUSE HE WAS INCOMPLETE OR lonely. The Westminster Catechism tells us, however, that "the chief end of man" is "to glorify God and enjoy him forever." God is a God of glory without the praise or company of human creatures. The glory of God is not that which he receives from his creatures but that which he himself is as the Creator and Lord of all creation. Human persons, in contrast, cannot be complete without "glorifying or enjoying" God, for that is their nature and their destiny as created "in the image and likeness of God" (Gen. 1:26-27). If there is a glory which comes to God from his human creatures, it is the reflection of his own glory which now returns, having been sent forth as Word and Spirit.

But is this "reflected glory" more than poetry? Is it human? Can we discern it in the face of the creature, if not in "skin and bones?" Certainly no attempt at a theological anthropology can ignore the superscription which biblical revelation places over the archway leading to the arena of the human: "Then God said, 'Let us make man in our image, after our likeness' . . ." (Gen. 1:26). This is the point of departure for all biblical understanding of the form of the human. There is no way to reduce this statement to a poetic glance away from the human. It stands as the Word of God, which determines that the human creature exists as a creature of the sixth day, in solidarity with all other creatures but in absolute distinction from them. While other creatures are created "after their kinds," the human is created "in the image and likeness of God." Taken in the most straightforward sense, this statement directs us to consider that if the human person exists at all, it is as a being created in the divine image. There is no room in this statement for understanding the divine image as merely a perspective from which God views his creature. Rather, the creative act itself is "in the image and likeness" of God.

WHAT IS AT STAKE?

Many theological issues are important only as issues over which theologians quibble (an exercise which may also say something about the value of theology, by and large). But the concept of the *imago Dei* is not one of those issues. It is the foundational concept for understanding the biblical teaching concerning the nature and value of human personhood. In taking up the question of what the *imago Dei* means for human personhood, we address an issue that touches virtually every other tenet of Christian belief. The essential nature of human being is determinative for our understanding of the kind of redemption God has wrought for human beings through his Son, Jesus Christ, who is the true Image of God (Col. 1:15). And though we know essential humanity only through the God-Man, we know the incarnate God only through his participation in our common humanity (Heb. 2:14-18). As Barth once said, "theology has become anthropology since God became man." In this context, the character of the *imago Dei* (as the essential determination of the *humanum*[1] which constitutes human existence as opposed to nonhuman) affects the entire spectrum of God's revelation. It is not too much to say that the core of the theological curriculum itself is contained in the doctrine of the *imago Dei*.

It is not our intent here to unfold the history of the doctrine of the *imago Dei*, nor even to consider this doctrine as our primary focus. Our concern is with the nature of human personhood itself based on the assumption that human beings are created in the image and likeness of God.[2] We must, however, discuss certain concerns which are relevant to our own objectives in setting forth the beginning of a theological anthropology.

First of all, does the concept of the *imago Dei* mean that there is a subtle "connective tissue" between the being of God and the being of the human person? Is the bestowal of the divine image and likeness in the human person a bestowal of "being in kind?" Most theologians have distinguished between humanity created "*after* the image of God" and Christ as "*the* image of God." Some distinction needs to be made between the *humanum* as a created essence and the *imago* as the uncreated being of God which is determinative for the *humanum*. A strict identity between the *imago* and *humanum* as the essence of personhood would imply either that the human person is in some way part of uncreated divine being, or that the *imago* itself is created and therefore different from the being of God. What is at stake here is maintaining the correspondence between human being and the being of God while at the same

---

1. As a technical term in this discussion I use *humanum* to denote the essence of the human which each person is, without regard to personality or other variable characteristics. The *humanum* is that in each person which makes him or her human.

2. For a brief discussion of *imago Dei* and a list of additional sources for study, see Appendix B.

time preserving the absolute difference. Most theologians will argue for correspondence rather than strict identity; what remains debatable is precisely how the correspondence is to be understood.

Second, are we to understand the *imago* as an imprint or endowment of the very character of God, or as an abstract idea of humanity, or merely as a goal. The intent of Scripture seems to be that no matter how one understands the correspondence between the *humanum* and the *imago*, the *imago* is a gift or an endowment which takes place in the concrete and particular existence of each person. It is not merely that "humanity" in the abstract exists as the ideal of true humanity, in the image and likeness of God; each human person exists in the image and likeness of God. As Emil Brunner put it, the *imago* is explicitly given to humanity as a gift, not simply as a goal; "it is something humanity is."[3] Two passages in the New Testament (1 Cor. 11:7; James 3:9) support this understanding of the *imago* as present in the actual existence of human persons. Precisely how we are to understand the concrete presence of the *imago* in a person's actual existence remains debatable. Our point is that we must understand it in the concrete and particular sense of being a person, not merely as an abstract principle of humanity.

A third question is whether or not the physical body is to be included in the *imago*. Early theologians of the church rightly rejected suggestions that the physical body of human beings was in any way identical with the *imago Dei*. But this led to a dichotomy between the physical and nonphysical aspects of human personhood, with the *imago* tending to be located in the mind or the moral nature of the person. If (as we indicated above) the *imago* corresponds to the *humanum* but is not identical with it, the *humanum* itself can be understood as including body as well as soul. And it also follows that, if the *imago* is present as a particular and concrete instance of human being, it can only be present as an "embodied" *imago Dei*.

Fear of anthropomorphism, which imports creaturely aspects of human being into a concept of God, threw up an almost insurmountable barrier to including the physical body in the correspondence between human being and God's being. The result was a destructive dualism between body and soul as constituent parts of personal humanity. So, too, because the human self relates to the world through bodily existence in the world, theology tended to ignore this important aspect of human existence as existence in solidarity with God's creation. So long as the *imago* is virtually identified with the spiritual, rational, or moral aspect of human existence, disregard for one's own existence as embodied person can lead to disregard of the personal existence of others

---

3. *Man in Revolt: A Christian Anthropology* (Philadelphia: Westminster, 1947), p. 104.

in their embodied form. From a biblical perspective, no fundamental distinction can be made between the human person as an embodied soul and as an ensouled body. Consequently, we conclude that the *imago Dei* is borne as a concrete and particular endowment of each person's existence as embodied personal being.

Fourth, how does the doctrine of the Fall, in which human nature became hopelessly enslaved to sin, affect the concept of the *imago Dei*? If the *imago* is correspondence between human being and the being of God, and if particular human being becomes alienated and estranged from God, how does the *imago* continue to exist in the sinner — if at all? If the *imago Dei* is essential humanity — even if expressed as correspondence to rather than identity with divine being — we must affirm its continuity through the fall: each person who is a sinner is also human. The biblical teaching seems to entail that sinners, even in their total depravity, remain human and are dealt with as such by God in judgment and in hope. Clearly there is some impairment or even "loss" of the power of the *imago* in the human who is also sinner with respect to relation to God; and theologians have debated how to understand this "loss" while maintaining the continuity of the *humanum* through the fall. Again, our purpose is not to judge in this theological debate, but to affirm the more general truth that there is continuity of the *humanum* in Adam through his fall into sin and subsequent alienation from God. Because we have insisted that the *imago* is present in the *humanum* as embodied human person, and because we view the person in a state of sin as fully human, we can only account for that continuity of humanity as a continuity of the *imago Dei* as constitutive of humanity, even in what becomes virtually a negative form. Later in this chapter we will show that humanity as response-ability is both a positive and negative form of humanity.

Finally, what is at stake here is the meaning of regeneration and renewal of humanity through the supernatural grace of God for our concept of personhood. Again the issue is one of continuity, though now in more existential terms. Granted that the sinner remains human even when in a state of sin, does the sinner as an existing self remain the same person through the process of moving from "death to life" in what the Scriptures call the new birth? To put the question another way: what part of my humanity is included in the regeneration experience — my soul alone, or both body and soul?

Those who deny that the effect of sin through the fall was pervasive, extending throughout the whole race and over every aspect of personal existence, will limit the doctrine of regeneration to what they see as having been affected by sin. What has not fallen need not be made new. On the other hand, those who deny that the *imago* includes both body and soul as the correspondence of the *humanum* to God's own being, will tend to think of salvation as a purely "spiritual" experience, not really affecting one's bodily existence in the world. This is reflected in terminology such as "soul-winning" or "saving souls" as against healing or recovering persons in a wholistic sense. Furthermore, if one does not see the *imago* as including embodied existence in the world, one will tend to view redemption as being "saved out of the world," rather than including the reconciliation of the human person to the world and to each other in the world, and of the world to God. In this sense, theological anthropology becomes a "theology of liberation" when it can take seriously redemption through Christ *as* historical existence, not merely as a primarily spiritual experience *in* history.

THE IMAGO DEI AS
ENCOUNTER AND RELATION

Since the biblical texts which actually speak of the image and likeness of God as constituting essential humanity are sparse and somewhat ambiguous, we have to be cautious about building theological anthropology on the concept of the *imago* alone. Three of these texts do occur as part of the narrative of the origins of the human in creation itself. In Genesis 1:26, 27, we read:

> Then God said, "Let us make man in our image, after our likeness: and let them have dominion over the fish of the sea, and over the birds of the air, and over the cattle, and over all the earth, and over every creeping thing that creeps upon the earth." So God created man in his own image, in the image of God he created him; male and female he created them.

It is instructive that the plural pronoun is used with reference both to God and to "man" as created in the image and likeness of God. One must be careful about inferring from the plural pronoun here a trinitarian concept of God as "three persons," but there is at least an intentional correspondence in this text between the intrinsic plurality of human being as constituted male and female and the being of God in whose likeness and image this plurality exists. Genesis 2 elaborates this further in its commentary on the existence of the solitary male, terming such an existence "not good." Adam has no fundamental "encounter of being with being" in his relationship with the other creatures such as occurs when the woman is presented to him as a "being from and for him." Quite clearly the *imago* is not totally present in the form of individual humanity but more completely as co-humanity. It is thus quite natural and expected that God himself is also a "we."

God exists as a being who encounters and relates to himself. Thus, God exists in an I-Self polarity of being. This is prior to and determinative of his existence as an I-Thou relation to the human person. This explains why Adam cannot exist in an I-Thou relation with God without also existing as an I-Self person in polarity of being with another. The *imago* is not first of all I-Thou (relation), but I-Self (self-in-relation). When the male encounters himself in the female, and when the female encounters herself in the male, each exists as I-Self but also as I-Thou. With respect to the world and other creatures, a man can say, "I am not this," and in this he knows what he is not. But in relationship to other persons he can say, "I am like this"; the man sees who and what he is in the other. In the particularity of co-humanity as experienced as male and female, however, the man can say with respect to his relation to woman, "I am not this, but this." Through the I-Thou relation, each person experiences himself or herself as a distinct I-Self, which is the fundamental expression of the *imago*. It is through encounter that the self exists "in the image and likeness of God." However, this encounter entails co-humanity, which is the I-Thou relation at the human level. This appears to make "relationship" the distinctive aspect of the *imago Dei*, whereas, in fact, relationship is a functional possibility and necessity of the *imago*. Encounter is more fundamental to the *imago* than relation.

This becomes clearer in a third text from the Genesis story (the second, Gen. 5:1, is more or less a restatement of the first). Genesis 9:6, which follows the judgment of the flood, says: "Whoever sheds the blood of man, by man shall his blood be shed; for God made man in his own image." Why is murder such an affront to both God and man? Because it is an affront to the *imago Dei* which is present as embodied humanity. God does not pronounce a judgment on murder because it involves the killing of a creature, but because we "encounter" the *imago Dei* in other persons in any act which affects their own existence in the world. Promiscuous killing of non-human creatures is certainly an offense against the sensibilities of humans with regard to creation as valued by God and upheld by human responsibility. However, it is not murder, because the life of a non-human creature does not bear the *imago Dei*. In the New Testament Jesus teaches that hatred of another person is tantamount to murder because it "despises" the image of God in another. In the same way, to withhold what another person needs for the well-being of his or her bodily or personal existence in the world is a denial of one's own participation in the "love of God," by which the redeemed humanity finds expression (cf. 1 John 3:17,18; James 2:15-17).

Despite variations in how early Christian theologians understood the *imago Dei*, we noted a rather uniform tendency to equate the *imago* with some faculty of the individual self which represented either a moral, spiritual, or rational superiority over non-human creatures. More than any other early church father, Augustine stressed the Godward orientation of the *imago*, and thus located the focus of redemption as the recovery of the whole person in his or her relation to God. However, Augustine's "relational" concept of the *imago Dei* includes little if any hint of what we have termed "co-humanity" as encounter of the other at the human level. Drawing on the rediscovery of Aristotle, Thomas Aquinas developed this concept of relation to God into a "natural theology" by which a more ontological connection between human and divine being could be posited, though by way of analogy of being rather than direct identification.

The Reformers set aside the Thomistic emphasis on "analogy of being" as constitutive of the *imago Dei* and concentrated more on its christological aspect as righteousness manifested in true faith and obedience. While the Reformers tended to be more Augustinian (in the sense of construing the *imago* as the orientation of the whole person to God) and thus "relational," they too failed to develop the implications of this relational concept for concrete human existence at the level of co-humanity.

What all these formulations of the doctrine of the *imago Dei* lack is what we have called the "encounter" of one with the other through which the I-Thou relation becomes differentiated more concretely in terms of the I-Self. Not only does this lack tend to reduce the *imago* as constitutive of the *humanum* to an individualistic ideal at the moral, spiritual, or rational level, but it also leaves no place for grounding ethics in anthropology. We will enlarge on this in Chapter Ten; suffice it to say now that if the I-Thou relation with God constitutes true humanity in an individual sense, an act against another person does not directly touch the *imago* except in an ethical sense. Because God, as the *Thou* who constitutes the true orientation of the self, wills that I also love that which he loves, my fellow human being, I have an ethical obligation to support the life of each person whom God loves. This, however, makes love first of all an abstraction and only consequently a matter of immediate and practical concern. Our approach has been to locate the *imago* in the demand which co-humanity places on me, so that my determination of the good of the other is first of all anthropological and only consequently ethical. My abstract obligation to humanity as a moral responsibility is primarily determined by my concrete and specific encounter of the *imago* in the other.

The tendency among contemporary theologians to abandon concepts of the *imago Dei* which define the *humanum* as an ontological structure of human being, in favor of a "relational" concept by which the *imago Dei* is more the "function" of relating, is subject to the same criticism. Where "relating" becomes the equivalent of "loving," situational ethics replaces theological anthropology as determinative of human responsibility. To be sure, there are severe problems with the medieval notion of the *imago* as a "substance" or "faculty" of human existence which can be identified and defined metaphysically; but to abandon any ontological basis for the *imago* in favor of an existentialist or sociological function is not only unbiblical but ethically impotent.

How can one deny that the *imago Dei* is fundamentally a structure of co-humanity? asks Karl Barth:

> Is it not palpable that we have to do with a clear and simple correspondence, an *analogia relationis*, between this mark of the divine being, namely that it includes an I and a Thou, and the being of man, male and female? The relationship between the summoning I in God's being and the summoned divine Thou is reflected both in the relationship of God to the man whom he created, and also in the relationship between the I and the Thou, between male and female, in human existence itself. There can be no question of anything more than an analogy.[4]

"Is it not astonishing," Barth exclaims,

> that again and again expositors have ignored the definitive explanation given by the text itself (Genesis 1:26-27), and instead of reflecting on it pursued all kinds of arbitrarily invested interpretations of the *imago Dei*? ... Could anything be more obvious than to conclude from this clear indication that the image and likeness of the being created by God signified existence in confrontation, i.e., in this confrontation, juxtaposition and conjunction of man and man which is that of male and female. . . .[5]

There is no "connective tissue" which ties human being to divine being, even by "analogy," Barth argues. One cannot ascend "hand over hand," by way of an ontological "umbilical cord," from human being to the being of God. Thus Barth not only rejects the Thomistic doctrine of the analogy of being (*analogia entis*), but he rejects the claims of a natural theology which attempts to begin with the assumption of correspondence between the human and divine and establish criteria for our knowledge of or relation to God independently of God's gracious act of revelation.

Barth does not deny that there is an analogical relationship or correspondence between human being and divine being. But he adds that "the analogy of relation does not entail likeness, but the correspondence of the unlike . . . a dissimilar repetition of the fact that the one God is in Himself not only I but also I and Thou. . . ."[6] From the revelation of God in Jesus Christ, Barth argues, we now can see the differentiation within the very being of God himself. God exists in a polarity of being, made visible to us in the relation of Father to the

---

4. *Church Dogmatics*, III/1, 196.
5. *Ibid.*, 195. For a criticism of Barth's argument at this point, cf. G. C. Berkouwer, *Man—The Image of God* (Grand Rapids: Eerdmans, 1962), pp. 93ff.
6. *Church Dogmatics*, III/1, 196.

Son and Son to the Father. In this relation, God encounters himself as Father, Son, and Spirit. In the humanity of God the Son, the true correspondence is established between human being as "image-bearer" and divine being as that which constitutes the objective content of the "image." Now we can understand Adam, Barth would claim; now we can see why Adam as the solitary male could never bear the divine image and likeness. There is no "correspondence" between Adam as solitary male and the divine being, because the image must also be experienced as differentiation of being. Thus Genesis 1:27 gives a true explication of the image as well as stating it as the basis of the human: "In the image of God he created him; male and female he created them." The woman "answers back" to the being of the man, even as the man "answers back" to the being of the woman. The correspondence between human being and divine being is not just a metaphysical or formal correspondence; it is a correspondence which is experienced as the material content of human existence.

The "dissimilarity" in the correspondence between the human and the divine is qualitative. *Being* is not a continuum with human being at one end and divine being at the other end. Human being is created being, and as such it stands in an absolute disjunction from the being of God who is the Creator. However, it is in the act of creation and not subsequent to it that God endows the human creature with his own image and likeness. This means that the *imago Dei* as a technical concept of the essence of humanity as *humanum* is first of all a differentiation between God and the creature who bears his image. Only in a secondary sense and as a consequence is the human person differentiated from other creatures.

Here we can see more clearly the significance of correspondence as the distinctive aspect of the *imago Dei*. Adam has a solidarity of being with the other creatures in that both are created and creaturely—of the dust of the ground. However, there is no "co-response" in Adam's relation to the creatures. There is no encounter of being in such a way that the other creatures differentiate the being of Adam in a subjective sense. Yet, between God and Adam, where there is dissimilarity of being rather than similarity, there is "co-response," correspondence of being. God speaks to Adam and Adam hears. The speech creates the hearing. The Word of God creates the response. Word and response to the Word thus constitute a single event, yet differentiated in terms of speaking and hearing.

One should not confuse communication with correspondence at this point. Humans can communicate with animals at a creaturely level, and one can suppose that there is a form of communication between animals—probably at a deeper level than ordinarily assumed. Communication presupposes similarity of being or of nature. Correspondence, however, as an event in which one being is differentiated from another and yet encounters the other in such a way that an I-Self emerges or is affirmed, is qualitatively different. Correspondence of being in this sense includes communication also. But communication based on similarity does not and cannot include correspondence. For correspondence must be established through the encounter of one being by another. The Creator can encounter the creature and in addressing the creature can differentiate the creature in terms of a subjective relation. Adam is the *thou* to whom God speaks, and thus becomes the *I* in correspondence to the *Thou* of God to whom he responds.

The Word which establishes this correspondence is therefore a gracious word. Its source is in the freedom of God, not only to create, but to give his own Word to the creature and thus create a response. The dissimilarity is never overcome, but rather continues as the "leading edge" of grace in every encounter between God and human persons. This is why Adam and Eve continue to bear the *imago* even after disobeying God and turning away from him. They have no power to efface that which is itself an endowment of grace. God continues to address the person who has turned away from him. The human can never become merely creaturely, for it bears the image and likeness of God, even in a state of alienation. The continuity of the *imago Dei* in the sinner does not condition grace, as though there remains some human "good" which grace presupposes. Thus "total depravity" does not exclude a concept of continuing to be a sinner and bearing the *imago*. This is how one can understand Calvin's concept of "common grace," by which the sovereign grace of God sustains all persons, even unbelievers, in their humanity.

We conclude this part of our discussion by reiterating the importance of the *imago Dei* as a fundamental assumption for theological anthropology. We have argued that the *imago* is essential humanity experienced concretely and particularly in terms of each person's human existence. The continuity of the *humanum* through the process of creaturely reproduction and despite the contradiction of sin can be accounted for by the fact that each human person bears this *imago Dei* as an indispensable structure of being human itself. In our discussion, we pointed out that we were more interested in exploring the significance of the *imago* for a theology of human personhood than in arguing an abstract and technical point. Being human thus means being in the image of God as a particular person. It is to this aspect of the *imago* that we now turn.

2. Being in the Image of God

FREEDOM IN DEPENDENCE

The divine Word came not to all creatures, nor to just any creature, but to Adam and Eve in particular. Yet it did not come to them as creatures; rather, in hearing the Word they became creatures who bore the image and likeness of God in their very creaturely being. In dependence on the divine Word for their very existence, they were free. The creaturely world does not know the words freedom and bondage, nor does it know that creaturely being is absolutely determined by a creaturely nature. It has no word or speech, but this silence is not experienced as absence of the Word. This is quite different from the alienation or sense of bondage the human person can experience. For the human creature, having been given the Word, cannot live humanly without it. It is free and knows that it is free, but this freedom depends on the source of the Word.

Philosophical anthropology, particularly that which is based on the motif of existentialist thought, posits a dialectical tension between a sense of freedom and necessity as the very core of human selfhood. Knowing oneself as unbound in spirit, the self also knows itself as bound in the flesh. Out of this tension the self is born in anxiety, and must pass through "dread" on the way to a higher self linked with the eternal by means of the passion of "faith." It was Kierkegaard who gave the most original and clearest articulation to this concept of human personhood; and Reinhold Niebuhr, drawing on his insights, posited human nature as essentially caught in this dialectic of freedom and necessity.[7] In this model, freedom is always in tension with necessity, the human spirit is always caught in the inescapable net of mortality, and the self is rooted in anxiety.

This is not the biblical concept of freedom as a distinctive component of the *imago Dei*. Freedom must be understood from a theological perspective before it can be discussed as an existential perception. Freedom does not happen in the way existential anthropology explains it — as a result of the entrance of sin into the world as the critical point of authentic selfhood. Before the fall, and in the person of Jesus Christ, freedom is expressed as instinctive response to the source of the Word, which comes to the human person and which becomes a human person. This freedom produced by the Word is not simply the spirit of the infinite "tugging at the human soul." Human freedom is not a freedom *from* that which binds the self, but a freedom *for* that which determines the self. Adam and Eve experience themselves in a freedom of fellowship and response to the very source of their creaturely life — the Lord God. There is no fundamental anxiety or tension which posits the self at the juncture of the infinite and the finite. Being the finite creature that he is, Adam has freedom which knows itself to depend on the source of life and being

---

7. Cf. S. Kierkegaard, *Sickness Unto Death* (Princeton: Princeton U.P., 1954, 1969); *The Concept of Dread* (Princeton U.P., 1944); and Reinhold Niebuhr, *The Nature and Destiny of Man: A Christian Interpretation*, Vol. 1 (New York: Scribners, 1943).

itself. It is the freedom to be for God — and therefore for all that is the deter-mination of God. Thus, Adam is also free for creation, and for his own crea-tureliness as the object of the Creator's determination.

For all creatures but the human, creaturely nature determines destiny. There is no way for creatures to escape being what their nature determines them to be. A creature's destiny is determined by a creaturely nature; and creaturely life itself becomes "fate," in the sense that whatever befalls the creature "naturally" becomes the fate of the creature. The human creature, in dependence on the determination of the Creator's summons to be in relation, escapes the blind determination of creaturely nature itself. It escapes existence under the edict by which nature becomes fate. It is given a destiny which lies quite outside the determination of its own creaturely nature. This destiny is the determination of the creative divine Word. Biblically, it is expressed by the summons into the seventh day, the day of God's own perfection and rest. No other creature of God's making participates in the destiny of the seventh day. This is the biblical concept of freedom: not to be determined by the creature of the sixth day, but to be drawn into the seventh day by a determination which is experienced as a creaturely life of solidarity with creation, but oriented toward fellowship and participation in the life of God.

The kind of freedom we are considering here is not the same as the autonomy of the human self — a kind of neutrality by which the self exists independently of God's determination, free to move one way or the other. Rather, human freedom is the result of a determination to be oriented toward God as an eternal source of life. In this determination to be free toward God, to be a creature in fellowship with God, the attribute of existence with the other is also given. One implication of the endowment of freedom as summons into the seventh day is freedom to be for the other. Even as God is in himself free to be for his own creation and for the human creature, to which he gives his own Word and Spirit, so the human person exists in the image and likeness of the Creator, which is the freedom of co-humanity. Adam knows this freedom in his discovery of Eve as the one who meets him in the reality of a truly personal and human relation. This freedom, which he could discover in no other creaturely being, came to him as a total surprise when he awoke. It came out of no presupposition within creation or within his own imagination.

Again it is instructive that the Genesis 2 account of creation offers an unsophisticated and yet profoundly theological critique of the concept of the image and likeness of God experienced as freedom for the other. In this second chapter of Genesis — which may be seen as an "as if" commentary on Genesis 1:26-27 — the implicit question is: what if the Creator had made the first human being as a solitary male, with no other being for him to encounter? Could the man have found within the possibilities of the created natural world a counterpart, or partner for himself?

And so the story of creation is told again, this time from the perspective of the sixth day looking backward into itself rather than forward to the seventh day. God's judgment on the existence of the solitary man is that such existence is not good. Consequently, other creaturely beings are formed out of the dust of the ground and brought to the man to see "what he would call them." This naming of the animals was certainly more than a task of sorting the creatures into zoological categories. In naming them, the man was searching for that encounter with his own being which would free him to experience himself as addressed and recognized by another, as a *Thou*, for which he could become the corresponding *I*. One way of visualizing the story is to imagine Adam as becoming more and more desperate and unfulfilled with each failure to experience this "image" in the animals he named. With each new animal that God brings to him as a possible "counterpart," we can think of Adam as experiencing deeper anguish of his own being—only to have it end with failure.

Finally, the story tells us, God saw that there was no "counterpart" to be be found for Adam. Even the Creator himself could not find any possibilities within the natural creation that would satisfy the need for the human to find completion in another. Putting Adam to sleep, God took his despair and loneliness, which had become intense and unbearable, and divided it. He divided the loneliness and he turned it face to face; and Adam, awakened, says at last: "This is bone of my bone and flesh of my flesh." The last conscious thought of Adam as he falls asleep under the divine will is of absolute hopelessness. How could he have fallen asleep with hope? The Creator himself had failed to find within creation a partner and counterpart to his own being. But then he awakens in the morning and reaches out and exclaims, "There is somebody in my bed!"

Certainly such a reading of Genesis 2 takes some liberties with the text! But we must insist on the point being made here. There are no possibilities for the completion of the human person within the first six days of creation. There is no source of freedom from this deadly determination of nature itself, from this hopeless fate. The true source of the human experience of freedom to be for another and to know oneself is in the divine determination to exist as co-humanity; or, as the basic text in Genesis 1:26-27 tells us, to exist in the image of God, male and female. This existence for and with the other is the source of the openness of being which issues in speech, hearing, and love. It is the freedom not only to exist, but to exist "gladly" as Barth puts it:

> This means that if we are to embrace human nature as such, as created
> and given by God, then we must grasp as its motivating element the

decisive point that man is essentially determined to be with his fellow-man gladly, in the indicated freedom of the heart. By nature he has no possibility or point of departure for any other choice. If we have to maintain that he has this choice in fact, it does not derive from his nature. For we cannot make God his Creator responsible for this fatal possibility. And it is even worse if we praise the Creator for obviously giving man the possibility of a different choice. For this is to praise Him for allowing and enabling man to choose in his heart inhumanity as well as humanity, and therefore to be in his heart inhuman as well as human, or both perhaps alternatively. And we then ascribe to human nature the strange distinction of a freedom for its own denial and destruction. We should not call this freedom nature, but sin.[8]

To esteem "freedom of choice" as an expression of individual autonomy and the basis of human dignity and responsibility is to miss the point. The so-called freedom to be the "master of my fate, the captain of my soul" is at bottom joyless and cheerless. For this is a freedom which denies dependence on the other as the source of one's own personhood. This "freedom of choice," Barth rightly reminds us, is what lies behind the fall of humanity, not its emergence into true personhood. We are not only determined by the other, and ultimately and originally by God, but we are made to respond in such a way that we do this "gladly," in joyful recognition of our own being. This is the image and likeness of God.

RESPONSIBILITY IN HEARING

As a second component of "being in the image of God," let us now look at the uniqueness of human being as that which is the consequence of "hearing" the Word of God. Earlier we said that speech creates hearing. It is not the case that the Word of God presupposes a possibility of hearing in the creature and then speaks. God addresses the creature in creating it, and it is created with the response-ability which appropriately constitutes it in relation with the Creator himself.

It is noteworthy that in the Genesis account of creation, the author tells us that the things created came into being as a result of a divine fiat: "Let there be. . . ." But on the sixth day, when God summoned the man and woman into being, he immediately addressed them as those who now have response-ability. The "hearing" of God's Word by the original man and woman is itself both a distinctively human quality of being and a mark of the image and likeness of God. Up to this point, there is no indication that creation or any

---

8. *Church Dogmatics*, III/2, 273.

other creature has this capacity or responsibility of "hearing." In a certain sense, creation is mute, it has no word of response; it hears no word or sound of the Creator. Creatures other than the human will never be judged for not hearing, for "deafness." However, the human person emerges from the event of the Word spoken and heard, which is given and received. It is not that the first human creature had the capacity to hear and then the freedom to respond to the Word addressed to it; rather, like Lazarus being raised from the dead (John 11), hearing one's name called is itself life in response to the calling.

This response-ability lies solely in being addressed, in being chosen and summoned into response. It does not lie buried in some prenatal or prepersonal moral or religious sense of the creatureliness itself. To be human is to be responsible to hear and follow the determination of the Word of God. Refusal to hear is disobedience. Consequently, because humanity exists only under the address of the divine Word, there is no authentic human disobedience. Disobedience is wilfully not to hear the divine command, and is therefore a denial of one's own humanity. There is no escape from this Word which summons into life:

> Thou dost beset me behind and before,
>   and layest thy hand upon me.
> Such knowledge is too wonderful for me;
>   it is high, I cannot attain it.
> Whither shall I go from thy Spirit?
>   Or whither shall I flee from thy presence?
> If I ascend to heaven, thou art there!
> If I make my bed in Sheol, thou art there!
> If I take the wings of the morning
>   and dwell in the uttermost parts of the sea,
> even there thy hand shall lead me,
>   and thy right hand shall hold me.
> If I say, "Let only darkness cover me,
>   and the light about me be night,"
> even the darkness is not dark to thee,
>   the night is bright as the day;
>   for darkness is as light with thee (Ps. 139:5-12).

There is no escape from the divine Word that forms us in the image and likeness of God. Wilfully or blindly to choose not to hear is disobedience more cruel and destructive than the natural deafness and muteness of the beasts. The grounds for human accountability do not lie in a natural capacity or ability to choose to hear, but in the knowledge of one's own unwillingness to hear and to respond. The muteness of my dog is no act of cruelty against me, but the silence and not hearing of my human friend is an offense to my very being.

This was brought to my attention quite forcefully during preparation for a family dinner. While I was preoccupied with slicing the Easter ham, my six-year-old granddaughter was constantly besieging me with questions which brought no response. Finally, she asked indignantly, "Grandpa, can't you hear?".

Without thinking, I responded, "I can hear, but I'm not listening." This provoked some laughter, but it struck me as a serious symptom of a deeper affliction. Were I deaf, she could not have been hurt. But for me to say, "Yes, I can hear, but I'm not listening," was a moment in which our common humanity was suspended. That is inhuman.

Perhaps we can now understand better the biblical reiteration that the Word of God "makes deaf." Isaiah was commissioned to go out and speak the message of God (Isa. 6), but this commission was accompanied by a strange instruction: this proclamation of the Word of Yahweh would "Make the heart of this people fat, and their ears heavy, and shut their eyes; lest they see with their eyes, and hear with their ears, and understand with their hearts, and turn and be healed" (Isa. 6:10). This Word, which is the source of human life itself, will, when addressed to those who are inhumanly turned against the one who speaks, produce deafness: that is, it will reveal the already existing deafness and hardness of heart. Jesus cites this passage as the purpose of his parables (Matt. 13:14), and John quotes it to account for the unbelief Jesus' ministry produced (John 12:39-40). It is used by Paul to explain why some resisted the Word of God which he taught (Acts 28:26); and in a letter to the Corinthian church, he suggests that this "hardness of hearing" is the veil which comes over those who refuse to hear the Word of God which testifies to Christ (2 Cor. 3:14-15).

Being in the image of God is not a religious overlay on our natural humanity. On the contrary, being in the image of God is itself fundamental to our true humanity. Without the freedom to be for God and the other, we are living in contradiction to our basic humanity. To live in such a way as to resist the Word and will of God in favor of our own instinctive rights and desires is to live inhumanly, not just nonreligiously. Later this will be the basis of our discussion of the implications of renewal and redemption through the grace of Christ. The removal of the "old nature" when a "new nature" is bestowed through regeneration of our humanity is not the taking away of our own humanity or personal identity, but the opening up again of our true self. It is like the restoration of sight to one blind from birth, like enabling one who is hopelessly deaf to hear, like calling Lazarus back out of the tomb into the bright sunlight of his own human life. Being in the image of God is being once again response-able in hearing and obeying the divine Word.

DIFFERENTIATION IN UNITY

The *imago Dei* is a personal and existential way of being in the world which is predicated on a specific endowment of creaturely existence. Responsibility and freedom are just two aspects of the multidimensional reality of the human person. This personal existence is contingent to the world; that is, human personhood is not supported by structures of reality inherent in creaturely nature itself. The divine Word summons the creaturely self into communion with God's own life in such a way that the human person never becomes divine. There continues to be a di-polar relation between the Word of God which creates and sustains human personhood and the existence of the self in its own being. Thus the human person never becomes an undifferentiated extension of divine personality. In addition to freedom and responsibility, therefore, the *imago Dei* is manifested as being-in-differentiation. This is a technical way of expressing the straightforward biblical statement that in the image of God he made them, male and female he made them.

The human self, experienced existentially as a particular expression of being-in-the world, is not differentiated merely by virtue of particularity. This is both the insight and the weakness of Kierkegaard's philosophical anthropology. Undoubtedly because of his "Cartesian" starting point, Kierkegaard saw clearly that particularity is essential to human personhood, for the self exists as a fundamental and concrete expression of human being. Despite his horror at the prevailing idealism of his own time (represented by the thought of Hegel), Kierkegaard began with the self as an existing subject — which is methodologically the same as Descartes' beginning with the self as a thinking subject. The existing self thus differentiates itself from all else, even other subjects, in order to reach the particularity of personal being so essential to being itself. Not only did Kierkegaard have no concept of the I-Thou relation, as it would later be developed by Martin Buber, but he also had a condescending attitude toward sexuality, to say the least. Kierkegaard viewed sexuality as a limitation of being at the creaturely level; and in particular he saw female being as the weaker and more ineffective form of creaturely being.

We will consider the implications of human sexuality for theological anthropology more fully in Chapter Eight. But it is important here to set forth briefly the fundamental polarity of personal being which is characterized by the *imago* as "male and female." God apparently exists as a differentiation in unity, revealed to us through the economy of redemption as God the Father, Son, and Holy Spirit. The essence of this differentiation is a polarity of being characterized by the presence of being at each point. Father and Son may be seen as the dimension of polarity, with Spirit being the dimension of presence at each point in the polarity.

Bearing in mind that an analogy is a relation of the unlike, we see a correspondence between the being of God and human being characterized as the *imago Dei*. Human being is also a fundamental polarity of being; the unity of being here, however, is not a third dimension (as in the being of God) but is God himself, as the three-beings-in-one who represents the "middle term" of human being. God is a triune being, human being is not. Yet, the *imago* which determines the nature of human being comes to expression as a polarity in which God himself participates. This is one way of understanding why Adam as the single human creature, despite his relation with God, is not complete in his creaturely humanity. Adam does not experience himself as a differentiation in unity, though he experiences the differentiation as a creature *vis-à-vis* the Creator. But this form of differentiation is more like that of existential anthropology, in which the existence of the self is itself the ground of the differentiation in an absolute sense. With the creation of the woman, as explained in Genesis 2, the differentiation of human being is now experienced at the creaturely level itself. However, this fundamental polarity of being would become a division of being, rather than simply a difference in being, except for the unifying structure of God's participation in the relation. The "two can become one" because this too is a determination of God.

It is crucial at this point to see that this fundamental polarity of personal being is experienced at the creaturely level as the only form of the differentiation. This means that the differentiation must necessarily be found in the creaturely form of male and female sexuality. For the human to exist at all it must exist as particular, concrete creaturely being. Thus, one is either male or female and must experience co-humanity as such. Male or female establishes the fundamental particularly of one's own being. Male and female expresses the polarity in terms of co-humanity. We can now see the implication of this for the concept of the *imago Dei*.

If we are to hold that the *imago Dei* is essentially relational with respect to "being in the image of God," then the relation itself must be ontological, not merely ethical or functional. That is, the relation must be an essential structure of being in which there is a polarity or differentiation capable of experiencing unity of being through relating. Therefore, we hold that human sexuality at the creaturely level — that is, being male or female — is linked in some way to the fundamental polarity of being which is the *imago Dei* itself. Subsequently we shall see how this can be held without projecting "gender identity" or creaturely sexual distinctives into God's being. The point here is that differentiation in unity is one significant component of the *imago Dei*, and that this differentiation cannot be viewed abstractly or ideally, but concretely and particularly in each individual person.

This, as we indicated at the beginning of the chapter, is something of what is at stake in the concept of the *imago Dei* for theological anthropology. Human persons are not identical with the *imago*, but bear the *imago* in the form of the human itself (the *humanum* which each person bears). This *imago* endowment, which causes the creaturely being that we call a human person to exist, is not a subsequent endowment on an already-existing human-like being. Because the *imago* is borne by the human person in the form of the human itself (*humanum*), there is continuity of the *imago*, even through the fall and as a sinner.

Being in the image of God, we have shown, is to experience the freedom and response-ability which the Word of God itself creates in and for the human person. There is, to be sure, a contradiction in the face of all that has been said. Human being is in some sense distorted being, even as and especially because it is human being. We would prefer to say that distorted human being is sinful rather than merely sick. For we believe that in the concept of sin there is more hope than in the concept of disease. To elucidate that hope we look directly at the contradiction as that which is, even in all of its sordidness and pitiableness, human — and therefore loved of God.

CHAPTER SEVEN

BEING HUMAN—
IN CONTRADICTION AND IN HOPE

> Almighty and most merciful Father: we have erred and strayed from thy ways like lost sheep. We have followed too much the devices and desires of our own hearts. We have offended against thy holy laws. We have left undone those things which we ought to have done; and we have done those things which we ought not to have done; and there is no health in us (The Morning Prayer of the Episcopal Church).

THERE IS NO HEALTH IN US! THIS IS THE REFRAIN WHENEVER AND wherever honest people take stock of themselves and of their own generation. In every story of the deeds and days of human beings on this earth, the powerful and sorrowful ingredients recur: grief, regret, contradiction, confusion. There appears to be something tragic about the human condition. The finest aspirations and the highest dreams are shot through with failure. Something is working against the human heart. There is something wrong.

Possibly it is we ourselves who carry the tragic flaw and spread the fatal disease like some virus carried unknowingly from one generation to another. Out of all creatures, the human person is most likely to foul his own nest. We do not live in some Garden of Eden, with innocence spilling over from every drink of the cup of life. Rather, as Arthur Miller tells us in *After the Fall*:

> We are very dangerous...! We meet unblessed; not in some garden of wax fruit and painted leaves, that lie of Eden, but after, after the Fall, after many, many deaths.... And the wish to kill is never killed, but with some gift of courage one may look into its face when it appears, and with a stroke of love—as to an idiot in the house— forgive it; again and again ... forever?

SIN AS A THEOLOGICAL PROBLEM

This fundamental flaw has not escaped the attention of theologians through the ages. Being human is being in contradiction and in hope. This is a theological statement of the problem. Being in contradiction is itself not a theological statement. We can document the contradictions experienced at both the existential and sociological levels of humanity as empirically true. The hope is not so easily documented. In fact, apart from a theological anthropology, it has no basis in reality. If people do hope, it is, in many cases, "against hope." Our concern in this chapter is not only to show that a theological anthropology can and must deal with the contradiction which being human involves as personal existence, but also to unfold the connection between hope and contradiction in such a way that both are seen as part of a structure of reality.

In the history of theology the doctrine of sin is a fundamental tenet of belief, in both the Jewish and Christian traditions. Even thinkers outside the biblical tradition have made some attempt to explain the origin and nature of evil to their contemporaries.

The Greek philosophers explained human disorder and contradiction in terms of the ignorance and finitude which clung to the immortal soul as it came into contact with the temporal and physical world through birth. In becoming enfleshed, the immortal soul is necessarily subjected to the limitations of finitude. Thus it exists in a state of ignorance, as the source of eternal knowledge and life are eclipsed by temporal limitations. The physical body, which seemed to constitute this limitation, was considered as a sort of "prison" for the soul, limiting it in a way that brought pain and frustration. The Greeks therefore looked on death as freeing the soul once more to become immediately aware of the eternal knowledge and life which constitutes the essence of reality. This gave death a "soteriological" significance, as it constituted the deliverance of the soul from its bondage as embodied person. And so Socrates could face his own death, which was meant as a punishment for subverting the minds of the youth, with a sense of hope and positive expectation. A true Greek philosopher, he could long for the freedom of his intellectual soul from the finitude and limitations of the human body.

This is in marked contrast with the Hebrews who were contemporary with these Greek philosophers. The person, for the Hebrews, includes both body and soul. Thus death was viewed as a dissolution of the basic unity of body and soul, and therefore as a loss of life. Far from being a deliverance from the contradiction of sin, death was seen as a punishment for sin which brings the sinner under divine judgment. "You shall die in your sins," is the biblical warning from beginning to end. Paul linked death with sin in his defense of the claim that all are sinners needing salvation through grace (Rom. 5:12-21).

As Christian doctrine developed following the New Testament period, however, theologians came under the influence of Greek concepts of sin. In the third century, Origen taught that the human soul existed prior to its embodiment in a human person. In this pre-existent state, he speculated, the soul acted in some way that incurred divine disfavor; consequently, it was "sentenced" to a life on earth and subjected to the limitations and humiliation of a human body. According to this teaching, there is a certain antipathy between the soul and the body. Rather than accepting the terms of its bodily existence as determining its own state of being, the soul must resist and seek a higher spiritual life.

Sin enters into the world, according to Origen, through the birth of the soul in the form of a human person. The material or physical form of life, then, is not the source of sin, but rather the punishment or judgment inflicted on the soul. Human existence under the conditions of bodily life must then become the occasion for the soul to "work out its own salvation," which will ultimately occur when it is released from the body through death to return purified and perfected to its original state. One can thus understand the theological motivation behind Origen's mutilation of his own body by castration: renouncing bodily pleasure is one form of "atonement" for sin, which has its source in some spiritual deficiency in the soul itself. As a result of his particular philosophical anthropology, he interpreted many New Testament texts in such a way as to support his attempt to "mortify the flesh" in hope of freeing the spirit (soul).

We see here the importance of the assumptions anthropology brings to the theological task. This, too, is why a theological anthropology is critical as a basis from which to understand the doctrines of the atonement, justification, and sanctification. Fortunately for the church, this particular teaching of Origen was discredited by other theologians and abandoned by the end of the third century. In fairness to Origen we must add that he expressed a firm commitment to the orthodox doctrine of salvation through Christ's work on the cross. Certain subtle influences remained, however, principally in the form of a dualism between the physical and spiritual aspect of human personhood, with a tendency to view the physical or bodily component as inherently evil, or at least an impediment to true spirituality.

Augustine followed more closely Paul's position that each person inherits a sinful nature as a result of the original defection of Adam from God's will. Because of this sinful nature, each human person is "born of sin" and actually does sin. Everyone, Augustine taught, is by nature depraved and incapable of restoring himself or herself to righteousness. Not that each person is as bad a person as he or she could possibly be; but each is totally incapable of restoration to an original state of grace through any effort of the self, including the good one might possibly do. This meant, according to Augustine, that each person is in a state of solidarity with Adam, who committed the original sin. Each person is guilty of Adam's sin in that Adam is supposed to have acted as the "federal head" of the entire race. Human persons do not have a "choice," therefore, when it comes to sinning. Each person will inevitably sin and thereby confirm his or her sinful nature.

Augustine's contemporary Pelagius denied that each person is formed with a sinful nature and thus inherits both sin and guilt. Rather, he argued, everyone is born into a state of innocence like Adam before the fall. No one is a sinner until he or she commits a personal act of sin against God. Sin is the result of a free act of the human will, rather than an inevitable act caused by an inveterate disposition of human nature.

The controversy between Augustine and Pelagius set the stage for the divergent views regarding sin and salvation which were to prevail through the medieval period and even into the Reformation itself. If sin is inevitable because it is caused by inheriting a sinful nature, as Augustine taught, then salvation will also be the inevitable and determined result of a divine act of grace based on God's predestination of the person for salvation. For Pelagius, who saw sin as the result of an individual act of rebellion against God, the possibility of not sinning at all is a very real one. He therefore argued that salvation is a possibility for each person based on a free decision to repent and seek God's favor.

The sixteenth-century Reformers, particularly Luther and Calvin, were Augustinian with regard to sin as a fundamental aspect of human nature. Both held that human persons, born with a fallen nature, cannot keep from sinning, because they are infected with the original sin of Adam. Every newborn infant inherits not only the guilt which accrues from Adam's sin but also a disposition which is itself "turned toward sin" and away from God. Consequently, each person is under judgment (and the penalty of death) from the moment of birth. This does not free a person from responsibility, but it does mean that at the age of accountability, each person must affirm for himself or herself that which has been affirmed on his or her behalf by the church — that one is saved only by the free grace of God given through the death and resurrection of Christ.

Opposing this teaching — and Calvin's formulation of it in particular — was Jacobus Arminius (1560-1609), who taught that persons were not born guilty of sin, but actually became guilty upon committing personal sin. Arminius, however, did not take the radical position that each person is born in the same state as Adam before the fall. Contrary to Pelagius, Arminius taught that there is a "spirit-given" freedom — rather than a natural freedom — not to sin. Everyone inherits some "corruption" of nature, expressed as a disposition toward sin. This "semi-Pelagian" position became the modern counterpart to the earlier Augustinian/Pelagian debate. Again the critical point is the anthropological one: is human nature essentially sinful and incapable of pleasing God, or is

91

human nature neutral with regard to sin and grace, with the result depending on "freedom of choice?"

To a large extent, whether one has a negative or positive view of human nature will determine many other doctrines in the theological curriculum. If one rejects the idea that human nature intrinsically lacks spiritual or moral worth, the concept of sin will be linked more with behavior than with being. This will also affect the concept of guilt and divine judgment, with guilt becoming more subjective than objective, and divine judgment coming under question itself as at least unfair, if not immoral.

This, of course, is exactly what took place during the eighteenth and nineteenth centuries. Under the positive mood of the Enlightenment and the Age of Reason there was a significant move away from the Augustinian concept of human nature as basically sinful. With the rise of rationalism and an evolutionary philosophy of human origins, the concept of sin as personal guilt tended to be discarded in favor of an impersonal concept of evil as that which is "alien to human existence." Viewed thus, evil must be dealt with by attacking those structures of thought and practice which limit or deprive persons in their growth toward maturity. Both Arminianism and Calvinism held to a concept of sin that had to do with personal moral agency. Transformed into a concept of impersonal evil, however, sin no longer issues from personal agency, whether a person sins "freely" because of an inherited disposition toward sin (Arminius) or necessarily because of an inherited sinful nature (Calvin).

Both Arminianism and Calvinism taught the necessity of personal salvation through the grace of God in Christ, including the atonement for sin which takes place through death and resurrection. However, when sin becomes impersonal evil, it is no longer seen as the act of a moral agent but as a metaphysical notion. It follows that guilt and atonement are reckoned to be crude anthropomorphisms which create an angry God in the image of the guilt-ridden sinner. The more positive view of the human person as intrinsically "reasonable" and thus capable of moral development through enlightened reason makes sin an unthinkable concept, an unwarrantedly negative view of human nature. Disorder at the human level comes to be attributed to sociological, psychological, intellectual, economic, or political structures which have become evil because they intimidate or suppress the development and freedom of the natural goal of the human self. And redemption from evil no longer has its roots in divine grace directly affecting the nature of a person, but is located in the process of adjustment, reorganization, restructuring, or even revolutionizing the conditions under which the human exists.

Here again, the radical break between the post-Enlightenment concept of sin and salvation and the traditional view, espoused not only by Calvin but also Arminius, is significant. The critical break, we will argue, is at the point of anthropology. How one views the nature of the human person will to a large extent determine one's explanation for disorder and contradiction as well as one's hopes for the achievement of a true order. Sin as a theological problem is essentially the problem of how one should account for the obvious distress and contradiction which exists at the level of human existence. Seeking to set forth the beginning of a theological anthropology, we must look more carefully at this distress and disorder as a symptom of true humanity.

SIN AS A SIGN OF HUMAN DISORDER

Sooner or later, everyone laments that there seems to be something wrong from the very beginning. "Behold," writes David the Psalmist, "I was brought forth in iniquity, and in sin did my mother conceive me" (Ps. 51:5). The Psalmist confesses that he is a sinner because he has done that which is wrong, but he also sees this act as an indication of a deeper disorder. Something has gone awry from the beginning. The defection is rooted in the very origin of his personal history. It is as though some dreadful thing has attached itself to the core of his being, and he can neither shake it loose nor forget it.

Certainly this sense of dread (or, to use a more psychological expression, "anxiety") is a more fundamental disorder — or at least disruption — in our being than an act of sin which may only be a symptom of that disorder. At this point one must ask the anthropological question, not just the ethical one. It is not merely, "Is this behavior right or wrong?", but, "Who am I to do this? Who am I to *wish* to do this? Who am I *not* to wish to do this but to do it anyway?" (cf. Rom. 7).

Following Kierkegaard's concept of the self, Reinhold Niebuhr explained the phenomenon of sin in terms of an intrinsic conflict or tension between the self as limited or bound to a physical existence and the self as unlimited and unbound as a free spirit. Niebuhr posits sin as the very presupposition of the self. He will not agree that the anxiety produced by this fundamental conflict and tension is sin; rather, he asserts that it is the constant state of temptation and is the inevitable source of sin as a defection of the self from its true origin and goal in divine love.[1] While the ideal possibility exists that faith will purge anxiety of the temptation to sinful self-assertion, this has been realized only in Christ, who was without sin. For every other human, sin is inevitable, but not necessary.[2] Sin presupposes itself, Niebuhr adds, thus identifying himself with the Augustinian position — though with an entirely dif-

---

1. *The Nature and Destiny of Man*, I, 182.
2. *Ibid.*, 251.

ferent concept of the nature of personhood. We could not be tempted except that we had already sinned. Temptation, thus existentially considered, presupposes sin as failure of the self to face the dread of existence as personal being responsibly—that is, with faith. Niebuhr argues that this concept of the inevitability of sin does not destroy personal freedom, for the self can contemplate this inevitability and acknowledge its own self-deception. Thus at the heart of Niebuhr's concept of the self is the paradox that the human person is most free in the discovery that he or she is not. We are responsible to have faith, even though that faith will carry with it the knowledge of our own failure. Thus, grace as the expression of divine love toward us is the basis for faith.

Although he is not a theologian, Ernest Becker gives a further theological exposition to this concept of sin in his book *The Denial of Death.* "Sin and neurosis are two ways of talking about the same thing," says Becker.[3] Neurosis is the result of our denying the reality or mortality of our creatureliness. Faced with the agonizing terror of being a self in light of the knowledge of ourselves as both a mortal body and an unlimited spirit, the existing self turns away from this task of becoming a person and reaches out for security in some manageable exercise with clearly defined limits. Faith, as the full expression of personal reality, means that one would be able to live before the divine Spirit in absolute freedom from this paralyzing conflict between the spirit and the flesh. One narrows down one's existence by identifying the self with what is within our grasp and control. In seeking to control our own existence and escape the terror of life, we become obsessed with what appears to give that sense of security and continuity. This, argues Becker, is not only neurotic behavior, but it is also a failure to become a person by risking oneself to the transcendent—to the idea of God. Therefore, sin and neurosis alike are symptoms of an underlying defection at the level of our true being.

We have referred here to Niebuhr and Becker simply to point out that there is an existential aspect to the question of sin which leads us to the question of what it is to exist as a person. It is one thing to define personhood in abstract or metaphysical terms. It is quite another to understand personhood from the perspective of an existing person. The closer one comes to the state of existing as a person, the more pronounced the connection between sin as objective behavior and sin as a state of being-in-anxiety (or, to use the biblical term, temptation). Is it really true that what theologians call sin is the same as what psychologists call neurosis? When we confess that "there is no health in us," are we referring to psychological distress as the source of all other distress, or is sin more "unhealthy" than sickness?

---

3. *The Denial of Death,* p. 196.

If anxiety or dread is a symptom of the disorder plaguing human persons, guilt can also be looked upon as a symptom. Feelings of guilt may certainly accompany a sense of existential anxiety or become the form in which "dread" is experienced. Is a sense of guilt evidence of sin, or is it also more a symptom of the disorder which afflicts most persons? From the perspective of ministering to persons in order to restore them to personal health or existential well-being, is guilt a positive motivation or an indication of the sickness and disorder itself? Will strong feelings of guilt drive one into the arms of God? I doubt it.

Note that we are speaking here of "feelings of guilt," not of the state of being which relates us objectively to the source of our being — God himself. Perhaps it would be helpful to see guilt as the symptom of being an idolater, rather than as a positive motivation toward grace and forgiveness. An idol is a "partializing" of the demand upon us to worship the transcendent as the source of our own being. Ernest Becker suggests that the transcendent comes to us as that which is holy or sacred. In the light of the demand to be holy, we seek something close at hand and manageable. And so we fabricate some object — or project on some other object or person — the worship we owe to the transcendent. Feelings of guilt now can become more negotiable in terms of payments we make to our "idol."

In this sense, guilt is a reminder of what is sacred to us and actually binds us to that object. Without a sense of guilt we would not need the "sacred object" as that which has the power both to give us life and take away our life. Guilt feelings then become embedded in rituals of worship. However, there is always a fundamental ambivalence about such worship. For the ultimate act of worship will be the destruction of the idol (god) which is the objectification of our guilt. Thus, the human person can finally become free from that debilitating guilt by destroying the god (idol) who is the source of it. Existentially, however, this cannot be sustained; and here lies the source of the ambivalence. Without a god upon which to project the need to be related to the transcendent, the terror returns; and so the guilt returns as a sense of existential inadequacy in light of the demands the transcendent makes upon us.

One could read the story told in Genesis 31 as a commentary on what we have just said. Jacob seeks to return home after twenty years of service for his uncle Laban. With two wives, two concubines, eleven sons, and one daughter, he sets out for the land of Abraham and Isaac. As the party was leaving — secretly, so as not to arouse Laban's attention — Rachel, unbeknownst to Jacob, "stole her father's household gods." When Laban discovers that the gods are missing, he overtakes Jacob and his company and demands the return of the gods. So confident is Jacob that no one of his company has them that he says, "Anyone with whom you find your gods shall not live" (Gen. 31:32). When a search is made of Rachel's tent, she successfully keeps them hidden, so that Laban returns empty-handed. Rachel is unable to let go of these gods and live out of the transcendent Word which is the source of the faith for Abraham, Isaac, and Jacob. After the return to Canaan, an unseemly incident occurs concerning Jacob's daughter Dinah, which results in the slaughter of an entire village by her two brothers. Jacob now understands that he must renegotiate the relation he has with God. Realizing now that Rachel has brought with her the household gods of Laban, he demands that these gods be destroyed before they go up to Bethel, where Yahweh must be approached as the holy one who cannot be manipulated or managed. The kind of unspecified guilt which causes a person to become "religiously" attached to idols is not an aid to true religion, but is a symptom of a deeper disorder which must be discovered and dealt with in terms of that Word of God which establishes the true order of our being.

As symptoms of disorder at the level of true humanity, anxiety and guilt are both more psychological than sociological, although they certainly have consequences beyond the individual's psychic distress. There is a symptom of the disorder of human persons which is manifest more as a sociological disorder, and that I will simply call inhuman behavior. Perhaps we primarily understand sin as this kind of inhumanity, particularly when it comes to expression as violent or cruel behavior. A crime of violence is a manifestation of sin, but also it is a symptom of much more. Behind the violent act which inhumanly affects other persons lies the kind of egocentricity which goes by the name of pride. Fundamentally this is a revolt against God at the I-Thou level, as is illustrated profoundly in Dostoevski's famous novel *Crime and Punishment*. Dostoevski shows that it is the murderer Raskolnikov who sins in the most horrible manner. He murders a pawnbroker because he is convinced that he, a brilliant student, will make a greater contribution to society than this worthless old woman. As Jaroslav Pelikan has put it:

> The murder of the old pawnbroker was a sin, but not merely because it was a breach of conventional morality. This made it a crime, not a sin. Raskolnikov's sin was brought on by his egocentricity, his assumption that his position in the universe was so important that he could suspend the existence of another person to advance his own ends. . . . Sin, therefore, was not the violation of some precept or prohibition, it was the assumption: I am God.[4]

---

4. *Fools for Christ* (Philadelphia: Muhlenberg Press, 1955), p. 74; cited by George W. Forrell, *The Protestant Faith* (Englewood Cliffs, N.J.: Prentice-Hall, 1960), p. 135.

No one can dispute that acts of violence against other persons are "crimes against humanity," not merely violent acts in and of themselves. What makes this particular form of violence so terrible is that it is a sign of a fundamental disorder of human being itself. Sociologists and psychologists can account for aberrant behavior as measured against a norm, but they cannot account for the fact that an inhuman act is also a sinful act. "Psychologically speaking," says George Forrell, "sin is pride. Theologically speaking, it is unbelief."[5] This is the basis for Paul's indictment of such behavior in the first chapter of his letter to the Romans:

> And since they did not see fit to acknowledge God, God gave them up to a base mind and to improper conduct. They were filled with all manner of wickedness, evil, covetousness, malice. Full of envy, murder, strife, deceit, malignity, they are gossips, slanderers, haters of God, insolent, haughty, boastful, inventors of evil, disobedient to parents, foolish, faithless, heartless, ruthless. Though they know God's decree that those who do such things deserve to die, they not only practice them but approve those who practice them (Rom. 1:28-32).

This is an accurate description of persons who live "inhumanly" and practice inhumanity in their relation to others. If one explains it by saying that it is egocentricity, or pride, is it enough to alter the behavior of such persons to bring them into conformity with society's standards?

In Peter Shaffer's gripping drama *Equus*, Alan Strang, a young boy, is placed under psychiatric treatment because he has driven a steel spike through the eyes of several horses under his care. This violent act was recognized to be as much a disorder of the boy's personhood as a crime against nature. Under psychiatric treatment, it is revealed that the boy is suffering a psychological-religious obsession; he believes that the god Equus looks out at him through the eyes of horses. A transference had occurred in this boy's religious life when his atheist father replaced a picture of Jesus hanging over his bed with the picture of a horse's head. When Strang is seduced by a girl in the stable in full view of the horses, he reacts violently, seizing a steel spike to blind the eyes of his "god," thus freeing himself from the guilt. As a result, he is left a seriously and mentally disturbed person.

As the psychiatrist unfolds the dynamics of the boy's life, he discovers that despite his psychotic nature Alan Strang is nevertheless in contact with a passion for transcendence and the holy totally absent from his own life. Bizarre and distorted though it may be, the boy worships and has passion. And the psychiatrist confesses, "When I in my comfortable, normal existence without any passion have not kissed my wife in years, this boy sucks the

---

5. *The Protestant Faith*, p. 136.

sweat off the flesh of his god. And I envy him." He goes on to say, "Yes, I can cure him, I can make him normal. He will only eat approved flesh at the end of his fork. His sexual parts shall become plastic and he shall ride on his mechanical horse over our paved streets."

But the psychiatrist still protests. There is no logic to curing. Even though a psychiatrist can remove passion he cannot create it. Worship cannot be transferred by removing a wire from one terminal and attaching it to another. Finally, however, giving in to those who urge him to make the boy well, the psychiatrist induces an abreaction; and Alan Strang is brought back into the reality of his life and his deed. As the boy lies shuddering on the threshold of his "healing," the psychiatrist stands over him and says,

> It's all over now, Alan, it's all over and he will go away now. You will never see him again, I promise. ... I'm lying to you, Alan, he won't really go that easily. Just clop away from you, like a nice old nag. Oh no, when Equus leaves, if he leaves at all, it will be with your intestines in his teeth. And I don't stock replacements. If you knew anything, you'd get up this minute and run from me as fast as you could.

Such troubled humanity is surely a symptom of some disorder — but what? Is it merely ethical deviance which has its source in some mysterious defiance of the will against what God has ordained? And why are some torments also so close to the truth of our humanity? "It is easier to lay down light burdens than heavy ones," Becker once said.[6] And somewhere in this mystery of human personhood, when we deal with the complexities of guilt, shame, and inhumanity, this morass of perplexity which accompanies us, we discover that there is more in that burden than mere psychological stress. Somewhere in all of this is probably our only touch with the sacred. And perhaps rather than us killing the god, perhaps we are the ones who are being "killed by grace." Stripped of our fig leaves, we can be clothed again and made whole. In the very midst of our contradiction, there is reconciliation. The burden that we cannot lay down is lifted from us.

SIN AS THE INVERSION OF THE IMAGO DEI

The image of God remains, despite the depths of inhumanity to which the human creature stoops:

> The fact that man sins does not mean that God ceases to be God, and therefore, man man. In this context, too, we must say that man does not accomplish a new creation by sinning. He cannot achieve any

---

6. *The Denial of Death*, p. 259.

essential alteration of the human nature which he has been given. He can only shame this nature and himself. He can only bring himself into supreme peril.[7]

However, this *imago*, which constitutes the *humanum* by which each person can be said to possess humanity as a creative work of God, becomes inverted when the human person turns away from God. We have already seen how this inversion works, as guilt becomes the basis for religious ritual as a way of self-reservation. Thus Barth concludes that the inverted form of the *imago Dei* is more pronounced in the religious form than in the nonreligious. "The religious relationship of man to God which is the inevitable consequence of his sin is a degenerate form of the covenant-relationship between the Creator and the creature. It is the empty and deeply problematical shell of that relationship."[8] From this perspective, we can now begin to trace out more clearly the nature of the disorder of which sin is the symptom at the existential and behavioral level.

Given our assumptions concerning the contingent relation of the human to the creaturely, it seems clear that this disorder is more than a sickness which can be cured by relieving a person from psychical distress. Voices within psychotherapy itself are expressing the same concern. Clinical psychiatrist O. Hobart Mowrer says:

> So long as we subscribe to the view that neurosis is a bona fide "illness", without moral implications or dimensions, our position will, of necessity, continue to be an awkward one. And it is here I suggest that, as between the concept of sin (however unsatisfactory it may in some ways be) and that of sickness, sin is indeed the lesser of two evils. We have tried the sickness horn of this dilemma and impaled ourselves upon it. Perhaps despite our erstwhile protestations, we shall yet find sin more congenial.[9]

Once we can deal with the category of sin, Mowrer continues, we are dealing objectively and not merely subjectively with distortion. Therefore, he says, we open up the possibilities of radical restoration and redemption.

Karl Menninger, another practicing psychotherapist, echoes Mowrer's opinion. "Sin is the only hopeful view. The present world miasma and depression are partly the result of our self-induced conviction that since sin has ceased to be, only the neurotics need to be treated and criminals punished."[10] The concept of sin as a "hopeful" perspective in treating people who suffer personality

---

7. Karl Barth, *Church Dogmatics*, III/2, 227.
8. *Ibid.*, IV/1, 483.
9. *The Crisis of Psychiatry and Religion* (Princeton: Van Nostrand, 1961), pp. 50-51.
10. *What Ever Became of Sin?* (New York: Hawthorne, 1973), p. 188.

disturbances is significant. Certainly accounting for personality disturbances as expressions of sin must be done with great caution. But the point both Mowrer and Menninger make is that the nature of the disorder may be such that a more radical confrontation with the very being of the person is required before true "order" can be restored. The possibility of this confrontation actually occurring and resulting in a restoration of personal existence under a proper order emerges only out of a theological anthropology. And such a possibility is implied by the actuality of personal being existing in a true order determined by the divine Word of God, experienced as the image and likeness of God in co-humanity.

Sin, therefore, originates in the inversion of the divine image. The human person seeks to set the self-conscious, subjective side of the self above its objective, unconscious side. A dichotomy emerges between the physical self, which is taken to be a blind and instinctual deterministic force, and the psychical self, with which one experiences the freedom of spirit. This disunity is the fundamental disorder, and from it flow both sinful actions and psychological disturbances. No longer can the *imago Dei* function as that which integrates the self in its orientation toward God and the other; instead the psychical energy of the self is used for self-defeating and self-destructive ends.

Both sinful actions and psychological disturbances are symptoms of disorder. But in the final analysis the nature of the disorder can only be accounted for theologically. Theological anthropology can explain why psychotherapy works to reduce the distortion when psychical energy has become a vicious tool of the inverted *imago Dei*. Knowing that sin does not result from distortions at the creaturely level alone, theological anthropology has the insight and resourcefulness not to label psychical stress as sinful. But it also has the courage to summon the person to accountability to the Word of God, which constitutes personal and human existence. In the Genesis 3 story of the temptation and fall Adam and Eve manifest the inversion of the *imago Dei* by no longer being able to exist in a relationship of openness and trust with each other and by avoiding God and hiding in the garden. Nevertheless, Adam cannot evade the responsibility for his own actions, though he protests, "It is the woman that you gave me." Nor can Eve evade her own responsibility by saying, "It was the serpent who caused me to sin." The true nature of the disorder which has plunged them into distress can only be revealed by this Word of God, which seeks them out and encounters them at the deepest level of their being — far deeper than any psychoanalysis can go. In being summoned to responsibility and accountability, each experiences his or her own authentic humanity.

Someone may ask, then, if the fundamental disorder is not psychological, is it ethical? Among modern theologians, Emil Brunner stressed that sin is a "revolt against God." Sin is rebellion against God and his command, which enters into the closed circle of creaturely existence and summons humans to accountability. Distinguishing between the *imago Dei* as a formal capacity for righteousness and as a material state of "being-in-righteousness," Brunner argues that accountability remains after the loss of the material state of righteousness because the human person is still capable. For Brunner a "point of contact" remains in the sinner. This point of contact makes it possible for that which is still human — because it is still formally the *imago Dei* — to respond; and therefore the sinner ought to respond. This freedom of response which can still be posited in the sinner, according to Brunner, is the positive aspect of the *imago Dei* which survives. However, because the material content of righteousness has been totally lost in the fall, this positive aspect of the *imago* is only an ethical possibility, presupposed by the Word of God when it is addressed to the sinner. The sinner alone is unable to activate that response and still depends on God's grace in order to respond in faith and obedience.

Barth of course had little confidence in this formal "possibility" remaining in the sinner. The *imago Dei*, he argued, cannot be posited first of all as an abstract formal possibility and then secondarily as a concrete and material reality.[11] What is at stake for Barth is the concreteness of the *imago Dei* as an actual human structure of reality. If the sinner is the actual person, not merely a hypothetical one, then the *imago* must be located in that actuality. But this means that the *imago* is actually inverted in such a way that, rather than forming a positive presupposition for obedience to the Word of God in faith, it represents as a presupposition the negative actuality grace must overcome to produce faith. This distinction is important for our discussion. If, as Brunner appears to hold, the actual disorder is a discrepancy between the ideal self and the actual self, then the "ought" will precede the "can."

This is what is meant by asking if the fundamental disorder is ethical. If the disorder is of this nature, then the possibility for healing rests with the ideal rather than the actual self. But as we have said before, the psychical energy by which the self actually exists is capable of being diverted into a religious (and also ethical) type of behavior which might be itself a monstrous and inhuman disorder. The Pharisees of Jesus' day were apparently so misled by their own zeal to perfect their behavior that they became caricatures of humanity. The authentic humanity of Jesus exposed this charade for what it was — an offense to God and a disregard for others. Brunner would of course protest that he has no intention of substituting an ethical existence for an existence in grace. Yet while we respect that protest, we must insist that the

---

11. Cf. *Church Dogmatics*, III/2, 128-32.

actuality of the sinner's human existence is a more likely presupposition for grace than a formal possibility which only exists as an ideal.

Let us press to the conclusion of the matter. Because sin is an inversion of the *imago Dei*, sin is itself an "inauthentic" form of humanity. We cannot say that sin is the result of a human intention, choice, or action. From a theological perspective, Barth is quite correct that sin is an "ontological impossibility."[12] Human personhood, as determined by the divine Word, does not include the possibility of sin among its formal components. The *imago Dei* is never a neutral ground from which the human person can contemplate the alternatives of obedience or disobedience to God. Rather, the *imago* is itself the basic response and obedience of the human to the divine Word.

Again we can take Lazarus as an example: when he heard Jesus call his name (John 11), that hearing was already the ontological reality and the content of obedience. Had Lazarus decided "not to come forth" out of his tomb, he would have "inverted" the ontological reality that constituted his own human life, using the life-force given to him for his own purposes. But this "sin" — this denial of the Word of God as constitutive of his life — would have no ground in the humanity of Lazarus, as it would have if he had "been alive" when he "heard" Jesus call his name. In that case, he would have had the possibility in his own being of responding or not responding. This was not the case with Lazarus, nor is it ever the case in Scripture. There is no authentic humanity except that summoned forth by the creative divine Word itself. There is no human existence which first of all is in a state of anxiety, indecision, or dread before it can actualize its own possibilities of response and faith. The fundamental order of humanity is one of rest, not unrest. It is an order which knows itself to be in correspondence to God, not estrangement from him. Therefore, disorder must be understood as a disruption and confusion of that which is actually the case. Health precedes sickness, it is not the result of a cure. Goodness is an orientation of the person toward the source of life, not the result of correcting deviant behavior.

Sin must therefore be assessed from the perspective of the relation of the person to the source of truth, rather than from the appearance of what is true. Thus Bonhoeffer could say, "What is worse than doing evil is being evil. It is worse for a liar to tell the truth than a lover of truth to lie."[13] The liar conceals his true nature when he tells the truth, and against such deception there is no protection. But when a lover of truth tells a lie, the contradiction will become apparent in light of the truth, and the person will be forced to deal with the ethical implications of that act. However, because the lover of truth is partic-

---

12. *Ibid.*, 139.
13. *Ethics* (New York: Macmillan, 1955), pp. 64f.

ipating in a true order of being (for love is of God), there are resources for renewal in that relation. King David was said to be a man after God's own heart. After he committed adultery, lied, and even killed, why was he still considered thus? It was because, when confronted by Nathan's "Thou art the man!", David agreed and replied, "You are right. I have sinned" (cf. 2 Sam. 12:1-15; Ps. 51).

Grace precedes sin and makes it possible. Strange as this may sound, it can be no other way. For if sin is the presupposition of grace, it must be intrinsic to the human person. Personhood, however, is itself a work of divine grace. Sin presupposes grace, says Barth,

> Not that it is grace which leads or compels us to sin. Sin resists grace. It affronts and betrays it. It has no basis in grace. It is in fact so terrible and infamous because it can have no basis for the grace in which God acts as Creator and in which man has his being as His creature. But its inconceivable reality can be grasped only when we see it as rebellion against grace.[14]

We can draw out the practical implication of this in quite another way. We might say that humanity presupposes and precedes inhumanity, and so the true order of being human presupposes disorder. There are many forms of sin and various levels of sin with regard to the seriousness of the consequences. There are deep disturbances of the human person which are not sinful, but are rather an impairment of or loss of psychical health. But there are also quite rational and apparently "healthy" forms of inhumanity.

There is some degree of contradiction in the way each of us experiences our own personhood. Left to ourselves, we would find comfort in either chronic sickness or in the presumption of health. But like Adam and Eve, who took refuge in the trees, we would have no hope. Theological anthropology dares to bring human disorder and contradiction before the Word which summons personhood into responsible existence. There is hope with the God who can kill and make alive. Even when we dare to pray, "and there is no health in us," the fact that this is a prayer rather than a complaint testifies to the true order of our humanity. And in knowing this, we are well.

---

14. *Church Dogmatics*, III/2, 35.

CHAPTER EIGHT

BEING HUMAN —
AS MALE AND FEMALE

"**M**ODERN MAN HAS SHIFTED THE FIG LEAF FROM HIS GENITALS TO HIS face. He has lost the mystery of his sexuality and in the process he has lost his own identity."[1] That perceptive remark by Dwight Small captures the dynamics of present-day culture, in which unisex has become a life style for some and feminism a new "liberation theology" for others.

The question of human sexuality has become as much a political and ideological question as a psychological one. When candidates for public office in San Francisco openly admit that the one who is able to secure the "homosexual vote" will undoubtedly be elected, the question of sexual preference is no longer merely ethical or psychological. When Christian bookstores report large and increasing sales of books which cater to what some have called the new evangelical eroticism, sexuality is seen to have economic implications far beyond the documented trade in pornography. When sexual preferences between and among men and women now are debated in the rhetoric of "human rights" and "liberation," we are not surprised that the church is unsure of its ground and embarrassed by its response. And when priests become advocates for "consenting adult relationships" and theologians the prophets of "gay liberation," all in the name of "authentic humanity," we know that it is time to look at human sexuality again, this time from the perspective of a theological anthropology.

SEXUALITY AS A MODALITY
OF PERSONAL BEING

In biblical theology the touchstone for any critical examination of what is human is the concept of the *imago Dei*. We have seen that this *imago* is an endowment the human person bears as a distinctive of creaturely being, but that it cannot be inferred or derived from creaturely being itself. There can be

---

1. Dwight H. Small, *Christian, Celebrate Your Sexuality* (Old Tappan, N.J.: Revell, 1974), p. 180.

no such thing as creaturely humanity apart from the image of God, but the human person does not possess intrinsic aspects of this *imago* by virtue of being a creature. The image of God is extrinsic, not intrinsic, to creaturely humanity. It has its source in that power which creates and constitutes the human, the divine Word. We cannot explicate the *imago* by analyzing the phenomenon of creatureliness itself, even though we have no other access to the human but through creaturely humanity. The contingent relation between the human and the creaturely constitutes an epistemological check on a methodology which does not take into account the revelation of God as a Word which determines and explains the *imago*.

The content of the *imago* is experienced as differentiation within unity. Or, one could say, human being is a polarity of being experienced as complementarity. Because the particularity of human being is always of a creaturely sort, this polarity and complementarity is expressed in terms of sexuality — male and female, male or female (Gen. 1:26-27). Thus the polarity is intrinsically one of sexual differentiation, for there is no other form in which it is manifest except through creaturely humanity, which occurs as either male or female sexual differentiation. Our basic thesis can then be put this way: the *imago Dei* is not intrinsic to creaturely humanity, but is contingently related to it; human sexuality, on the other hand, is intrinsic to the *imago Dei* expressed as polarity of the human at the creaturely level.

The differentiation between Creator and creature is not a barrier to relation; indeed, that which is totally "other" *constitutes* the basis for relation of persons and is the source of true intimacy. Intimacy is intensified by otherness. This is true for the human relationship with God as well as for the relationship of human persons. The assumption, of course, is that this "otherness" is part of a basic modality or complementarity. Because the *imago Dei* is a correspondence between God and human persons, even though it is a correspondence of the unlike, there is actually a true encounter and meeting of being in it. If this differentiation is blurred, so that an absolute distinction between God as Creator and human as creature no longer remains, there can no longer be true encounter of being.

This polarity or modality of being — in which differentiation is experienced as complementarity, correspondence, and encounter — is the basis for a theology of human sexuality. We may consider the sexual differentiation between male and female to represent, but not to constitute, personal differentiation. That is, male and female seem to be concrete manifestations of the essential polarity of being. To put it another way, we are not in a polarity of being simply because we happen to be male or female. Other creatures of the sixth day have sexual distinctives, but they do not have the differentiation which constitutes personhood. Personhood is not the result of being male or female.

Rather, for the human person, creaturely maleness and femaleness is a manifestation of the fundamental polarity of personhood. It is a sign of personhood, in which the sign reveals the true differentiation of being which is essential humanity — the *imago Dei*.

Purely sexual differentiation is shared in common with other animal creatures. However, the sexual differentiation between humans, unlike animals, is a unique differentiation and the only differentiation of personhood.[2] Animals do not experience differentiation of being by virtue of creaturely sexuality. With animals there is no modality in which correspondence and encounter emerge. Through their creaturely sexuality, animals do not experience the other as total "other" in the sense of the mystery of encounter with being. The sameness of creaturely nature does not disclose being to being in such a way that encounter and relation occur. Within the species dog, there is an instinctive and natural drive to mate, but the mating of dogs does not produce relations which transcend that natural and instinctive drive. Its result is the perpetuation of the species, not differentiation of being. After the maternal instincts which seem to bind the mother to her young disappear when the pup is weaned, there is no recognition between them, but only the future possibility of mating as members of the species. This takes place without embarrassment and apparently without shame or guilt.

Human persons, however, not only mate but they "meet" — and meet again, or fear meeting again, or meet with guilt and shame. For human persons, sexuality becomes a disclosure of the "other" being in such a way that a complementary relationship results, which both intensifies the "I-Self" and enhances the "I-Thou." Thus there is a conjunction between the creaturely aspect of male-female sexuality at the biological or natural level — which has to do with the replenishing of the species — and the meeting of persons. The biblical mandate for human persons is mate as well as meet. Adam and Eve, addressed as those who bear the image and likeness of God, are told to "be fruitful and multiply . . ." (Gen. 1:28).

The business of mating, it seems to me, must be taken as seriously as meeting. Deliberately not to mate is a serious decision which must be made with responsibility. It appears that we cannot dissociate the *imago Dei* in its polarity of sexual being from the creaturely responsibility to mate and to reproduce, that we cannot be responsible persons in our sexuality without taking responsibility for the implications of our sexual being, that is, the capacity and responsibility to reproduce. I make this observation tentatively, and I would emphasize that this cannot be taken as an absolute necessity. It is one thing to determine as male and female that mating should not in every case

---

2. Cf. Karl Barth, *Church Dogmatics*, III/1, 186.

result in reproducing another human being; it is quite another to deny that mating and reproducing is in any way associated with our human sexuality, and therefore with the *imago Dei*. I am not only thinking of the extremes to which some religious groups have gone, such as the Shakers in late-nineteenth-century America, who encouraged and even mandated sexual abstinence between husband and wife on spiritual grounds. I am referring to situations in which couples view child-rearing as an inconvenience and hindrance to their own personal gratification and pleasure.

I say this only to try to provide a meaningful commentary on the implications of mating as well as meeting. The decision not to mate, like the decision to mate and not reproduce, must take into consideration our accountability to God as creatures who bear his image. There is no sanctuary from the problems and responsibilities of human sexuality in either platonic love or erotic spirituality.

To return to our basic argument, there is an intrinsic distinction between male and female personhood, not merely an accidental or acquired one. The modality of personal being at the creaturely level is essentially one of differentiation from and with the other, and the only point of reference by which to enact that polarity is through one's identity as a male as contrasted with a female, or as a female as contrasted with a male. To break that modality by denying the fundamental distinction of sexual orientation with regard to one's own identity is to conceal the *imago* itself. If that happens, frustration and limitation of personhood will result. As we shall see, this is *not* a matter of setting up sexual stereotypes by which to identify masculinity and femininity in terms of personality characteristics.

The point is that what we call human personhood or selfhood is not a self-contained faculty expressed as abstract individuality, but an openness of being which stands out of itself towards the other as the source of our being. This modality of relation, which can be called co-humanity, is linked with creaturely sexuality in such a way that a theology of human personhood is also a theology of sexuality. To be a person is to be essentially a man or a woman in terms of creaturely humanity. Because this modality, expressed in terms of sexuality at the creaturely level, is itself an endowment of the *imago*, rather than the result of any determination of creatureliness itself, there remains a mystery of human sexuality which is the mystery of personhood itself. This mystery is the connection between the *imago* and creaturely being which cannot be explicated in a way that will make it self-evident or obvious.

This is why we have said that human sexuality at the creaturely level is a "sign" of the fundamental polarity and complementarity of being which is constituted by the *imago*. As we shall discuss later, human sexuality thus has a certain "sacramental" dimension, as the mystery and reality of the being of another are disclosed through sexual relation (what we have called meeting rather than merely mating). John Zizioulous speaks of an "ek-static" dimension to personhood, which is represented by differentiation in unity.[3] When this differentiation is affected by sin, division results, so that one person is separated from the other as a discrete individual, with an autonomous ego to protect and sustain. Psychical energy which should be building up the "corporate" ego of the modality is then diverted to maintaining the private ego. Theologically stated, the division which produces this individualizing tendency and its consequent tension and conflict is a perversion and distortion of differentiation. Thus, problems in sexual relationships between people come to manifest this division rather than enhance differentiation. In such a situation, eliminating sexuality as a factor by attempting to operate on a level of trans-sexual being is a great temptation, but of no help. Nor will it do to intensify sexuality into an ideological or political struggle for equality. While that may temporarily redress perceived injustices committed in the name of sexual superiority, one must in the final analysis be affirmed in one's sexuality by the other in order to be affirmed as fully human and equally as person. Only when sexuality is understood as a modality in which there is true correspondence and encounter of being can this take place.

SEXUALITY AS ORIENTATION TOWARD A GOAL

The divine Word which summons personhood into being constitutes a continuing summons. The Word is never merely past tense. It always enters the present from the perspective of the future. It is always ahead of us, though it is there with us, and was there from the beginning. Its very nature determines that human personhood also exists as an orientation toward its goal, its true destiny in fellowship and participation in the life of God. This is why we referred earlier to the seventh day rather than the sixth as the theological term which establishes the uniqueness of the human creature.

Because human sexuality is intrinsic to human personhood, it is an orientation toward this goal, experienced as differentiation in unity. It follows that sexuality cannot be completely understood on the basis of a doctrine of origins, by way of a kind of "archeological" study. But the same Word which summons personhood into being summons it into existence in a modality of being experienced as creaturely sexuality, male and female, male or female. Hence that very creaturely sexuality which is a sign of this modality is also

---

3. "Human Capacity and Incapacity," in *Scottish Journal of Theology*, XXVIII (1975), 401-48.

summoned toward a goal, rather than merely working out the possibilities of its origin in a creaturely nature. To be male or female, then, is also a goal of personhood, not merely a present with a past. It is an orientation toward that which is the source of our being as correspondence to God.

In a certain sense, then, one could say that human personhood is a penultimate experience at the creaturely level; but the next-to-the-last word gains its significance only from the last word, which must be spoken, heard, and understood. The possibilities of our personhood will emerge out of this fundamental structure of being. Because we are sexual beings in terms of creaturely sexuality, we are oriented toward a goal in which the differentiation presently experienced will be completed in a perfect modality of personal being. This is the basis for what — in psychological terms — is called gender identity.

In terms of my own personal being and identity as a person, what does it mean to say that I am not only a person, but a man? What does it mean for another person to say, I am not only a person but a woman? Do these mean fundamentally the same thing, the only difference being a cultural perspective due to acquired characteristics? Is it a purely functional description of my life, so that I can work within certain role formations? On the basis of our assumptions and argumentation, the gender identity which is expressed in terms of male or female personal being must be seen as an "ontological" rather than a pragmatic or social distinction. That is, to be male or female in terms of gender identity is to know oneself in the essential differentiation which constitutes personhood itself. We are committed then to hold that sexuality, as intrinsic to the image of God, also entails that gender identity is rooted in an ontological determination of personal being.

I recognize the perils in this position. Paul Jewett, for one, has considered this option and rejected it because of what he sees as unresolvable difficulties.

> It should come as no surprise that some, at least, among contemporary theologians are not so sure that they know what it means to be a man in distinction to a woman or a woman in distinction to a man. It is because the writer shares this uncertainty that he has skirted the question of ontology in this study. Whether or not the entire effort to deal with sexual polarity in theological categories is a *cul-de-sac*, surely much of the traditional effort has proven to be so.[4]

---

4. *Man as Male and Female* (Grand Rapids: Eerdmans, 1975), pp. 178-79. In my judgment Jewett's book will be a classic in the field of theological anthropology. No one who writes in this area can afford to ignore his significant contribution to the discussion of what it means to be fully human as male or female. My questions concerning his methodology or hermeneutical assumptions should not obscure the fact that I agree wholeheartedly with his objective of arguing for the full equality of man and woman, both in the marital role and in the life and ministry of the church.

How helpful this decision will prove to be is a subject to which we shall return later.

We can put the ontological question this way: did the divine Word that summoned me into being as a human person — and therefore determined that I would be either male or female at the level of creaturely being — also determine an essential sexual polarity for me? Is there an intrinsic order to sexual identity? Is maleness or femaleness essential to and intrinsic to personhood, or is it an acquired characteristic that belongs entirely to the provisional period during which we exist as earthly and temporal creatures? If gender identity and the polarity of male or female are acquired and accidental aspects of our personhood, we should leave sexuality to the psychologist and the ethicist, and go on about the business of a theological anthropology. However, if sexuality is indeed an intrinsic polarity of being expressed as gender identity, then we can identify the true order of human sexuality as an order of being human itself. Sexuality, then, is an order of personhood in terms of a fundamental polarity of being.

Certainly the position for which we are arguing does not have modern social science on its side. E. Mansel Pattison, a practicing psychotherapist and a professor of psychiatry and human behavior, identifies eight variables that go into the formation of sexual identity: (1) chromosomal sex, which has to do with the type of chromosomes one has genetically; (2) gonadal sex; (3) hormonal sex; (4) internal sex organs; (5) external genitalia; (6) assigned gender identity; (7) core gender identity; (8) gender role identity.[5] The first five variables are secondary sexual characteristics with regard to the formation of gender identity, while the last three are primary. Assigned gender identity is the gender assigned to an infant by those who provide parenting; core gender identity is the biological self-image that results through the growth of one's own perception of self in relation to others; and gender role identity is the function performed in society which carries the label of masculinity or femininity.

Pattison concludes that gender identity results from a combination of all of these variables, none of them essential to the person. As a behavioral scientist with a commitment to Christian theological assumptions, he holds that gender identity is accidental to personhood, and not essential. But he adds, "In a basic sense we can only be men or women in terms of our cultural existence. There is no universal identity of masculine or feminine; gender role

---

5. From a paper on "Women's Role and Status in Western Society: a Psychological Perspective," delivered at the Second Annual Conference on Contemporary Issues, Conservative Baptist Theological Seminary, Denver, 1973.

6. *Ibid.*

identities are culturally relative."[6] For all practical purposes, Pattison concludes, child-rearing must be sexist if gender identity is to develop. A non-sexist environment will seriously obscure and confuse gender identity, and gender identity is essential to a healthy self-image and to one's function in society. Thus, while Pattison argues that gender identity is not an intrinsic quality or component of personhood, he agrees that it is indispensable for the healthy development of personhood. Despite the fact that great damage has been done through abuses in stereotyping gender identity through particular cultural patterns, one must still expect that a concept of being either male or female is important, if not necessary, for the identity of each person. To abandon such gender formation would result in greater confusion and greater problems.

From the perspective of theological anthropology, how does one respond to this? Having argued that creaturely sexuality at the level of human personhood is a "sign" by which the essential polarity of being is experienced, we may view gender identity itself as such a sign. That is, there is no apparent reason why one cannot accept the conclusion that there are a number of variables at the creaturely level which go into the formation of gender identity. For the essential polarity of being which constitutes the differentiation of human personhood is not a determination of creaturely being or of creaturely sexuality. It is not necessary that gender identity itself be intrinsic to creaturely sexuality, only that it be intrinsic to the *imago Dei* which is experienced as creaturely sexuality.

This is a subtle but important distinction. I agree with Pattison that gender identity, viewed from a perspective of creaturely sexuality, is a relative and not an absolute determination, and that each person will nevertheless develop a healthy and authentic self-identity only when gender identity is fixed in terms of that self-identity. Pattison cannot explain why this is so (nor should he as a social scientist have to); it is enough for him to point to the empirical results when gender identity is not a positive aspect of one's self-identity. But the theologian must account for that in terms of the assumption that human being is created in the image of God as the concrete and particular person that he or she may be. Thus, "he" and "she" belong to the same theological dogma as *imago Dei*. To fail to be able to relate "he" and "she" as specific instances of created humanity to the *imago Dei* is to cut the *imago* out of this historical and creaturely level of human personhood, with the result that the empirical self is surrendered to the social scientist while the theologian can only attempt to describe the ideal self. For this reason some theologians resort to ethics when dealing with matters pertaining to human sexuality. But such "theological ethics," not properly grounded in theological anthropology, has recourse only to abstract values such as "human good," or "liberation," or "social justice" in deciding particular instances of human behavior.

Helmut Thielicke, for example, appears to waver at the critical point of grounding sexual polarity in the ontological differentiation of personhood itself. In *The Ethics of Sex* he argues that human sexuality is qualitatively different from animal sexuality.[7] While human sexuality is also biological sexuality, Thielicke says that the biological aspect of human sexuality is integrated into the *humanum*, and that the *humanum* is integrated into the *divinum*.[8] Apparently human sexuality at the biological level is grounded in an ontological differentiation intrinsic to the *imago Dei*. But Thielicke is nervous about drawing such a conclusion. The "sex character" of individuals as male and female is not an "absolute." There is what he calls an essential "plasticity" about sexuality which leaves the individual free from ontological determination. This is confirmed by his assertion that sexual differentiation is a "medium" through which personal differentiation is expressed, but in the ultimate "immediate" relationship of the human to God sexual orientation as a component of differentiation will dissolve.[9]

What the nature of this eschatological experience of personhood will be, when there is no longer an ontological differentiation, Thielicke is unable to say. It is clear, however, that this distinction between the "mediate" and the "immediate" orientation of the self to God enables him to posit quite specific attributes to the temporal "vocation" of being man and woman. It is, so to speak, says Thielicke,

> the "vocation" of the woman to be lover, companion, and mother. And even the unmarried woman fulfills her calling in accord with the essential image of herself only when these fundamental characteristics, which are designed for wifehood and motherhood, undergo a sublimating transformation, but still remain discernible, that is to say, when love and motherliness are the sustaining forces in her vocation.[10]

Our assertion that gender identity is intrinsic to human personhood does not entail a set of stereotyped characteristics by which to identify masculinity

---

7. *The Ethics of Sex* (Grand Rapids: Baker, 1964), p. 20.
8. *Ibid.*, p. 19.
9. *Ibid.*, pp. 6-7.
10. *Ibid.*, p. 81. George Carey argues that "man is not psycho-sexually neutral at birth" and that "difference is an essential part of complementarity"; *I Believe in Man* (Grand Rapids: Eerdmans, 1977), p. 152. Citing Margaret Mead, Carey suggests that there are basic similarities in which men and women have experienced being male and female, hinting that sexual differentiation is a transcultural given of human experience (p. 151). For a more recent argument, drawing on both social science and biblical texts, see Stephen B. Clark, *Man and Woman in Christ* (Ann Arbor: Servant Books, 1980), where it is argued that the sexual differentiation between male and female is "created into the human race" (pp. 440f.) and that men and women are not "interchangeable units" (p. 394).

and femininity. Such stereotypes almost invariably attempt to describe the female in terms of the male, either as the "weaker vessel" or as the "intuitive" one as opposed to the rationality of the male. Barth vigorously protests this categorization of masculine and feminine traits, and labels Brunner's depictions of them as preposterous.[11] But Barth is not of much help when it comes to saying what it means to be male as opposed to female. Whatever it means, he suggests, must be determined by the man and woman in pursuing the concrete instance of their own humanity through their sexual identity, not by attempting to rise above sexual identity in search of true humanity.

Perhaps that is as good an answer as any. But it can be argued that it is still meaningful and helpful to be able to affirm that there is a permanent aspect to the present differentiation as male and female, even though one cannot give account of it in terms of descriptive content. But this is true only if one agrees that gender identity is an ultimate — and therefore eschatological — orientation of the self. One can no more describe the appearance and form of a resurrection body than explain what it means to say that the polarity of being we know in terms of gender identity will be part of that eternal experience. What is important for the existential self is that despite a radical change in form, there is continuity between the penultimate and the ultimate. Paul assumed that this was a sufficient answer to the question concerning the nature of the resurrection body (1 Cor. 15); and we affirm the same in this case.

Despite the potential confusion about gender identity and sexuality as a present experience, being oriented toward a goal where the polarity is one of differentiation and complementarity through perfect unity is a source of comfort and courage. In the midst of such confusions and even disorder, it is helpful to believe that one is being determined by something beyond biological or social history. We shall have more to say about this later.

SEXUALITY AS COMPLEMENTARITY
OF PERSONAL BEING

We have asserted that sexuality is essentially a polarity of being experienced as differentiation within unity. It may be helpful to extend that discussion by thinking through the implications of gender identity as at least one form of the complementarity which that differentiation entails. In Genesis 2, the lack of complementarity in terms of creaturely humanity was announced in the form of divine verdict: "It is not good that the man should be alone." There must be some essential "other." But the content of the word "other" must be sexual, not asexual; for any "other" human creature must be either male or

---

11. *Church Dogmatics*, III/4, 152ff.

female. Theologically, one could argue that the *imago Dei* could be completed only by the subsequent creation of a female as a partner for Adam — though this has little if any exegetical warrant. However, in light of the basic text in Genesis 1:26-27, which posits male and female as created in God's image and likeness, it seems reasonable to conclude that it is significant that it was Eve who emerged from the rib of Adam, not John. It follows from this that the complementary aspect of the *imago Dei* is not a reciprocal flow of "humanity" which takes no regard of creaturely sexuality, but is necessarily related to sexuality, and thus to gender identity. Intrinsic to the "Thou" by which I am known to another, is also "he" or "she."

But now let us think of this reciprocity in terms of what we know about the ultimate Word which is determinative of the penultimate. The complementarity by which gender exists as "he" or "she" also corresponds to the divine modality of being if it is rooted in the *imago Dei*. God reveals himself through the incarnation as a reciprocity of being-in-relation, expressed as Father, Son, and Holy Spirit. God the Father is consistently revealed as the source of all God wills and determines to be. God the Son is revealed as the source of all God is willing to be as perfect response to his own determination. The Father ordains, and the Son subordains his own will to that of the Father. This subordination of the Son to the Father is as important to the modality as the ordination of the Father. As a modality of divine being reciprocity is not merely functional and ambiguous, but ontological and discrete. God's being is always revealed to be "being-as," rather than mere being.

Unless one wishes to say that God, in his eternal being-in-himself, is only accidentally and not necessarily related to God in his being-for-us through the economy of salvation history, we can ascribe content to the modality of God as "three-in-one." It would then follow that subordination, as one aspect of the being of God the Son (Jesus Christ), is ontological and not merely economical, with respect to our understanding of God. Theologians who, because of the unfortunate implication some have drawn that women are inferior to men, are uncomfortable with the concept of subordination, may take the desperate expedient of suggesting that the modality of ordination and subordination as an aspect of God's being is provisional and temporary, limited to the economy of salvation history. But this would mean that any or all aspects of God's being as disclosed through the economy of salvation history might be provisional. For example, the assertion that God is love would not then assure us that the actual content of love as an ultimate form of God's being bears any resemblance to love as revealed in the penultimate. Scripture does not encourage us to go in this direction.

Some, like Paul Jewett, would substitute "partnership" as a concept of a reciprocal modality for correspondence between the ordaining and subordaining polarity in God as the basis for this reciprocity. The concept of partnership, however, lacks ontological significance. There are destructive partnerships as well as edifying ones. What is meant by partnership in this context, I suppose, is a complementary relationship in which good is the result rather than evil. But to denote the being of God as three-in-one as partnership appears to say nothing about the being of God, whereas the concepts of "son" and "father" do say something.

If Jesus is the Son of God, and if this sonship entails a partnership in which the Son is God "being willing" in conjunction with the Father who is God "willing to be," we are speaking of more than a function of divine being within the economy of salvation history. We are talking about what ordinarily is called the pre-existence of the Son of God prior to the incarnation. That sonship which comes to expression in Jesus of Nazareth in salvation history is itself a mode of being for God. The being of God expressed as "willing to be" we call God's sovereignty, by which he calls into being that which is not and sustains what he creates through his divine power. God as Father wills and sustains being through his sovereign power. However, that which we call "being willing" as the life of God the Son is equally a sovereign power of God, expressed as the power of unfailing love even as obedience unto death on the cross (Phil. 2:8). There is no less sovereignty in God the Son than in God the Father, though in each instance God remains differentiated in an absolute and not a relative sense. Because the ultimate being of God is disclosed through Jesus Christ as such, there is reason to believe that the penultimate humiliation the Son experiences is not determinative of what either "Son" or "subordination" means. The "self-emptying" of Jesus is not an emptying of sovereignty, but a manifestation of the sovereign God in his activity of reconciling the world to himself.

If there is correspondence between the being of God and human being — despite the fact that human being is more unlike than like divine being — we should expect that there will be a polarity of being with its own reciprocity. The fact that this polarity must be experienced through creaturely sexuality links gender identity with that polarity by means of the complementarity of the sexual relation. Clearly the biblical authors understood the modality of male and female relationship in terms of a hierarchical complementarity. Paul expressed this most pointedly in speaking of the natural "headship" of the husband (male) with respect to the wife (female). If we account for this teaching by attributing it to a culturally biased male chauvinist attitude on the authors' part, we may disregard its significance for theological anthropology. Or, if one wishes to argue, on the basis of a transcending theological principle (as Paul

Jewett does), the language of hierarchy can be consistently transformed into the language of partnership.[12]

But what would the source of such a hermeneutical principle be? Is an abstract concept such as "analogy of faith" more inherently theological, and therefore more normative, than the words which denote the concrete event of creation and revelation itself? Why is it necessary that Paul be "wrong" when he teaches that wives must be subordinate to their husbands, despite the fact that this is expressed in the language and thought-forms of his own tradition and culture? Is it because the concept of subordination has itself become culturally despised and incapable of restoration in its essential theological sense? If so, this might be a premature conclusion, and a dreadful expedient with far more serious implications than has been bargained for.

Theology's difficult task is to clarify — and perhaps even resurrect — biblical concepts, not to substitute more congenial alternatives. For our part, aware of the pitfalls, we choose to continue to explore the implications of the biblical teaching of a specific order of male and female relationship in terms of what may — for lack of a better expression — be called the hierarchical modality. In the case of the modality of Father and Son, the terms ordination and subordination appear to be ontologically equivalent, and thus neutral so far as quality of being is concerned. In the perfect complementarity one expects of the divine being, so freely does the reciprocity of ordaining and subordaining spin on its axis that there is no apparent distinction between the two. In seeing the Son who subordains, one also sees the Father who ordains (John 14:9). This differentiation is itself a perfect unity of being, with no advantage or disadvantage. Whatever disadvantage accrues to the Son because of the task of being servant of all for the salvation of the world, is itself gathered up into the ontological joy of sonship. Rather than abandoning this theological dogma as a positive content for the *imago Dei* in favor of some other expedient such as partnership, it seems more fruitful to pursue it as a clue to the ultimate orientation of gender identity as a component of human sexuality.

If we were to call the polarity by which human persons exist in the image of God essential sexuality — as distinguished from creaturely sexuality — we could argue that the former is more related to the ultimate determination of our personhood and the latter to the penultimate. Creaturely sexuality necessarily includes all that goes to distinguish us from each other as male or female, all the variables that go into gender identity. At the level of creaturely sexuality, "he" or "she" has a relatively distinct meaning in terms of sexual differentiation. We even use these pronouns to refer to nonhuman creatures. However, we are more than creaturely beings. We are human beings endowed with the

---

12. *Man as Male and Female*, pp. 134ff.

imago Dei, which is a differentiation which includes the creaturely "he" or "she" but expresses much more than that.

Essential sexuality, as that fundamental polarity of being which differentiates us as persons, may then be said to exist coincidentally with but not identically to creaturely sexuality. We cannot equate the differentiation of the *imago Dei* with creaturely sexuality as absolutely identical, any more than we can equate the *imago Dei* as absolutely identical with creaturely being, for that would mean that everything that had creaturely being would also be the *imago Dei*. However, because we have no other way of speaking about the essential polarity of being which is the ultimate determination of our being human, we continue to speak of it as essential "sexuality." And we continue to speak of that essential polarity as a differentiation of "he" and "she," that is, in terms of gender identity. This is quite the same as attempting to speak of the "resurrection body"; we continue to think of ourselves as having "hands" and "feet," though we are not sure that we will need them or that our body will actually have appendages.

Creaturely sexuality, even as human sexuality, exists as a penultimate form of essential sexuality. There will be a time when the penultimate will give way to the ultimate. This is how one could understand Jesus' teaching that "when they rise from the dead they neither marry nor are given in marriage, but are like angels in heaven" (Mark 12:25). Obviously, if they do not marry, there are no brides or bridegrooms, no husbands or wives. And possibly there are then no fathers or mothers. One could speculate that the only designation which will still be appropriate will be brother and sister! The role relationships represented by terms like husband, wife, mother, father, are not eschatologically determined; therefore, these roles, with all their biological, social, and cultural implications, are only coincidentally joined with our essential personhood. The fact that I know myself to be a male is also related to the fact that I am husband and father; but in that correspondence there is not an exact identity but a coincidental relation. There is no way that the present roles can be absolutized so as to determine my essential being, any more than the scars I bear in my present body will determine my resurrection body.

This theological perspective seems to liberate us from the tyranny of role-relationships as determinative of our personhood far more effectively than the concept of partnership, with its asexual implications. There will be and is a tension between the ultimate and penultimate. If gender identity does determine one's specific part to play in the present outworking of co-humanity as a sexual being, and if the Scriptures speak truly of that order when they speak of "submission" and "headship," we can only submit these terms and our own part in this complementary relationship to the judgment of the ultimate upon

117

the penultimate. It is possible that Paul knew very well what he was doing, but that we have lacked the courage to think and to live together in this way.

Some may protest that this theological exercise is a thinly veiled attempt to justify discriminating against women and even treating them as inferior persons. (After all, it is a male who is writing these lines!) In any case, it may be argued, the position developed here plays into the hands of males looking for an excuse to continue their domination of females. This charge cannot be taken lightly, and we cannot in fairness excuse ourselves from answering it on the ground that we have a different agenda in this book.

We have used the concept of a hierarchical modality to express first of all the "ordered equality" of the Trinity, and secondly Paul's teaching concerning "headship" and "submission." Although "hierarchical" is not itself a biblical term, it does express the differentiation which exists between Father, Son, and Spirit within the unity of divine being. The subordination of the Son to the Father is a modality of being which has a certain order but does not entail inequality of being.

Now, does this concept of "ordered equality," with terms like "headship" and "submission" as the Apostle Paul uses them, necessarily involve the subordination of women as persons to men as persons? I think not. The essential modality of co-humanity — which we have called an essential sexuality — clearly has an eschatological dimension. The command of God which summons the human creature into existence and which determines the order of existence is not identical with creaturely origins or even a creaturely order of existence. "When they rise from the dead they neither marry nor are given in marriage." On the other hand, the relationships of husband and wife, mother and father, appear to be temporal and provisional in light of the eschatological order. Though we often use the word "role" for these relationships, they are more than mere sociological functions. In some way they point to the eschatological order so that experiencing oneself in terms of such a temporal order can be understood as living under the command of God. On the other hand, precisely because these temporal orders are eschatologically relativized, they cannot be determinative for personhood nor for existence as co-humanity in its ultimate intentionality. To live as husband or wife, mother or father, is to live responsibly under the command of God, but the sociological role order itself cannot be determinative of the command of God.[13]

---

13. In my judgment this is a weakness in Stephen Clark's *Man and Woman in Christ*. Clark argues that the differentiation between male and female at the creaturely level is "God's purpose for the human race" (p. 447), basing this on Gen. 2, which, he says, teaches a subordination of woman to man for the sake of complementing the man and enabling a true human unity to exist. Clark buttresses his argument with largely inconclusive social science data. Thus the biological differentiation of male and

Here we must see that God's command summons us to think, act, and live so as to be accountable to God himself, not merely in conformity with an abstract principle or rule. Thus, the command of God comes to us as the Word of God, the Bible. However, as Geoffrey Bromiley has helpfully reminded us:

> The Bible does not replace God. He has not just given us the Bible and left us to it. He himself is still the one with whom we have to deal. ... Even as we consult holy scripture, we are really consulting God himself in his self-revelation as he came and comes to us through holy scripture. God indeed says what scripture says, but this does not imply a direct equation of God and scripture.[14]

We must not misunderstand Bromiley at this point. He is not suggesting that there is any other access to God than through Scripture. What he is arguing is that God holds human persons accountable to himself, not merely to a law or principle which may be abstracted from him — even if that law is supported by biblical prooftexting.

The command of God is always the work of God, even though it comes to expression through a temporal order or a regulative law. When the regulative law is used so as to oppose the work of God, one is accountable to God himself, not to the law. This is what lies behind Jesus' statement that "the sabbath was made for man, not man for the sabbath" (Mark 2:27). The significance of this is heightened when we remember that violations of the sabbath law were punished by stoning (Exod. 31:15). When Jesus saw that carrying out this law without regard for God's purpose for human healing and hope was itself contrary to the work of God, he brought to bear the command of God in such a way that the person caught in the "legal trap" was freed and restored to life.

"The kingdom of God does not mean food and drink but righteousness and peace and joy in the Holy Spirit," Paul taught (Rom. 14:17). Yet the Old Testament set forth precise laws concerning food, and these regulations carried the force of divine commands (cf. Lev. 11). In the light of the "theological

---

female is taken to be the essential structure of the social order, in which subordination of the woman to man in both the family and people of God is achieved. Because this order of natural creation is taken as God's intent for the human race, the redemption of humanity through Christ restores this original order and confirms it as a human social order, determinative for both family and church. Missing in this argument is the eschatological determination of human being, in which the "new humanity" can point beyond the natural determinism of the biological and the social. Clark tends to link the *imago Dei* too strongly with the creaturely differentiation of human sexuality. I would argue in response that the true nature of the differentiation is not determined by the biological-social order of nature, but rather comes to expression through this order, thus leaving room for a transformation of the natural order without destroying the differentiation and complementarity of true humanity. The church then as expressive of this new order does not simply rest on and confirm the natural order, but reveals the natural order to be a penultimate order.

14. *God and Marriage* (Grand Rapids: Eerdmans, 1980), p. 2.

principle" Paul establishes in Romans 14:17-18, was Moses wrong in promulgating these laws? Not at all. These laws are the very ways in which God's command was to be heard and obeyed. However, in a pastoral situation, when Paul saw that the command of God was directly related to the work of God, he admonished, "Do not, for the sake of food, destroy the work of God" (Rom. 14:20). Against those who argued that they were no longer under any regulations because of their freedom in Christ, Paul taught that they were still subject to the command of God, and the command of God is to "walk in love." Against those who argued that the regulations concerning food constituted the command of God in an absolute sense, Paul taught that "he also who eats, eats in honor of the Lord, since he gives thanks to God" (Rom. 14:6). Though Scripture regulates life in certain specific situations, the regulations themselves cannot become the Word of God (in the sense of God's command) in such a way that God's work is destroyed. In the same context as he says, "Do not, for the sake of food, destroy the work of God," Paul argues that "it is wrong for anyone to make others fall by what he eats; it is right not to eat meat or drink wine or do anything that makes your brother stumble" (Rom. 14:20-21).

To be sure, the laws governing eating and drinking in the Old Testament do not address the same order as those concerning the sabbath or male and female relationships. But our point is that when Moses gave specific laws to Israel, including the law of the sabbath, these laws had the effect of ordering their temporal life in such a way that they were brought under the command of God. The laws concerning foods and the sabbath are not relativized because they are cultural, temporal, or provisional. Rather, they are relativized by an eschatological order which, when it breaks in upon human life, radically qualifies existing orders by that final order of which the temporal and provisional orders are a sign. The temporal order and regulations derive their meaning and purpose from the eschatological order, not the reverse.

The order of male and female, as Paul teaches, is grounded in a modality which is eschatologically revealed through the coming of Jesus Christ as the Son who is subordinate to the Father. In dealing with what is no doubt a matter of some confusion and even disorder in the churches, Paul expresses the command of God in terms of an "order" in which the husband is to be the head of the wife and both are to be submissive to one another (1 Cor. 11:2-16; Eph. 5:21-33). Later, he even goes so far as to suggest that women ought to keep silence in the church and not have authority over men because woman is actually "second" to Adam in the order of creation (1 Tim. 2:8-15). To be a Christian man or woman, wife or husband, in churches under Paul's apostolic authority was to live under the command of God precisely as he articulated it. It is doubtful that one could appeal to a "theological principle," even spoken by Paul himself in another context, to argue that Paul was "wrong" in teaching thus. Nor is such an expedient necessary. Jesus' action in liberating men and women from a life-defeating principle of the sabbath did not make Moses wrong in teaching that one who violated the specific law of the sabbath should be put to death. Nor did Paul's teaching concerning the kingdom of God and laws concerning the eating of meat mean that Moses was wrong in originally issuing these specific laws.

The temporal order which establishes the relation of male and female in the "roles" of husband and wife is itself provisional. It is subject to the eschatological order, which will end certain aspects of it (in heaven they neither marry nor are given in marriage) while affirming the essential order of co-humanity as relation in perfect fellowship. The same command of God which stands behind Paul's injunction concerning submission of wives to husbands is found in his teaching that in Christ "there is neither Jew nor Greek, there is neither slave nor free, there is neither male nor female" (Gal. 3:28). The same command of God which releases the human person from a tyrannical and life-defeating principle occasioned by a law concerning food is also the command of God which occasioned the law in its own time and place. One is not "wrong" and the other "right."

Paul rightly considers the eschatological order, as revealed through Jesus Christ, as relativizing the temporal ordering of human sexuality as male and female (Gal. 3:28). But it would be a source of theological confusion to conclude from this that the fundamental polarity of being as expressed in the image of God is thereby dissolved. We cannot be sure, of course, what it means to say that the "ordered equality" of the eternal Son constitutes eternal subordination to the Father. But it is of no help to us to suggest that what we know of that modality of being as a differentiation within God himself is itself only provisional and not essential.

In the *eschaton*, we learn in Scripture, all forms of the temporal order through which the command of God is heard and obeyed will pass away (Luke 21:33; 1 Pet. 1:24-25). This surely means that whatever existing temporal forms negate the work of God are already relativized and transformed through the coming of Jesus Christ. Here is at least the suggestion of a hermeneutical clue to the vexing problem of how to take Paul's teaching seriously when he gives the command of God in the form of a temporal order alongside his teaching about the essential order. In the end, this surely does not mean that a new "law of marriage" or "law of the sexes" can be developed which merely replaces one that is considered outmoded. It does mean, however, that each person must determine for himself or herself how the command of God is to be fulfilled through these present structures of man and woman, husband and wife, parent and child. There is a tension between the eschatological structure of the modality, including that which gender identity represents, and the present and provisional form of the modality.

The "liberation" which the command of God brings to men and women is not a liberation from discovering one's own essential personhood through role structures, but a liberation from the power of the role structure itself to determine absolutely one's being. To the degree that the existing relationship — say, of husband and wife — can be mutually suspended as a "law," so as to permit the eschatological reality of personhood as "partnership" to be experienced, there seems to be no theological basis for denying permission to do so. Women are not consigned to being homemakers and mothers as the only way of achieving true personhood, any more than they are disenfranchised from being full partners in the ministry of the gospel with men. What we are arguing here is a theological assumption: that the divine order for male and female relationships is an ontological structure of personal being, with Christ as the middle term. In this modality, hierarchy and subordination are both radically qualified by the middle term. The true "partnership" and experience of equality between Father and Son in the Godhead are the result of that ontological order of "Father" and "Son," not the suspension of it. The Son does not have to be liberated from that order which entails subordination in order to have full equality and freedom of being, he has this freedom and this joy in being the Son.

Some will no doubt retort that this is no perfect world in which we live. We are all sinners, and sin has corrupted and distorted every relationship, so that it is too much to expect for that ideal and ultimate order to have any effect on the existing order. Thus women must be free from men and men must be free from women if true partnership is to be achieved. But this surely is a counsel of despair! It makes too much of the power of sin to destroy what the Word of God determines, and it makes too little of Christ's power to transform the existing order sufficiently so that we can "work out our own salvation" in the confidence that God works within us and for us (Phil. 2:12-13). Where situations are bereft of God's grace, one or the other person may have to surrender the role relationship itself to the death and resurrection process, but what cannot be surrendered is one's own being as male or female. If being "woman" is impossible in a situation where there is only unrelenting inhumanity, then one must not consent to the destruction of a "work of God."

Here is where the true hermeneutical task begins — where individuals in concrete and specific situations must discern the distinction between a regulation which seeks to become the Word and the Word of God which seeks to edify and build up human being as the "work of God." In this case too, it may be said: "The sabbath was made for man, not man for the sabbath" (Mark 2:27).

SEXUALITY AS A BASIS
FOR LOVE AND MARRIAGE

We have deliberately discussed human sexuality apart from marriage as the basis for human sexual identity. We hold with Barth that human sexuality is intrinsic to the *imago Dei* and must therefore be understood in terms of co-humanity — rather than in terms of marriage as an ethical containment for what would otherwise be an unbridled instinctual impulse. As the covenant relationship between man and woman, marriage is a possibility because of the intrinsic sexual nature of human persons. But marriage is not necessary in order for persons to become fully male and female in terms of gender identity. Unmarried persons, whether never married or formerly married, are not denied full completion of the *imago Dei* in terms of co-humanity, even though they are excluded from the provisional and temporal experience the marriage relationship offers.

We have already argued that marriage relationships, in terms of the role relationships of husband and wife, are provisional and not determinative of our fundamental humanity in the *eschaton*. However, it is a bit more complicated than that. Marriage is not simply an "alternative social form" which may be elected as a style of life purely for what it offers in the present. It is in some way, to use Paul's terminology, a "mystery" by which the uniqueness of the covenant relationship between men and women can be experienced (Eph. 5:31-32).

While we could say that marriage is not necessary in order for a person to experience his or her own fulfilment as a person created in the image of God, we must add that marriage is an "order of creation," and as such is given to men and women as a fundamental structure by which love and sexuality can be consummated freely and fully. The "mystery" of which Paul speaks when he recalls the language of Genesis 2, which speaks of this consummation as "becoming one flesh," is a mystery not merely of sexuality, but one by which the divine covenant (Christ and the church) joins with the human covenant (the two shall become one). While we do not believe that this language warrants the medieval concept of marriage as a sacrament of the church, it does suggest that the consummation of human love through sexual encounter is itself a "sign" of the *eschaton*. There is a "meeting" of self with self which is both temporal and provisional as well as ultimate and lasting. Because marriage is not an institution which survives into the *eschaton*, it must be a sign of something else that does survive. We believe that marriage is a sign of that essential sexuality which we spoke of earlier. As such a sign, it joins creaturely human sexuality with essential human sexuality as no other human experience does.

Having said this, we should comment on Brunner's rather strange view that marriage is also the ethical containment of what would otherwise be "unsanctified" sexuality. In this view, marriage is the ethical custodian of human sexuality, and thus a haven for those who would otherwise have no sexual restraint.[15] Barth, on the contrary, says that sexuality is sanctified by humanity, not by marriage.[16] Of course Barth does not mean to say that free rein can be given to indiscriminate sexual needs or impulses. Humanity for Barth is always co-humanity, and as such bound in covenant relationship to manifest the order that the divine Word establishes. In any event, both Barth and Brunner would agree that sexual encounter at the physical level between man and woman should take place in the context of covenant commitment, ordinarily of a public nature such as takes place in the wedding ceremony.

This raises difficult questions in regard to the unmarried and sexual fulfilment. If abstinence is the only style of life permitted for those not bound to another in "covenant commitment," how can such persons realize the full meaning of being either male or female? Again, the tension between the provisional and temporal life of human persons and the eternal and essential order of being is a source of wisdom at least, if not much comfort. To paraphrase Paul, one might say, "If there is no resurrection of the dead then let us eat, drink, and copulate, for tomorrow we die." The power of sensual needs and drives is always strongest when informed by a sense of immediacy — there is no tomorrow. If one chooses a celibate life, that can always be understood to be a gift of God (1 Cor. 7:7). There is the wisdom. And I suppose that for such who know the unmarried state to be a "calling," there is also some comfort. For those who do not accept that an unmarried state is a "gift from God," there is not such a clear answer.

Certainly this is a pastoral situation which requires great wisdom and understanding. But it does appear to me that there are more resources for that person in being helped to see that sexuality is intrinsically human — and therefore intended to come to expression through the "meeting of persons" rather than only through "mating" — than in being told that there are no resources outside of marriage itself. I doubt that the church has explored this dimension of human sexuality sufficiently, being more preoccupied with marriage as the ethical solution to the "problem of sex." Having said all this, we have only set the agenda for what would surely be a book in itself on the subject of a theology of marriage and family.

---

15. Brunner, *Love and Marriage* (London: Collins, The Fontana Library, 1970), pp. 183, 195.

16. "The command of God ... sanctifies man by including his sexuality within his humanity"; *Church Dogmatics*, III/4, 132.

ORDER AND DISORDER
IN HUMAN SEXUALITY

Disorders of human sexuality can only be understood with respect to the true order of sexuality. We have argued that since the true order of sexuality is rooted in the *imago Dei* as constitutive of human personhood, sexuality is primarily a subject of theological anthropology, and only consequently a subject of theological ethics. Of course, there are always ethical implications when one discusses the order of true being. One *ought* to live in accordance with what *is*; and what *is* can only be determined by what the divine Word has established as true and good.

We have seen that human sexuality serves as the creaturely form of differentiation, in the sense that personhood is concretely experienced as male or female, male and female. When this differentiation becomes division through a denial of the covenant relation which constitutes the true order of human being, a fragmentation occurs which leads to autonomous sexuality. Each person views himself or herself as male or female in an egocentric fashion. Sexuality becomes an instrument in the service of the self, and the other becomes an object of manipulation for one's own interest. Autonomous sexuality therefore becomes anonymous sexuality. The self is not revealed to the other in a true order of differentiation and complementarity, but is concealed in the sexual relation. This first step in disordered human sexuality is pictured in Genesis 3, where the man and the woman become aware that they are naked and cover themselves from each other with fig leaves.

It is not surprising, then, that human sexuality is a source of frustration and confusion at both the individual and social level. Sexuality does not come under an ethical mandate of its own as mere "behavior." It is intrinsically bound up in the order or disorder of personhood itself. Because personhood is experienced intrinsically as sexual orientation in terms of male or female, sexual disorder is a critical indicator of the level of personal disorder.

Because of this, I am not comfortable viewing marriage as an "ethical containment of sexuality." The wedding ceremony has no power to legitimize that which itself violates the true order of personhood. Pastors and marriage counselors often encounter "anonymous sexuality" within marriage relationships. Persons conceal themselves through sexual encounter, thus detaching their sexual identity from love and even from the other person as a counterpart in being to oneself. A possible consequence of such alienation of sexuality from the marital relationship is that one will seek sexual experiences outside the relationship, where there is greater anonymity and no accountability to the other. At the same time, sexual encounter within the marriage becomes physical recreation at best and a humiliating and devastating travesty of the relationship at worst. Heterosexuality as practiced within the legality of the marriage relationship may indeed be the most prevalent form of sexual disorder — and the one which has the greatest personal consequences in terms of marriage and family life.

The offense in this concealment of one's own person in sexuality goes beyond the harm done to the human partner. There is a presumption in such a concealment of the self which is rooted in the autonomous nature of the self attempting to serve its own ends. When the fundamental order of cohumanity as differentiation is denied and deliberately set aside in favor of a "personal independence," this too assumes a sexual form. Thus, when Paul in Romans 1 recites the indictment against those who have usurped the prerogative of the Creator in attempting themselves to be a "creator," this presumption against God is said to take the form of sexual confusion.

As Paul sets forth sexual disorder — including the exchange of "natural relations for unnatural" — it is sinful because it is contrary not only to the will of God but also to the *work* of God. Human beings are created in a true order of being, male or female, male and female. As they relate to one another, the differentiation of being essential to the *imago Dei* is constructed out of the sexual differentiation, which Paul calls "according to nature." What is sinful is not so much the disorderly behavior of the physical act itself as the presumption against the fundamental order of being in the form of a concealment of that order through one's sexual behavior.

We acknowledge that creaturely sexuality is constructed of a set of variables liable to some degree of alteration and even confusion. Gender identity is not a biological given in any absolute sense. Ordinarily, gender identity is firmly oriented in biological sexual identity, but this does not seem to be the case for every person. Some persons appear to suffer confusion and disorder of sexuality at the creaturely level itself. In recent years so-called sex-change operations have attracted a good deal of attention. From the perspective of a theological anthropology, some of these cases at least may be viewed as attempts to seek a true order of sexuality, aligning gender identity and biological sexual identity so that a true differentiation of personal being as either male or female may take place. Many such medical reconstructions have resulted in apparently healthy and meaningful heterosexual relationships. We point this out in order to clarify the point of sexual confusion and concealment. There is a distinction between a presumptive disorder of personhood, which conceals personhood in the sexual relationship, and a disorder of creaturely sexuality itself, in which the variables that go into the gender identity are themselves out of alignment. The one is presumptive and therefore sinful, the other may not necessarily be.

Many if not most moral regulations society imposes on sexual behavior are direct implications of the true order of personhood as we have outlined it. However, we do not relate the command of God by which human sexuality is ordered only or primarily to these moral regulations. That which is immoral or even illegal by society's standards may not yet approximate what the Word of God terms sinful and disordered. "The command of God," says Barth,

> will always point man to his position and woman to hers. In every situation, in face of every task and in every conversation, their functions and possibilities, when they are obedient to the command, will be distinctive ... and will never be interchangeable. ... But there are real violations and offenses. They arise where the one sex or the other sex forgets, or for any reason refuses to acknowledge, that it has its right and dignity only in relation to the opposite sex, and therefore in distinction from it. ... The root of fellow humanity and of humanity generally is thus affected.[17]

The denial of one's own sexual orientation as either male or female, or the attempt to detach the differentiation of the self as person from the sexual encounter with the other, violates the divine command. From this we can see why no ethical value can be placed on relationships which appear to enhance the quality of personal and mutual love but deny the intrinsic order of sexual love as male or female, male and female. The attempt to argue for the freedom of sexual encounter in terms of "sexual preference" alone does not accord with our understanding of theological anthropology, nor does it become more acceptable when presented under the ideological flag of "human rights."

We agree that all sexual disorder must be treated as a disorder of personhood, whether it occurs within heterosexual relations or homosexual relations. Homosexual relations are not a disorder of human sexuality merely because they are not heterosexual. There is no intrinsic moral good which occurs merely through heterosexual relationships at the physical level. Such relationships must be accountable to the true order of human personhood and find their dignity and validity in this accountability. We are simply contending that heterosexual relationships can have that dignity and validity because they are an orientation toward the essential sexuality intrinsic to the image of God.

Can we then say that homosexual relationships are impossible in the same sense? Perhaps we should turn the question around and ask, what could serve as the ground of the dignity and validity of homosexual relations? To what intrinsic order would a homosexual orientation look in being accountable? None appears in the biblical account of human sexuality. To argue that differentiation is still possible at the personal level is to detach physical sexuality from personal being, so that a non-differentiated sexual relation can still sup-

---

17. *Ibid.*, 154.

port and enhance a differentiated personal relation. One might argue that many homosexual relationships appear to be more "human" in terms of personal sensitivity and support of the other than many heterosexual marriages, but this would require a theological anthropology which unravels everything which has been said to this point. It is not enough to interpret the biblical texts which speak judgmentally against homosexuality in such a way that they do not speak against non-promiscuous homosexual attachments. Even if this would remove the ethical onus from some homosexual relationships, it would mean abandoning theological anthropology, not to mention a theology of sexuality.

We speculated earlier about whether Paul Jewett's reluctance to take an ontological approach to sexual polarity would be helpful in the end. Now we can see the implications of this decision for dealing with homosexuality. Perhaps this is why any reference to the question of homosexuality is conspicuous by its absence in Jewett's book, *Man as Male and Female*. Given the assumption that sexual polarity is itself a variable, with no ontological link to the *imago Dei* in terms of differentiation, one is not surprised at such silence. If one wishes to discuss homosexuality as unwarranted sexual behavior one has recourse only to theological ethics, supported by the biblical prooftexts which mention homosexuality. In light of the contemporary debate over the hermeneutical implications of texts which can be shown to have a distinct cultural overtone, it is understandable that one would be reluctant to pin the issue on such an ambiguous exercise.

A theology of human sexuality has led us to doubt that an argument can be made for homosexual orientation as a possibility fully equivalent to heterosexual orientation in terms of human personhood as created in the image of God. This is in our judgment the inescapable conclusion drawn from the assumptions established as fundamental to theological anthropology. Many forms and levels of disorder find their way into sexual orientation and behavior; and from the perspective of theological anthropology homosexual orientation is but one of these. From the perspective of pastoral care, a theological anthropology provides its own orientation, which again does not resort to abstract ethical principles but acts from the perspective of the eschatological nature of human personhood itself.

The true order of human sexuality is an essential polarity by which differentiation is experienced in a reciprocity of being. This is the image and likeness of God. The divine Word which determines that this is the ultimate goal of human persons accompanies each person in the pilgrimage toward that goal. The ultimate Word reaches into the penultimate and gives direction and wisdom, but also compassion and encouragement. The particular responsibility of God's people who live under the authority and wisdom of that ultimate

Word is to contextualize disorder for the sake of a reconciliation to the true order of being.

This is what it means to speak of justification by faith. God does not abandon the human creature when it falls into disorder; rather, he approaches it and contextualizes that disorder with his own structure of grace. For the sake of reconciliation to the true goal of human personhood, God brings that which is under the power of disorder into a higher authority. God creates the space and time in which disorder can learn of the wisdom of that divine Word.

To some extent, the people of God as the eschatological sign of the kingdom of God are that space and time in which the divine Word has come, in all of its eschatological power, as the final and true Word. And yet that Word comes among us and is with us "full of grace and truth" (John 1:14). In a lecture on grace and the Word of God, Thomas F. Torrance once identified the interval between the declaration to the paralytic (Mark 2) of the Word of forgiveness and the Word of physical restoration as the "eschatological reserve" by which God creates space and time for faith and repentance. The healing of the paralytic's body is a sign of the ultimate Word of restoration, healing, and perfection of all things. Before that final Word comes in its absolute and transforming power, the paralytic is held fast by the Word of forgiveness, which is the same Word. This is what I mean by the contextualizing of disorder for the sake of ultimate reconciliation to the true order of being. Theological anthropology brings with it the wisdom of this eschatological reserve and puts it to the service of pastoral care. In this wisdom, there is a "teleological suspension of the ethical," to borrow Kierkegaard's phrase. No one dares to raise a charge against God's elect, those who are loved by God (Rom. 8:31-39). But this is true only where there is a space and time in which God's grace is proclaimed and practiced. This is the business of the church. It really has no other business. It is responsible to know the difference between order and disorder, but wise enough to contextualize disorder with grace and truth.[18]

Through skilled psychotherapy from a Christian orientation, through authentic community in which love is shared in practice as well as in pronouncement, through the presence of Jesus Christ in Word and Sacrament, all of us disordered human creatures can discover the wisdom and truth of God's order. Sexual disorders are not of a different kind. They are first of all human disorders, and there is a place for being and becoming human in the space and time of God's Word.

---

18. An excellent treatment of the role of the church in dealing with disorder from a perspective of theological anthropology is Richard Crane, "Problems of the Homosexual in Relation to the Church," unpublished dissertation, Fuller Theological Seminary, 1977.

CHAPTER NINE

BEING HUMAN—
IN LIFE AND IN DEATH

ERNEST BECKER SPEAKS OF "HEALTHY-MINDED" PEOPLE WHO INSIST THAT fear of death is an acquired instinct. The healthy-minded person maintains that we are born with a natural confidence in life. Our anxiety and dread result from nurture and not from nature. Becker himself does not subscribe to the philosophy of healthy-mindedness. He argues that the fear of death is intrinsic to our nature as persons and that all sickness of the soul is rooted in the denial of this reality.[1] For Becker this denial takes the form of a heroic trans-ference, in which one achieves immortality by divinizing some object near at hand—or even the hand that manipulates the object. The larger canvas of life is really a portrait of our death, and we will expire before tracing out all the possibilities that confront us. The "normal" person survives by partializing life and narrowing that "terrifying vision of life" by concentrating on an accessible object or a manageable task. And it is this task which then becomes the heroic endeavor.

It does indeed take a good deal of heroism to live life. And not just on a grand scale, but in facing the commonplace routine of daily living with hope and courage. The heroic person is the one who gets up in the morning and does not commit suicide—or go back to bed. When a perversion which requires some kind of specialized treatment appears, it is a form of a failure of the "heroic" impulse, according to Becker. Too much reality has seeped in, and the unblinking eye of death paralyzes the hero. Sickness overcomes the soul. With penetrating insight (despite some tendency to fasten on the pathological side of human existence) Becker shows that the reality of death reaches into every nook and cranny of life, casting a shadow over the cheerful play of the child as well as the optimistic and idealistic dreams of the youthful. Being human is a matter of life *and* death. Even the stubborn insistence that one is in good health is a form of heroism in the face of the inevitable and capricious plague which infects every cell of creaturely existence. "The outer nature is perishing,"

---

1. *The Denial of Death*, pp. 13ff.

Paul concedes, even though the "inner nature" is being renewed every day (2 Cor. 4:16).

But what is the cure? Certainly not stripping away illusions, for that is itself unbearable. Life is much more than the mask which hides death. Life must have its own value as a form of "being human." But what is normal? If the illusions by which we face each day with hope and confidence in our "health" are functions of normal persons, are they really illusions? Is it altogether good to remove these illusions and produce a stark and unrelenting knowledge of our own mortality for the sake of a "cure?" Quoting a contemporary psychiatrist, Becker tells us, "It is not so much a question as to whether we are able to cure a patient, whether we can or not, but whether we should or not."[2] Becker's logic would argue that life itself is the terror, because it confronts us with possibilities which cannot be actualized. And even worse, those possibilities which are actualized are already doomed to extinction because we cannot give immortality to our own deeds and days. How does one live a "normal" life under such conditions?

Peter Shaffer creates this same dilemma in his play *Equus*. Martin Dysart, the psychiatrist, questions whether he has the right to restore a psychotic boy to normal life at the risk of destroying his perverted passion. "The normal," says Dysart,

> is the good smile in a child's eyes—all right. It is also the dead stare in a million adults. It both sustains and kills—like a God. It is the Ordinary made beautiful: it is also the Average made lethal. The normal is the indispensable, murderous God of Health, and I am his Priest. My tools are very delicate. My compassion is honest. I have honestly assisted children in this room. I have talked away terrors and relieved many agonies. But also—beyond question—I have cut from them parts of individuality repugnant to this God, in both his aspects. Parts sacred to rarer and more wonderful Gods. And at what length. . . . Sacrifices to Zeus took at the most surely, 60 seconds each. Sacrifices to the Normal can take as long as 60 months.

And, one might add, at $60.00 an hour!

But our purpose is neither to caricature the professional healer, whether priest or psychologist, nor to probe the ethics of professional therapy. The issue is anthropological. The question is this: is this sickness unto death our nature, and is normality the illusion of our immortality? Or is it the reverse? Which are we, mortal or immortal?

---

2. *Ibid.*, p. 270.

CREATURELINESS AS NATURAL LIFE

According to Genesis 1, we are sixth-day creatures. We came into existence along with all the other animal creatures. Taken from the dust of the ground, we experience solidarity with all that is of nature itself. Yet our creaturely nature experiences a tension between the material and immaterial. In our solidarity with other creatures, we share the same cyclical natural life. We come from the dust and return to it. We are animated beings with instincts as well as a "human soul"; but the nonhuman creatures also have a "soul," even though there is a qualitative distinction between human and nonhuman (see Appendix A). The divine in-breathing produces a creaturely soul which is human, as distinguished from all other creaturely beings who have life (*nephesh*). So, on the one hand, our creatureliness in its solidarity with all nature binds us to nature with its blind instincts and its unrelenting cyclical destiny. But, on the other hand, as human creatures, our existence is tethered to some other source of life, something that makes us always more than mere object, something which posits subjectivity and selfhood as the core of human personhood.

From the perspective of these two extremes one can understand how Becker can argue that the fundamental human condition is one of anxiety, dread, even terror. Personhood exists as the tension between these apparently contradictory forces. Despite the fact that we value our subjectivity and freedom of selfhood as at least an "intimation of immortality," our creaturely nature seems to be more determinative of our end than our human and personal aspirations. There is always a certain "wistfulness" about the brute fact of death, even when it is being met with resignation. In an interview on his deathbed, not many months after *The Denial of Death* had been published, Becker responded to Sam Keen's remark that this interview was an extraordinary event:

> I am sorry I probably won't get to see it. It's funny, I have been working for 15 years with an obsessiveness to develop these ideas, dropping one book after another into the void and carrying on with some kind of confidence that the stuff was good. And just now, these last years, people are starting to take an interest in my work. Sitting here talking to you like this makes me very wistful that I won't be around to see these things. It is the creature who wants more experience, another ten years, another five, another four, another three. I think, gee, all these things going on and I won't be a part of it. I am not saying that I won't see them, that there aren't other dimensions in existence but at least I will be out of this game and it makes me feel very wistful.[3]

---

3. *Psychology Today* (April 1974), p. 80.

Being human is also part of creaturely being. Our bodily existence is itself part of how we experience the differentiation so essential to community of being, human relationship, and fellowship. Co-humanity, as the concrete form of the *imago Dei*, is also being with and for the other person in terms of creaturely existence. I cannot be without or against, but only for my own body. And my body can only be for me; it cannot live or exist without me. I am embodied soul and ensouled body. Apart from my human soul, my body is merely a material object and thus impersonal. But also apart from my body, my soul is elusive and abstract and just as impersonal. The impersonality of dis-embodied soul is itself a breaking of the bond of co-humanity, and thus is a violation of the *imago Dei*.

Paul can only speculate apprehensively — and with some degree of horror — about the possible state of disembodied existence. Even thinking of being "absent from the body" and "present with the Lord," he shivers with discomfort at the idea of being "unclothed" (2 Cor. 5:4). Therefore, we conclude that it is unnatural for the human person to experience separation of the soul and body, for it leads to a depersonalization of the self. No doctrine of immortality of the soul will suffice to assuage this anxiety, nor will it be any comfort to conceive of death as a freeing of the soul from the body. "I will be sorry not to be around" is more than a narcissistic preoccupation with one's own embodied existence. It is a confession that "being around" is not all that bad, even under the conditions which often exist.

But Christian theology has often been tempted to surrender the body to the fate of the dust and pin its hopes on the immortality of the soul. More than once it succumbed to that temptation. In the fourth century St. Basil of Caesarea wrote:

> We should not be slaves of the body, except so far as is strictly necessary; but our souls we should supply with all things that are best, through philosophy freeing them, as from a prison, from association with the passions of the body. . . . In a single word, the body in every part should be despised by everyone who does not care to be buried in its pleasures, as it were in slime; or we ought to cleave to it only in so far as we obtain from it service for the pursuit of wisdom, as Plato advises. . . . And we ought to recall Pythagoras, who, on perceiving that one of his followers was putting on superfluous flesh by exercises and heavy eating said to him, "Pray cease making your prison house more wretched for you to live in!" It was for this reason, in fact, that Plato also, as we are told providing against the harmful influence of the body, deliberately occupied the pestilential region in Attica, the Academy, in order that he might prune away, as one prunes the vine of its excessive growth, the too great well-being

of his body. And I myself have heard physicians say that extreme good health is even dangerous.[4]

Preoccupied with cosmetics, natural foods, and physical health centers, we may find Basil's concerns ludicrous, but I suspect that we too experience an uneasy alliance between our body and our soul. Not many of us like our body as well as our "real self"; or, to put it another way, many of us would like ourselves better if we had a body that looked, performed, and lasted longer than the one we own.

But this is to capitulate to nonbiblical ways of thinking. The body is not a lower and mortal aspect of the person, while the soul in its abstraction from the body is a higher principle of personhood. To stress immortality as an abstract psychical experience of the self apart from the body is incompatible with biblical anthropology. This is not what the Bible means by eternal life and fellowship with God through the resurrection of the body.

Recent accounts of people who have apparently "died" and then experienced "out of body" sensations have caused many Christians to wonder if this is indeed some evidence of an "afterlife." Elisabeth Kübler-Ross documents many instances of persons who say that they have experienced a conscious state of existence outside of their bodies at a time when they have been pronounced medically dead, but then subsequently recovered. This, she suggests, is empirical evidence of "life after death."[5]

How do we respond to this phenomenon from a theological perspective? There is no reason to dispute the reliability of the testimony of everyone who has had such experiences nor of the documentation of the testimony. But we should be cautious about what conclusions we draw from these experiences. We could conclude that the relation between the "psychical" and the "somatic" aspect of personhood is in some degree of tension, and that the two are even capable of "drawing apart" from one another. Within the created order of creaturely being there seems to be no reason why this might not take place. Paul himself speaks of being "caught up to the third heaven — whether in the body or out of the body I do not know, God knows ..." (2 Cor. 12:2). As a purely "psychical" phenomenon, we would conclude that there is indeed a more tenuous relation than we ordinarily assume between the self and the body, which, under extreme stress, might give way to such a separation, even if it be a temporary one. But it would not be right to infer that this is then evidence of a "life after death" in biblical terms, or of the immortality of the soul. Quite the contrary. The concept of immortality as a self-conscious psychical expe-

---

4. Loeb Classical Library, *St. Basil Letters*, Volume IV (9).
5. *On Death and Dying* (New York: Macmillan, 1969); *Questions and Answers on Death and Dying* (New York: Macmillan, 1974).

rience apart from the body has nothing to do with immortality as a theological concept. This is more in line with a Greek way of thinking than with the Hebrew concept of the self, as we shall see. The Bible does not give us any assurance that what is meant by eternal life is the extension of psychical consciousness beyond the limits of bodily existence. The promise of the gospel is the resurrection of the body and the reuniting of soul and body in an imperishable state.

THE DYING OF THE BODY
AND THE DIGNITY OF THE PERSON

But what then is death? What is mortality? What is it to be a mortal being while at the same time bearing the promise of immortality? Certainly we know that death is a universal experience for all that is human. What is more, death brings the threat of separation between the soul and the body, if not the annihilation of the soul, and thus the end of personal existence. What is the meaning of the inevitable and universal experience we call death?

The Hebrews understood death as the loss of life, the attenuation of the life force that integrates soul and body. Thus, death was explained in terms of life. Death is the weakest form of life, a scattering of one's vital powers, a pouring out of the soul (Isa. 53:12; Job 30:16). One who dies is like water spilled on the ground, not to be gathered up again (2 Sam. 14:14). In the underworld, in Sheol, there is no real life, even though persons continue to "exist" as shadows of the real self. There is no praise of God in Sheol; and the dead have no memory of the living (cf. Ps. 6:5). The idea of separation predominates in the Hebrew view of death. The unity of the body and the soul is broken and the person is cut off from the "land of the living" (Isa. 38:11). In this sense, the Hebrew viewed death very existentially. It is a losing of one's powers, a final surrender to that which has the power to overtake the self. Yet this surrender is also a submission to what God himself has determined, so that the dead are not beyond God's concern and power. Whatever hope there is, is a hope in God, not in personal immortality as a clear concept of "life after death."

Some theologians distinguish between "dying" and "death." The former is defined as the natural process of all that is creaturely in nature. Because we are taken from the dust and return to it, nature itself seems to include this process of "corruptibility." The inevitable passing away of the temporal is due to the limitations of creaturely being appointed by the Creator. So far as we can see, God has not determined that creaturely being, as an expression of created natural existence, should exist in that form eternally. Mortality is a divinely determined characteristic of the sixth day. Before the fall Adam was already in a state of mortality. As a creature of the sixth day he shared with all other natural creatures this inevitable process of "dying."

On this view, there is a cycle of coming into being and departing from being at the level of nature. We were created mortal, and "dying" is the process through which every mortal creature must pass. If there is a different destiny for the human creature, if there is immortality as a gift of life shared with God the Creator, this is due to God's sovereign determination, not to some intrinsic human possibility. Immortality is a characteristic of God's own divine being, and belongs only to him. Even if Adam had not sinned, he would still have had to be transformed to reach a state of immortality (eternal life). Karl Barth argues that death belongs naturally to the human creature:

> This means that it also belongs to human nature, and is determined and ordered by God's good creation, and to that extent right and good, that man's being in time should be finite and man himself mortal. The fact that one day he shall have been answers to a law which does not inevitably mean that we are imprisoned, fettered and condemned to negation by its validity. Death is not in itself the judgment. It is not in itself and as such the sign of God's judgment. It is so only *de facto*. Hence, it is not to be feared in itself, or necessarily, but only *de facto*.[6]

Fear of death, Barth is saying, is not necessarily the condition of the creature. The fact that dying as a divinely determined order of creaturely existence also becomes the occasion for coming under divine judgment is a *de facto* situation, not a necessary one. Nonhuman creatures also experience death as a process of dying. But there is no divine judgment attached to this process. Only since dying has become judgment for the human person under the penalty of sin, has it become "death."

Here then is the distinction between dying and death. Dying can be said to be natural. In itself it is no threat to the human person. It has no power over us because creatureliness itself cannot determine human personhood. The divine Word determines that the human person should exist as a creaturely being, but that creaturely being has power only as a *de facto* situation in which the human is also a sinner, estranged from God and now subject to the limitations of the sixth day. Death, then, is a more theologically oriented word which denotes the judgment which accompanies the creaturely experience of dying.

For all creatures but the human, dying is itself a natural "fate." For the human creature, dying is to be a "transformation" by which the mortal puts on immortality — to use the language by which Paul speaks of the resurrection

---

6. *Church Dogmatics*, III/2, 632.

(1 Cor. 15:54). But with the act of sin, the human race is now subjected to dying as a judgment. "Death" thus enters the world and spreads to all persons (Rom. 5:12). It is this death which becomes the enemy of the human. It is this death which is to be feared; and it is this "death" which Christ came to overcome in order to liberate human creatures from dying without hope. Again, Barth makes the point clear:

> In the judgment of God man is in fact a sinner and a debtor, and therefore by divine sentence subject to death, i.e., to death in the harsher sense, the "second death." And Jesus Christ has actually gone in our place to death, to death in this second sense, in this absolutely negative sense of the term. ... We know the end of our temporal existence, our death, only as it is overshadowed by His death. Even though those who face death with their hope fixed on God ... know that death is vanquished in virtue of the death which Jesus Christ suffered in our place. ... The death which is behind them is an evil, an enemy of man. In the light of this fact there can be no doubt as to the unnatural and discordant character of death.[7]

On the one hand, Barth has argued that dying is natural and mortality an intrinsic aspect of creatureliness; now, on the other hand, he can say just as strongly that death is unnatural, a judgment against the sinner, an enemy of that which is human.

We said earlier that theologians disagree as to the state of creaturely humanity before the fall. Some have held that Adam and Eve were created as immortal, or with a kind of "natural immortality" which was lost in the fall and had to be restored through Christ. Luther and Calvin followed Augustine in teaching that prior to the fall a state of immortality was posited for the human person as a determination of God. Through the fall this "immortality" was forfeited and could only be restored by the gift of eternal life in Jesus Christ. Medieval theology, as it was represented by Thomistic thought, tended to see the human creature as mortal by nature; except for the infusion of eternal life through a gift of grace it would never experience immortality. The fall represented a loss of this *donum superadditum* which subsequently was restored through Christ. Modern secular thought rejects such a divine infusion of grace, and accepts the natural mortality of the creature as a universal fact of human existence. Death is thus seen as natural, not unnatural.

Kübler-Ross reflects this position. She holds that dying is a process quite natural to the human person as creature. She outlines five stages through which persons ordinarily go to reach some acquiescence to the process — denial, anger, bargaining, depression, and finally acceptance. Acceptance of death

---

7. *Ibid.*, 628.

is the goal, because it represents a coming to terms with what is natural. Death is not something ultimately to be resisted and denied, but a process of nature finally acceptable as basic to our humanity. For all of the valuable insight she contributes to our understanding of the psychological process of facing death, Kübler-Ross's basic assumptions concerning the nature of death *vis-à-vis* the human person lack the discrimination outlined above between dying as natural and death as an enemy of the human.[8]

We believe that humanity as originally created was not immortal by nature, though it was under the determination of immortality by virtue of being summoned into fellowship with God, whose own eternal being constitutes the basis for an immortal destiny of the human. This position avoids the problems created by suggesting that there is a "natural immortality" as contrasted with divine immortality; at the same time it does not surrender the human person to the deterministic and fatalistic process of dying as mere creature. To use Barth's language, being human is *de facto* being a sinner. Therefore, dying is itself a *de facto* state of being under condemnation and judgment. Death, therefore, is unnatural and is the "last enemy" to be destroyed (1 Cor. 15:26). Quiet and submissive acquiescence in the face of death is not the model Scripture gives us. The author of Hebrews tells us that Jesus, though he was the Son of God in the flesh, prayed "with loud cries and tears" that he might be saved from death (Heb. 5:7).

In the Old Testament death is never preferred to life, except in exaggerated, rhetorical expressions such as Job. What is natural is the endowment of life, the giving of the breath of God which constitutes the soul of the body. What is natural to the Hebrew person is being in the land of the living and not being in the underworld (Sheol). What is natural is life and not death. Death is the epitome of what is contrary to human nature; and one is not expected to welcome it with open arms. In the New Testament Jesus engages in open combat with suffering, sickness, and death. Sickness itself is unnatural and death is an enemy to be destroyed.

Here is no romantic glorification of heroic death, no toleration of death with stoic patience. However, because there is faith and trust in the God who brings forth life from death, another strain running through the Bible recognizes the limits of mortal existence. That is, life is both bodily and temporal in its creaturely form. It is experienced within divinely ordained limits, which can be accepted. We are not compelled to take death as an unqualified evil. The Psalmist tells us that persons acquire wisdom of heart by numbering their

---

8. For a critique of Kübler-Ross's concept of death, see the article, "Is Acceptance a Denial of Death?, Another Look at Kübler-Ross," *The Christian Century* (May 7, 1975), 464-68.

days (Ps. 90:12). Realism about the fact that we cannot live in this state forever has some value. David says to Solomon, "I go the way of all flesh" (1 Kings 2:2). The memory of the departed as God's anointed may be perpetually blessed in contrast to the way in which the name of the ungodly shall perish (Ps. 1). God's people can confess, "Blessed is he who dies in the Lord" and "Precious in the sight of the Lord is the death of his saints" (Ps. 116:15). Balaam's wish can make perfectly good sense: "Let me die the death of the righteous, and let my last end be like his" (Num. 23:10).

The remarkable circumstances which accompanied the death of three of the Old Testament saints point us toward the eschatological nature of the transformation death entails. God himself buried Moses, and his natural force was not abated (Deut. 34:5-7). We are led to believe that Moses could have gone on living had the termination of his life not occurred as an act of God's will. God brought about the transition and transformation without waiting for a natural process infected by sin to make it inevitable. Earlier, in anticipation of the inevitable and as an immediate effecting of that transformation, Enoch "walked with God and was not" (Gen. 5:24). And Elijah was taken up in a whirlwind (2 Kings 2). Elisha sees him in death; that is, he sees immortality swallow up mortality (1 Cor. 15:54). Once more, the transition is effected by a sovereign act of God, not through what we call the natural process of dying.

These Old Testament accounts hint that mortality can pass into immortality without the pain and shuddering shock of dying. Thus Paul sees quite clearly that we do not die as those who have no hope, for Christ has taken the sting out of death, which is sin (1 Thess. 4:13; 1 Cor. 15:54-56). Again we see the merit of distinguishing between dying and death. As a process which belongs to our creatureliness, dying continues even for those under the sovereign determination of God's power in Jesus Christ. But death as the enemy has been conquered. Because we die as sinners, even though we are under the law of life in Christ Jesus (Rom. 8:2), our dying reminds us of the death we deserve. Even in dying, death continues to be challenged.

On behalf of those who are dying we cannot consent to death as though it did not matter. It matters terribly, and the person who is dying is walking "through the valley of the shadow of death" (Ps. 23:4). We do not, as Christians, merely trust in immortality; we trust in the one who alone is the immortal God, and who has given his assurance through Jesus Christ that he will be present in life and in death.

The integrity of human personhood is inextricably bound up with physical existence. Our bodies are not cruel jokes played on us by the inevitability of death. The Hebrews saw a mystery in the relation of the soul to the body which was respected in death as much as in life. Without knowing why, they allowed the mystery and dignity of personhood to survive in the blood, bones,

139

physical history, and memory of the departed. A stock Old Testament phrase for impending death is "to sleep with one's fathers," which means: "My bones are mingled with those of my ancestors." That is a comfort, a basis for hope; for there is belief in the sovereignty of God's election of his people for his own purpose and glory. The New Testament person meets this mystery from the other end, from the eschatological perspective of the resurrection of the body and the certification of the dignity of the person in the body. In the Old Testament, one could only believe that the bones themselves, in a sense, continue to carry on this fragile life force. In the New Testament we see flesh and blood transformed through Jesus Christ, and yet, the reconstitution of the very same body with its familiar features.

The Christian can face death squarely, even as the enemy, for its sting has been removed. The dying person can be affirmed in his or her dying. Fear, pain, and even anger can be validated as personal experience without denying the ultimate reality of the resurrection of the body and freedom from suffering. Bonhoeffer spoke of his own ministry to the dying as a presence of the reality of God, even in silence, which did not violate the penultimate for the sake of the ultimate.[9] This is instructive for us: the presence of faith in the act of dying is a context in which dying becomes a pilgrimage rather than a dead-end. There is a "living end" which reaches back into the experience of dying. The seventh day breaks into the sixth.

CONTEXTUALIZING DEATH IN A COMMUNITY OF FAITH AND HOPE

These theological reflections lead to some practical considerations. The first is that death does not devalue or cancel out the life lived in our bodies. We are told that we shall be rewarded at the judgment seat of Christ for the deeds done in our body (2 Cor. 5:10). On the one hand, that can be frightening or discouraging, but we can also understand this teaching as an affirmation of the integrity of our human historical life. Our life is not some monstrous irrelevancy, as though death could unravel all its significance. On the contrary. Our real selves are historical, and we can take the things done in the body and to the body with utter seriousness. To clothe, to feed, to caress — these are things of deep personal and eternal significance.

The loss of consciousness does not entail a loss of subjectivity. The Hebrews knew that loss of consciousness meant that subjectivity, as the essence of personal existence, must now be considered to have continuity in the blood

---

9. *Ethics*, p. 126.

and in the bones. Otherwise why would Jacob and Joseph both have been so concerned that their bones be taken back to the Promised Land for burial (Gen. 47:29-30; 50:24-26)? The curtailment of the function of the body through suffering or injury or disease does not reduce the quality of a person's life. The fact that we sometimes suffer limitations of the functions of our body in no way diminishes our subjective value as a person.

Granted there is a mystery here. At a certain point we begin to ask how *much* of the body must remain in order for it to be a body? To lose an arm or a leg is to lose nothing of personhood: we are still "I," or "he" or "she." We can lose two arms; we can be quadriplegics and we can lose all of our extremities and continue to have full value as a person. But there is a continuum here. A point can come at which too much has been carved away, and the body can no longer support the life of the person. There is a sense in which everything which is contained in my physical body is "mine" by virtue of its function in supporting and sustaining my life. Yet at the same time, no single element of my body as a purely physical or chemical element is necessary to my existence as a person. Take the calcium out of my body and I no longer say that it is "mine" in the same way that it was when constitutive of my body.

The value of the body is not in its intrinsic worth as a physical and objective element in the world of things. Rather, its value is in its relation with the self as an indissoluble unity of personal being. The "body," therefore, is more than the sum of all its parts. It is a state of existence in which personal and human being is extended to all of the parts in their being contiguous to one another. Body, then, is not mere *soma* as distinct from *psyche* — though it is always that too. Paul speaks of a "natural body" and a "spiritual body" which have continuity and similarity, yet discontinuity and unlikeness (1 Cor.15). On the continuum of personal existence as embodied soul and ensouled body, there is a point at each end in which the contingent relation between human being and creaturely being becomes more pronounced, though, as a specific point, it remains essentially ambiguous and imprecise.

At what point does a mass of cell division at the biological level become a body, or even a person? At some point, surely. But is one cell a "body," or are two or more cells a "body?" Is the last heartbeat, or the last breath of a human person the death of the person or merely the cessation of "bodily function?" If other "bodily functions" — such as cell division — continue after the last heartbeat, is what remains the body of a person, or merely a corpse? In the process of being creaturely humanity, a person experiences a beginning and an end. Both are posited in mystery. Personhood, to use Barth's language again, may be considered to be a *de facto* existence. Death is a *de facto* determination. There is a point when the evidences are sufficient that "life has

141

ended." At that moment, a body becomes a corpse. To make that decision prematurely is murder, the taking of a human life. There is, however, by common consent, a threshold beyond which the connections between "body and soul" do not exist, and the body is placed in the earth from which it came. For many people, dying is not a sudden loss of bodily power but a slow and ongoing process. But there is still the reality of a bodily presence of the person, even when the body is losing its own power to sustain life.

It follows from this that the indignity of death is the loss of the use of the body. Dying involves an approaching disjunction between body and soul at the functional level, not the theoretical level. Thus, death is a final indignity because the body becomes a mere object over which the person has no control, and in which the person has no power of presence. The absolute objectivity of body when it becomes corpse entails a loss of subjective presence on the part of the person. A so-called "vegetative" state of bodily existence is virtually a form of death, and can itself become an indignity if artificially prolonged as a monument to medical technology. When a machine and a body have more of a necessary relationship than do the soul and the body, what is being sustained is not life, but a process of dying.

The presence of another person to us is unavoidably bodily, but not necessarily linked to the body. That is to say, to maintain functions of the body does not necessarily maintain the reality of the person as encounter. Here again is a mystery. For an incredible span of time and attention, the other person can continue to have personal presence to us even when in a coma or state of suspended bodily functioning. But a point can come when one person's control over the bodily existence of another as a form of sustaining the life of the other becomes itself inhuman and even monstrous. We are well aware that we now have the technological knowledge and equipment to sustain the function of the human body as a biological organism far beyond what is necessary for the sake of humanity itself. In the next chapter we shall see how theological anthropology can inform medical ethics in this area. Even when we consent to the disposal of the body, we are concerned for the dignity of the person. We do not ask that the mortician be sentimental; we value professionalism in the act of preparing for burial. But the community to which that person *still* belongs will contextualize the event of death and burial with a dignity which sheer professionalism cannot render.

The community — whether represented by the congregation of God's people, or a family, or a friend, or the lover of the one who has died — must assume subjective responsibility for the body in the death of a person. To allow the body to become a mere impersonal object is to commit an indignity against the person. In my dying, I will lose power over my own body, and yet it will be "my body" to the end. The natural transition from mortal creatureliness to immortal communion with God is meant to be a pilgrimage which is accompanied. Dying is meant to be contextualized in the form of a processional. Death is not an end, but the transition to a new beginning. To die without a processional which manifests that transition through the presence of a human community under the power of the divine Word is to be abandoned at the moment when one is weakest and most vulnerable. And so, that which is *professional* in the service of burying the dead must be continually contextualized by that which is *processional*. That which is mortal is being escorted to the very threshold of immortality and surrendered to arms which are prepared to embrace and preserve the form of the personal. At that threshold we say "dust to dust, ashes to ashes," and we give that body back to the earth, tenderly, even as we give over the person, confidently and in hope, to the resurrection of the body from the dead. We who are a subjective community of human existence give over the person to another community of divine fellowship. When we let go of the hand we do so with the deepest conviction of our souls that without faltering or fumbling someone else is taking that hand.

Upon returning from a period of study abroad, I learned that a member of the church I had formerly pastored was dying. As the choir director, she had shared with me a mutual ministry of proclamation of the Word of God. Now, through a freak of medical technology in a routine operation, she had developed cirrhosis of the liver. She became one of the "statistically few" who are destroyed through the very technology which cures. And she died in a year's agonizing, prolonged, and unrelenting suffering. All that could be done by the people who loved her was to make out of that entire year a processional of companionship and communion in faith, a manifestation of presence, one to another and both to God. Before the funeral service, her husband told me of the circumstances of that suffering and death. He said, "You know, Clara probably weighed only 60 pounds when she died in her own bed at home. I could lift her up in one hand when I bathed her emaciated body." During the hours preceding the service, I pondered the significance of what we were about to do in light of that conjunction of torment and love. It became clear to me that the processional had begun with his caring for her, body and soul. Upheld by the Word of God, within the context of a believing community, I could announce that to those assembled for the service of commitment. I spoke as much to all of us assembled as to him. This is a processional, and we have had Clara's body entrusted to us during these long months in preparation for this event. We who have bathed her with our own hands, who have held her emaciated and broken body to our breast, we are going to go forth from this place and place her body in the earth from which she was taken. We are going to do it with love and gentleness, as a community of which she is a member.

To us her body is still the person we know and love, and we are going to give her over to God, tenderly and with the confidence that he will keep her, restore her, and present her to us when all things are made new.

The truth of those words was not only in their power to sustain and comfort those who mourned her passing. The truth was, in a deeply theological sense, a truth of our own human being. We who live are part of such a processional in which eternity touches time through the enactment of this ancient ritual of living and dying. In death there is a meeting of persons that must be sustained. At the tomb of Jesus we see enacted this fundamental recognition of the mystery of the human person as embodied soul. The women came to the tomb to anoint the body, not as professionals who had learned how to mask the reality of death from the eyes of the living, but as those who know that the dead need the living to hold them in community. They came out of an ancient tradition that was as theologically sound as it was psychologically healthy. They came as those who could not so quickly surrender the body of the one who had been so personally present to them. They came to work out their own grief and to continue to give expression to their love by ministering to the body. Not just to a *body*, but to *him*. To wash away the blood from those wounds in his body was to minister to him. To bind his body in fresh linen, to anoint it with fragrant spices, was to hold him present to them during the time when he was most vulnerable, in that transition from life to death, until finally the earth itself should receive his body.

There is something destructive of our own personhood when we look away too quickly from the presence of the body of another in death. We ought not to try to mitigate our grief by removing the body of the other as an object of our love. Often we tend to anticipate even this, and so to turn away from the body of a person who is dying, as though in the grotesqueness of suffering the body has already become as alien to us as it is becoming to the one who still is present to us in it. Of course, a morbid preoccupation with the body as a way of denying the reality of death is as theologically unsound as it is psychologically unhealthy. Yet the mystery of the person as an embodied soul is not broken instantly by medical death.

There is no way to acquire an absolutely precise insight into the mystery of death. The mystery of the soul's leaving the body so that it can return to the dust does not correspond exactly to the sudden disappearance of blips on an oscilloscope. There are rituals that belong to dying as well as to living. We who are living are still connected, for at least a brief interval, to the other. The rituals of dying connect the ensouled body of the other with our own embodied soul. The processional is not long; it ends when the earth has claimed the body. But this is no time for awkwardness or fumbling. With keenness of insight as to the mystery of personhood even through the valley

144

of the shadow of death, we act with the certainty and freedom of those who know what they are doing.

When my father died after a prolonged struggle against cancer, I was summoned to his bedside for the final hours. As he moved fitfully in a deep coma, our family sat with him as he lay on his own bed in his own home. Occasionally during those 36 hours we ministered to him, wiping his forehead, touching him lightly, speaking softly to him. Shortly before he died, after he had been lying motionless for several hours, the Lutheran minister stopped by the house. Not saying a word, he walked over to the bed and began to read the 23rd Psalm. At the sound of his voice my father, who had not moved for hours, moved his hands and folded them on his breast. An incredible sign of the fact that, while we had given up attempting to communicate with him, he was a person in whom the Word of God could provoke and summon forth a response of hearing. Somewhere there was a connection that we had forgotten.

A short time later, my father expired. His sister, my aunt, took his false teeth out of the glass, adjusted them in his mouth, and closed it. Taking a dish towel, she wrapped it around his chin and forehead, tying up his face; and suddenly his humanity was restored, as though she were creating him again out of the lump of clay that God originally wrought into a human face. Asking for two coins, she closed his eyes gently, placing them on his eyelids to keep them closed. I was a silent participant in an ancient processional that knew instinctively and certainly what it was doing. Something deep inside of me knew that this was good, and I now knew that what she was doing was training me to do as much for her.

There is co-humanity, even in the process of dying. The eschatological reality of the resurrection of the body is grasped from this side of life and the divine Word which sustains the human person in unity of body and soul is made manifest. There is no room for illusion in that moment. Faith must be clear of mind and centered upon the one in whose Word and Spirit the human pilgrimage begins and ends. Only this time, the end is not a fatalistic or fearful conclusion to a life that has become a bad dream. Faith, then, finally, is more fundamental than fear.

Ernest Becker said of himself that he is not one of the healthy-minded. He distrusted that illusion of eternal life as a sick hope. But there is a healthy-minded hope. "Why are you troubled?", asked Jesus. "And why do questionings arise in your hearts? See my hands and my feet, that it is I myself; handle me, and see; for a spirit has not flesh and bones as you see that I have" (Luke 24:38-39). This was *after* his resurrection. Hands and feet are no illusions; they belong to the new being. Most of all, I would want to say that to Ernest Becker.

CHAPTER TEN

BEING HUMAN —
IN FEAR AND TREMBLING

FULL HUMANNESS, ERNEST BECKER ONCE WROTE, MEANS FACING UP TO life with fear and trembling.[1] Becker seemed to see this as an acute psychological state produced by the need for faith as an integrating and unifying concept of the self. Soren Kierkegaard, who wrote a brilliant essay on *Fear and Trembling*, saw the crisis more in theological than psychological terms. The paradox of faith, he wrote, is precisely that it is a temptation (*Anfechtung*) which comes on a person when confronted by the demand of God as the absolute as over against one's duty toward the universal as the ethical.[2]

Being human is surely a duty toward God, who is himself the one who summons the self into existence, but how is this duty to be recognized and discharged? If duty to God on behalf of "being human" and affirming the humanity of others is first of all understood as one's responsibility always to acknowledge that which is universally held to be good and true, one's first responsibility is to that which is "in principle" the right thing to do, and only consequently toward the concrete situation. However, as Kierkegaard shows, God's demands on us are in the form of absolute demands rather than universal principles, and these demands confront us in the concrete and particular situation of our own human existence. Abraham loved his son Isaac, Kierkegaard says, but this love as a universal and ethical principle of love was intersected by the command of God to offer him as a sacrifice. This is the "temptation" (*Anfechtung*); it is the irreconcilable discrepancy between the ethical (universal) and the act of faith (absolute) as an immediate and concrete demand on one's life. Thus, to live humanly, to be human, is to experience those critical moments in the vulnerability which comes to one who acts absolutely out of faith in God, yet in fear and trembling.

As part of a class assignment, one of my students once turned in a written paper which included a personal account of an experience which she now identified as being of profound theological significance to her. At the age of 40

---

1. *The Denial of Death*, p. 59.
2. *Fear and Trembling and Sickness Unto Death*, pp. 79ff.

she had become pregnant. An amniocentesis disclosed that her unborn child suffered chromosome abnormalities which indicated that the child would be micro-cephalic, mentally retarded, and neurologically handicapped. She and her husband, in consultation with their parish minister, decided on a therapeutic abortion.

> As the doctor infused my uterus with a natural hormone designed to bring on labor, I felt so terribly sad, yet very much at peace. That peace sustained me, as a very difficult labor ensued. I took no anesthetic, because I wanted to experience this child as I had experienced my others. When the child came, I felt tiny legs kicking my legs, and I asked the nurse to hand me my baby. She cut the cord and put my little girl on my breast with great tenderness. She tried to breathe and I held her as she left this life and went on to Him. She was a person. She was conceived in love and created by God. She deserved to be treated with utmost respect and humility. For she was an enigma, as all of us are who are persons, . . . all of us human beings created in the image and likeness of God, and redeemed in our Lord Jesus Christ. I thank God for the opportunity to have experienced her life and her death, and I look ahead with certainty to the time that I will know her face to face. We did not have the church's liturgy that day, but our own enactment served the same purpose. She was held in love as the transition from this life to eternal life was made.

People will read this testimony with a variety of responses. Some will be angry and horrified with such an act. Others will question the case on ethical grounds, arguing that taking a life is no less murder in the case of an unborn child than of an adult person. Some may understand and accept her decision, yet uncertain as to what justification there can be for it.

When the sun is bright upon our backs and life is normal and everything apparently in order, it is not difficult to know what is good and what is evil. It is good to be human and to support human life. It is wrong to destroy and to torment human life. But at the margins of life, when there is disorder and distortion, where disease and death become imbedded in the creaturely being itself, who or what is the destroyer, and what finally is our responsibility to be human?

HUMAN BEING AS A
MARGINAL POSSIBILITY

In developing our theological anthropology, we explored at some length the concept of a contingent relation between the human and the creaturely. By contingent, we mean that the distinctive reality of being a human person is determined and sustained by some power and source beyond creaturely being itself. Though never less than a creaturely being, the human person is not an extension of a possibility of creatureliness in some necessary form. This, of course, is a highly theoretical discrimination between humanity and creatureliness. It is a conclusion reached by giving serious consideration to what Scripture has revealed. While nonhuman creatures are created "after their own kind" out of the elements of created material itself, human creatures are created "in the image and likeness of God." There is a divine inbreathing which penetrates this dust out of which the human is formed. Further, we argued that, despite the solidarity of the sixth day, which binds humans and nonhumans together as creaturely beings, the human person is destined to share fellowship with God and is therefore a creature of the seventh day.

Not everything which comes from the body of a human person is human — but some things are. Children born through a human sexual act are considered to be as fully human as the parents. Nor is there any doubt that what is conceived through this act can become human. The divine determination which constitutes humanity is, as far as we can see, joined to the human process by which children are conceived and born into this world. To call the relation between the creaturely and the human contingent is therefore not to risk the possibility of sheer randomness. The joining of the divine determination to be human with the creaturely process of producing another being can be assumed to coincide so closely that for all practical purposes they are identical. It is the task of a theological anthropology, however, to know the difference between what is coincidental and what is identical, for only by being able to posit the contingent relation between humanity and creatureliness can we hold in check the fatalistic determinism of creaturely nature itself, so that the human person is free to have his or her own destiny beyond the possibility of creaturely nature.

Most people agree that the distinctive quality of human life is that it is an existence characterized by freedom and not by determinism. To be sure, some would side with B. F. Skinner, for example, in arguing that there is no such thing as freedom or dignity as an intrinsic quality of the human. Human persons are themselves under complete determinism and do not exercise "free choice." Perhaps Skinner has read too much bad theology at this point. We would agree that the human person has no intrinsic dignity and freedom by virtue of being a human creature. Freedom and dignity are the result of a divine determinism which acts so as to suspend the natural determinism of creaturely existence itself. The fact that this divine determinism is experienced as personal freedom and dignity is a moot point in the debate.

Our point is that human personhood emerges out of the conjunction of a creaturely, biological process and the divine determination. Because the biological process itself has a "margin of error," there is a certain marginality which accompanies the possibility of being human. Ordinarily we do not see the margins of this determination and process exposed. Normal and healthy children emerge with sufficient regularity that we can almost assume that the process itself is determinative of humanity. But the creaturely process has its own order and consequently its own disorder. When the margins of the order of nature are broached, nature becomes problematical. The possibility that recognizable order will emerge can become marginal. A two-headed calf, for example, has no practical value to the farmer (except perhaps for sale to the circus as a "freak"). At the creaturely level alone, there is a certain degree of tolerance for such "marginal" creatures. If a monstrosity is produced instead of a normal creature, some utilitarian value is lost in the process, but no essential loss to creaturely being itself.

However, although the human occurs as a phenomenon on this field of creaturely being, these "marginal" cases are quite a different matter. The value at stake is far more than the utilitarian value of a creature. There is the quite real possibility of a loss of human being and therefore a loss of that which bears the image and likeness of God. The assumption that everything which results from the creaturely process of human reproduction is for that very reason intrinsically human entails that the image and likeness of God is identical with that which is potentially human as a biological organism as much as that which is actually human in the form of a living person. This would mean that the divine determination does not distinguish between order and disorder at the creaturely level. If that theological assumption is correct, one should be prepared to live with its implications, which are very close to a natural determinism according to which creaturely nature itself is endowed with the possibility of the *imago Dei*, so that being human is identical with a biological process of the minutest scale.

Consider for a moment the other end of the continuum. Most Christians would agree that at some point the creaturely (biological) form of human existence loses the power to determine the state of the person. A corpse which shows some remaining evidence of cell division due to chemical processes going on in it is nevertheless not a "person." Otherwise an autopsy would come under the same category as "surgery," the cadaver would still be accompanied by members of the family, and the burial of such a corpse would be an act of "burying a person alive." For life in this case would be necessarily related to biological process.

On what grounds do we consider these implications mistaken — even grotesque? Is it not clear that we have by common consent agreed that the life of the person is contingently, not necessarily, related to biological process? When the margins of life as a unity of biological and personal existence are broached so that we conclude that there is no longer personal being but rather

149

a corpse, then we say that the possibility of that specific human person does not exist in that same creaturely form. A theological anthropology such as we have developed shows why this commonly accepted practice is not an offense to human persons. That is, the ethics which control the treatment of a corpse as against the treatment of a person are fundamentally determined by conclusions drawn from theological anthropology.

However, it does not follow from this that it is ever within our power of determination to say that a malformed infant, no matter how deformed or deprived of what we consider to be normal human capacity, is less than human. In this case, the medieval theologians were not wrong in arguing for the validity of baptism for the insane or for extreme unction for those who were already (presumably) at the point of death. To say that human life is on some occasions "marginal" is not to say that we should actually make the determination that some are human while others might not be. The concept of marginality is merely to demonstrate what is meant by the theological construct of contingency. There is no necessary connection between the creaturely and the human so that the creaturely has the power of sustaining the human apart from the sovereign power of God.

We need not appeal to the grotesque or the exceptional to establish this point. I was once approached by a parishioner whose wife had just lost the child she was carrying: a stillborn male in the fifth month of her pregnancy. "What shall we do?" he asked me. "She feels that she has lost a child." My immediate response was that they should name it and that we would bury it as a person who belongs to God. This little Jonathan we laid to rest; he never squalled on earth, but will sing in heaven! I do not believe that anyone would take offense at this. The event of becoming a human person is in clear enough focus to make a decision about what is human. I doubt that there are any legal or ethical criteria to help answer the question, other than the moral responsibility not to offend human sensibilities.

Now consider another example—an hypothetical and extremely unlikely one. A woman approaches her pastor with a container in which there is a mass of thick blood. She reports that she has apparently suffered a miscarriage after being pregnant for possibly four weeks. What should she do with it? Wouldn't the proper response be to dispose of it in the quickest and most efficient way—as one would do with any body fluid? Would anyone suggest that the responsible thing to do would be to have a laboratory examination to see whether or not there has been, in fact, fertilization and cell division, and if so, schedule a funeral service and have an interment? I have never heard of such a case. But if human life is identical with fertilization and cell division as a biological event, as some would argue, such a miscarriage would also constitute the death of a person.

The issue in this case is more complex than the question of determining the point of death. But setting aside the question of motives, and even the ethical question of a theoretical "right to live" on the part of that which is not yet living, is there not some fundamental question here as to what constitutes a human person as a marginal possibility? No doubt we feel more comfortable allowing room for "marginality" when deciding the point of death than when deciding the point of "humanization" of a mass of cells. The implications of acting presumptuously in the latter case are so horrendous that we will ordinarily give the benefit of the doubt to the point of assuming that fertilization of the ovum itself is the beginning of human life. This is quite understandable, but it should not be the basis for making theological judgments about the nature of the human itself. Quite possibly that would lead to sheer natural determinism, and when natural determinism is linked with ethical absolutism it becomes the basis for an ideological mandate that all but eclipses the real issue. It is not surprising when such ideological presuppositions also became the basis for political opportunism. This is dangerously close to a twentieth-century equivalent of the first-century "Sabbath principle," in which technical discussions about the legality and morality of an issue left the actual human being bereft of the divine wisdom and grace which must accompany persons in their awe-ful decisions about what is right and good.

It is not our objective here to decide or even discuss the issues of abortion, the right to die, the right to live, or the right to exercise one's sexual preference in accordance with what seems "natural." We are attempting to lay the groundwork in theological anthropology for discussing the moral and ethical implications of these issues. There are ethical implications for the issues we have listed, but these issues must be decided on the basis of what is human in order to render a decision as to what humans ought to do in these situations. These critical issues are fundamentally anthropological before they are ethical. What one decides as to the state of the human person will ordinarily determine the weight of the ethical imperative.

This should not be construed as a campaign against ethics. As Barth has clearly pointed out in his treatment of true humanity (*Church Dogmatics*, III/2), the ethical imperative issues from the command of God by which real humanity is set forth as a created order and as an eschatological goal in Christ. Thus, "wrong-doing" is disobedience to the divine command (not being what we are divinely determined to be), not merely the violation of a legalistic principle. The same divine order which graciously summons forth the true order of humanity as command of God calls for judgment against that which is contrary to this true order. The church, established by the Holy Spirit as the community of Christ, bears the responsibility of exercising its knowledge of the grace of God both as the affirmation of real humanity and as judgment for the sake of repentance on disordered humanity. (We will be reminded of this again later when we discuss the community of God as the custodian of the mystery of life.)

If one holds that a human person must be virtually identical with the biological process which sustains human life, then one has an ethical mandate to sustain the process of life even to the point of using extraordinary measures to do so. One could not be relieved of the ethical imperative to preserve human life merely because doing so required extraordinary means, especially if those means were technically possible. This assumption removes the responsibility and freedom from human persons to intervene at any point in that process. One is always ethically responsible to maintain the biological process as a commitment to the preservation of human life. On the other hand, if one assumes a *contingent* relation between humanity and creatureliness, it is irresponsible to surrender the determination of the dignity of a human person to a biological and technological process. Thus, what is responsibility for one becomes irresponsibility for the other, which is why responsibility itself is not primarily an ethical (universal) category in regard to determining the status of human life.

If one holds that human personhood as an inviolable right to life is identical with the possibility of human life at the lowest level of organic existence, one will assume that there is an ethical mandate to preserve the existence of a fertilized ovum in the name of the potential human person. In this view, personhood is itself a derivative of humanity as a principle of life. The ethical mandate is rooted in the principle of human life, which laboratory analysis can determine with technical precision to be identical with biological life. On the other hand, if one assumes that there is a contingent relation between the human and the creaturely, identifying humanity with biological existence is dangerously close to "worshipping and serving the creature rather than the Creator" (Rom. 1:25). There is a semblance of idolatry in the glorification of the creature as an object of technological fascination. As technological competence proliferates, the line between "nature" and "technology" becomes blurred. The person whose anthropological assumption requires a contingent relation between the creaturely and the human has a crucial responsibility to recognize and protect what is human — and that responsibility cannot be delegated to a technician. The cry of a newborn baby brings relief as well as joy: we know what to do when we hear it. We are not always so sure when there is merely the possibility of that life. We only know that we are bound to recognize and love that which is determined to be human by the sovereign power of God. This is an absolute demand on us which (to use Kierkegaard's phrase) becomes a "temptation," a trial, by which we stand poised between conformity to the universal principle or obedience to God in faith, even at great peril.

If one holds that human sexuality is merely a creaturely form of being human, and that there is no intrinsic order to sexuality as it relates to the *imago Dei*, then one will see no ethical mandate in the matter of sexual preference in relating to others physically. There can be no such thing as right or wrong sexual order in human relationships; there can only be relationships which enhance the human quality or diminish it. Responsibility, in such cases, will be determined by mutual consent and mutual edification. The basis for the ethical mandate is again humanity as a principle of love and life rather than a recognition of the other as an absolute demand upon one's own being in terms of a fundamental sexual polarity. However, those who hold that sexuality is intrinsic to the *imago Dei* but only contingently related to creatureliness will feel that it is irresponsible to confuse the order of one's own being in terms of sexual polarity. But at the same time homosexuality, for example, can be considered from the perspective of the marginality of being human. Cases in which the creaturely sexual order and gender identity are themselves confused and complicated can be dealt with, not in terms of ethical behavior first of all, but in terms of what is possible as a true order of co-humanity.

The issue in these examples is not what the right or wrong decision is — as though we could determine that by theological analysis and then submit it to others as a standard for Christian ethics. Rather the issue is the relationship of theological anthropology to the ethical imperative. A commitment to the nature of the human as related to the creaturely process is the basis for responsibility in determining one's moral obligation. The position we have taken emphasizes that a fundamental ambiguity at the point of creaturely humanity makes it impossible to substitute ethical principles for personal decisions and actions. The very fact of this ambiguity does not conceal the definite connection between the human and the creaturely process. It simply means that in being confronted with the inescapable responsibility of acting humanly before God in certain critical situations, we are placed in "temptation" (*Anfechtung*). We do not decide these issues so as to be ethically innocent and receive the praise of others; we face these issues so as to be faithful to God and receive his blessing and know his peace. This can only be done with "fear and trembling," for the absolute certainty that one is right is perilously close to being wrong (cf. John 9:16).

THE COMMUNITY OF GOD AS CUSTODIAN AND STEWARD OF THE MYSTERY OF LIFE

We have stressed that humanity as a marginal possibility is not first of all settled as an ethical principle, merely to be applied in specific cases as uniformly as possible. Rather it presents itself first of all as a demand on those close at hand, a demand that human being as determined by God the Creator be recognized and affirmed as a possibility emerging from creaturely being. Is it realistic to assume that such a great responsibility can be borne by fallible human beings? Can individual persons be trusted with such responsibility? Would the more objective norm of ethical principles as a universal standard not provide some protection against an arbitrary, immature, or hopelessly subjective decision? The temptation which such questions present is that of seeking the security and comfort of an ethical principle or a religious law rather than existing before God unsheltered from his holy demand. The testimony of Scripture concerning the fate of those who seek such sanctuary is not encouraging. Those who became the victims of such laws have suffered an inhumanity greater than the sins meant to be regulated or corrected.

The determination of humanity is a function and therefore a responsibility of human persons. But human persons do not first of all exist as discrete individuals with an ethical conscience. They exist first of all as co-humanity, in a polarity of relation through which the image and likeness of God is discerned as responsible love. The differentiation essential to humanity is knowledge of oneself in terms of the other. While the Genesis creation account does not refer explicitly to the term "covenant" (*berith*), it does make it clear that existence in community (as co-humanity) is actually and logically prior to existence as a discrete human individual.

The biblical concept of covenant gives historical meaning to this fundamental order of humanity. Consequently, the people of God come into being as a covenant community, and as such they are responsible for serving as the custodian and steward of the mystery of human life. Cain protests that he is not his "brother's keeper," but he surely is his brother's brother (Gen. 4:9). He is responsible for Abel's life, because both bear the *imago Dei* as a concrete and social structure of their human existence. The killing of Abel is also a moral outrage, but it is first of all an act against the *imago Dei* which cannot be destroyed in one without damaging the other. Cain has suffered damage to his own personhood before he comes under ethical guilt.

The rituals by which the covenant community enacts its own existence are anthropological rather than ethical or religious. The community knows what it *is doing* in bringing forth and sustaining life before it knows what it *ought to do*. It is responsible to be human, to be what it is determined to be. Thus the contingency of human existence as an occasion which occurs on the broad field of creatureliness is preserved, and the continuity of human existence is maintained at the same time. The human community under the determination of covenant love acts responsibly to recognize and preserve human life with a knowledge which is hidden to creaturely existence alone. At the margins of human existence, when the contingency is exposed most nakedly, the community undertakes the determination of whether human life is present or not, and it does so humanly (that is, theologically), not merely ethically.

Even the disorder of human being through sin does not destroy the covenant basis on which the human exists. Indeed, the covenant becomes even more explicit as the gracious provision by which human life is supported. When Cain kills Abel, he comes under the universal and ethical principle of being a murderer. Under this principle, some might have warrant for exacting vengeance in the name of justice. But the divine covenant love, concerned to uphold humanity, anticipates this ethical absolutism and neutralizes it. The "mark of Cain" is a gracious act by which the Creator upholds Cain's humanity and warns those who would attempt to destroy him as a "favor to divine justice." One cannot use human sin as an excuse to transfer the responsibility for stewardship of the mystery of life from persons to abstract principles. Even as sinners, the community of God's people are a human community. As such they are responsible to recognize and exercise that humanity in obedience to God. Thus faith becomes the source of obedience, not conformity to ethical principles — though it must be added immediately that ethical principles are entailed in faith. It is just that faith is not entailed in ethical principles, nor is obedience to God.

The original contingency between true humanity and creatureliness, experienced as differentiation (co-humanity), was resolved into creaturely determinism at the fall. But divine reconciliation reintroduces the contingency and thus liberates humanity from this fate. Through the covenant love now expressed as reconciliation, humanity is once more set within the limits of divine determination as a creaturely order of being. The Ten Commandments are premised upon the law of covenant love (Rom. 13:8-10) and are themselves based on a divine act of reconciliation which restored the humanity of Israel through the Exodus (Exod. 20:2). The Commandments reflect the two-fold law: "You shall love the Lord your God with all your heart, and with all your soul, and with all your mind ... and your neighbor as yourself" (Matt. 22:37, 39; Lev. 19:18). Love of God entails love of neighbor. This has never been repealed in favor of a more abstract principle of human responsibility. Accordingly, the people of God became the custodians of the mystery which represents human life.

At an earlier stage of human knowledge, sheer naivete about the process of life permitted more tolerance with respect to locating human personhood in the life process. Life and death were once primarily observational, *de facto* determinations. But today we know too much about the biological process that sustains life, and how to either initiate or prolong the process, to allow this kind of tolerance. Since human life has been demythologized, more precision is required. Naivete permitted mystery to be embraced as a ritual of community, where decisions regarding personhood were made on nontechnical grounds. But with the loss of naivete came also the banishment of mystery. Modern science knows too much about life to entrust it to the rituals of community. A new order of priests has arisen, who are pledged to serve the laws of natural life. Only recently — and, it appears, reluctantly — has the sterile environment of the delivery room been opened up to permit parents to experience the mystery of birth together. Only recently has dying come to be recognized again as a ritual appropriate to a hospice setting, if not a home.

The very nature of human personhood is linked to the human community as determinative of its existence. This determination is not arbitrary, but accords with its understanding of the divine determination by which human life is in conjunction with but not ultimately determined by creaturely existence. The conception, embryonic existence, gestation, and birth of a human person is as much a ritual of the human community by which it is responsible to recognize and affirm humanity as it is a biological process. It is both, of course, but here is precisely the mystery which the community can grasp in a knowing and responsible way. The loss of naivete does *not* entail the banishment of mystery. The organic death and expulsion of an embryo is not an event in the process of human existence that can be determined to be either human or anti-human on the basis of either ethics or biological science alone. Both must participate in providing insight and information, but neither can fully grasp what is at stake with regard to human personhood. For neither can comprehend contingency and mystery as a state of being.

The claim that an individual has a *right* over his or her own body and is therefore free to decide for or against the beginning or ending of human personhood does not accord with the theological anthropology outlined above. This concept of "human rights" is alien to a biblical understanding of human life. Human personhood is a determination of creaturely being in such a way that co-humanity is the fundamental structure of personal existence. What is called a decision in regard to particular case situations in which human personhood is at stake is actually a theological determination which the community is prepared to support and enact as an affirmation of the true order of personhood.

In a certain sense this constitutes a limitation on human rights expressed in the form of autonomous, individualistic actions. Yet at the same time, it liberates the person from the tyranny of a deterministic morality, which measures the personal against an abstract principle, and from the tyranny of a naturalistic ideology, by which the personal is subordinated to an impersonal technocracy that measures human life in terms of electrical impulses on a scope. Recognizing the mystery which clings to the contingent relation by which humanity exists in creaturely form, the human community will not surrender personhood to unrelenting disorder, but dares to exercise its responsibility to affirm the true order of personhood by liberating persons from sheer disorder — for example, existence as a mere "vegetable" connected to a machine. However, the determination to permit the termination of creaturely life for the sake of personhood by removing extraordinary means for survival is a responsibility that can only be rooted in a theological understanding of human existence as co-humanity. Such a determination must be rooted in a profoundly "liturgical" act of the community itself, by which its own existence is determined by the reality of God. Only here can fear and trembling lead to faith and conviction.

Legal and ethical concerns are by no means irrelevant in critical cases where human life becomes marginal. But these concerns are insufficient to safeguard the mystery of human existence when it is subjected to situations which jeopardize not only its existence but its dignity. The concerns of which we speak ought not to be excluded in determining the fate of human life in extraordinary situations. And on occasion only the community of God's people will have the courage and faith to do what must be done, even at the risk of becoming an accomplice in ethically ambiguous actions. Earlier in this chapter we suggested that the church, as the community of Christ, exercises its knowledge of the grace of God so as to bring humanity under obedience to the divine command — the source of real humanity. Here again we must be reminded that this involves an (ethical) judgment against that which is disobedient and in disorder as well as a summons to repentance and faith. Were the community of Christ to assume that it can merely act for the "good of humanity" in general, it would fail to understand its own theological structure as a community also under judgment, which through faith and the gift of the Holy Spirit exercises a true knowledge of God and thus of real humanity.

One Sunday afternoon the father of a four-year-old boy called me as his pastor. The boy had been struck by a car and was in a coma. The father — who was also a medical doctor — was at his side in the hospital. I joined the vigil, waiting for some sign of hope that the boy's life would be preserved, despite a crushed skull and the resulting swelling of the brain under the effects of a serious contusion. After thirty-six hours, the father spoke to me quietly. "I am going to take one more EEG reading," he said, "and if that shows no sign of life then I would like to disconnect the machines which are keeping him breathing. We can keep the body functioning for a few more days, at least, but I believe that we should release him to be with God if that is his will."

This father was not asking for my opinion. He was seeking a confirmation that what he believed about the nature of human personhood is true. To allow a person to die, even a four-year-old boy, was not the end of his life but the beginning. Should we prolong or hinder that transition, or accept it with faith? As a minister of Jesus Christ and a representative of the community to which the family belonged, did I or could I affirm a truth in that situation in which the mystery of that boy's life could be sustained, even through death? Was I willing as such a representative of the community of Christ to become an accomplice of this event, or would I abandon the father to his scientific training and his tormented love? In prayer and faith, we agreed that extraordinary measures to prolong the mechanical functions of breathing were beyond that which was demanded by the dignity of the person in that boy. There was a deeper sense of the dignity of honoring the sovereignty of God, even in death. And so together we began the processional which led to the grave.

This is an "awe-ful" responsibility, and it can only be done with fear and trembling. The church as the community of God's people must have the theological nerve to enter into such an act on the part of one of its members. One could speculate endlessly on the ethical implications of the act without coming to a conclusion that would guarantee the innocence of those responsible to decide the issue. Perhaps ethical innocence is not even an option when human existence becomes marginal. One is responsible to do the will of Christ; but that is ordinarily not for the individual to decide, but for the community itself — or for its members who act in complicity with each other.

"We did not have the church's liturgy that day," wrote the student I quoted earlier, "but our own enactment served the same purpose." Who am I to challenge that? On what grounds would anyone wish to challenge it? I allow Abraham to ascend Mount Moriah, though I cannot explain to others why I do not try to stop him. His act of faith is too terrible for me to comprehend, yet I bow before his act as a manifestation of the power and reality of God in his life. Being human is no easy task, for our own humanity is at stake when another's is called into question.

Being human is ultimately a theological form of existence. It is one thing to have delineated the form of the human, and quite another to grasp my own humanity in the concrete moment in which it is put under trial. It is one thing to have outlined the reality of being human under the various aspects of the theological curriculum; it is quite another to become human through the labyrinth of errors that confronts us without and within. The community which serves as the context of human personhood must define itself in accordance with the theological and liturgical framework of its own existence as the people of God. It is from the perspective of this theological perspective that we will finally be able to consider what is involved in the "cure of souls."

PART THREE

PERSONHOOD AS ACTUALITY AND POSSIBILITY

CHAPTER ELEVEN

A THEOLOGICAL PARADIGM FOR AUTHENTIC PERSONHOOD

D IETRICH BONHOEFFER, THE GERMAN PASTOR AND THEOLOGIAN, arrested in 1943 for conspiracy against Hitler and executed by the Führer's order on April 10, 1945, sent a blank-verse poem from prison to his friend, Eberhard Bethge:

WHO AM I?

Who am I? They often tell me
I would step from my cell's confinement
calmly, cheerfully, firmly,
like a squire from his country-house.

Who am I? They often tell me
I would talk to my warders
freely and friendly and clearly,
as though it were mine to command.

Who am I? They also tell me
I would bear the days of misfortune
equably, smilingly, proudly,
like one accustomed to win.

Am I then really all that which other men tell of?
Or am I only what I know of myself,
restless and longing and sick, like a bird in a cage,
struggling for breath, as though hands were compressing my throat,
yearning for colours, for flowers, for the voices of birds,
thirsting for words of kindness, for neighbourliness,
trembling with anger at despotisms and petty humiliation,
tossing in expectation of great events,
powerlessly trembling for friends at an infinite distance,
weary and empty at praying, at thinking, at making,
faint, and ready to say farewell to it all?

Who am I? This or the other?
Am I one person today, and tomorrow another?
Am I both at once? A hypocrite before others,
and before myself a contemptibly woebegone weakling?
Or is something within me still like a beaten army,

fleeing in disorder from victory already achieved?

Who am I? They mock me, these lonely questions of mine.
Whoever I am, thou knowest, O God, I am thine.[1]

As a theologian Bonhoeffer realized that one must come to terms with the ambiguities of human existence: the need for affirmation, for belonging, for restoration and healing, for being a significant person, and for not being forgotten. But because he is a *Christian* theologian, he realizes that these human needs and his existential situation drive him directly to God as the source of his own personhood. But Bonhoeffer does not consider God a crutch for the weak; rather, God is for those who live fully in the world, who dare to look life squarely in the face and raise the most difficult questions a human can ask.

In elaborating on this thesis as a theological basis for achieving human personhood, we shall set forth selected theological motifs as a paradigm of personhood. By paradigm we mean a representational model of the reality of personhood. Personhood is considered to be a structure of reality, contingently related to the world and therefore determined and upheld in its being by the divine Word of God. The theological motifs selected are not the only ones pertaining to personhood, and we are not attempting to discuss these in the context of the history of dogma.

Our purpose is to suggest at least tentatively a fundamental integration between the basic human social and psychological needs and the core of the theological curriculum. Theological anthropology itself may in this way be considered the core theological dogma. To ask "Who am I?" is already to ask the fundamental theological question: "Is it true that God has created, spoken, come to us, provided healing and hope and, finally, will he be there for us in the end?"

ELECTION—
AFFIRMATION OF THE SELF

What is it that says "yes" to my condition, to who I am? What power or presence saves me from the blind and instinctual determinism of nature, from the capricious and heartless "accidents" which toss me about on the surface of life like a leaf caught in a raging torrent of water? In the face of what seems to be absurd and meaningless, I can affirm the value of my own existence, even if only to deny the conditions under which I exist. But this defiance of

---

1. *Letters and Papers from Prison*, enlarged edition (New York: Macmillan, 1972), pp. 347f.

the dark, this human cry that shatters the infinite silence, has no power to create an answer. Where is the original Word to which I can respond with my own AMEN?

The doctrine within the theological curriculum which corresponds most closely to this existential need is election. The popular mind has unfortunately caricatured this doctrine as teaching that God takes delight in creating and predestinating some human creatures to eternal torment and some to eternal bliss and salvation purely for his own glory. Here we cannot trace the development of election in the history of theology, but neither are we prepared to abandon a word and concept so fundamental to biblical theology. Election, put quite simply, means that God acts out of his freedom to create, sustain, and reconcile his creation to himself, and furthermore that he does this on his own terms and in his own way.

Genesis tells us that, after each movement of creation, God paused and declared that what he has made is "good." God affirms what he himself creates. It is good because he has created it and now wills it to be what it is by his own free act of creation. It is not as though he is bound by some abstract principle or decree residing in his being prior to his Word and will. Rather, his Word and will issue from the freedom of his own being, first to love and then create and then, having created, to love and affirm his creation. Election does not mean that God himself is free to love only that which he has eternally decreed, or that he must then hate that which he has eternally decreed, and consequently create it in order to hate it. No dualism within the being of God is implied by the duplicity within creation. Scripture offers no warrant for accounting for good and evil, belief and nonbelief, by positing a deterministic principle within the being of God. Election as God's act of love and affirmation of the creature which he has predestined for eternal life and fellowship with himself does not presuppose reprobation. Rather, affirmation presupposes the freedom of love which comes to expression through creation and reconciliation.

Election as a theological doctrine expresses a divine intentionality which determines that creation and the creature should be what it is. Thus, the grace of God is manifest in his election of the human creature not only to exist but to exist as one who bears the divine image and likeness. Election means that God's Word is operative on both sides of the human situation. God not only summons forth from among the possibilities of creatureliness the human creature as the one uniquely endowed with this *imago*, but God provides the appropriate and the only possible human response to that original summons. Not only does he say of his own creation that it is good, but he enables the creature itself to respond to that Word. To the creature which he divinely ordains to be human, he gives a name and a word. He gives this person a likeness, an image of God himself.

Being human, therefore, is not an actuality which may or may not emerge out of a creaturely possibility, either through a natural law, or through some "accidental" mutation, but being human is first of all an actuality which only then becomes a possibility. How does Adam know that of all the creaturely beings Eve is the one who completes his own being? This is not by "accident," but through a divine provision and determination. Adam's own *response* to another creature is not a possibility within himself or in creatureliness. But the response is *given* to him in the form of the human partner. When he can say "At last!" and receive the woman as his partner in co-humanity, he is giving his AMEN to God's determination and provision. Thus, election is first of all experienced by Adam as his own freedom to respond to and accept God's gracious provision. As God is free to create and to love his creation, Adam becomes free as one created to love the Creator and his fellow human creature. In their mutual love and knowledge of each other, the man and the woman thus express and experience divine election as the actuality of being human.

This principle of divine election is revealed most graphically through Israel's emergence as God's chosen people. Israel is the reaffirmation of the way of the human with respect to God. The true Israelite is restored to creation and is liberated to know creation as that which expresses the glory of God. The concept of *shalom* is the structure of wholeness and harmony which exists as the result of the divine Word. This peace is first of all a structure of reality before it becomes an existential experience for the human community. Experiencing God's *shalom*, the Hebrew is saved from the fatalistic and self-destructive principle of sin and restored to true community with God and with nature. For the Hebrew person, full creatureliness is now restored as a "liturgical" expression of this *shalom*, manifested in festivals of thanksgiving and praise offerings to God the Lord and Creator. All of this is the experiencing of divine election as the affirmation of human life as against death.

Offerings not authorized by the divine Word are rejected. The story of Cain and Abel portrays this. Abel's offering is acceptable; Cain's is not. The former accords with the way of true humanity, the latter does not. To take Cain's side, and argue on the basis of human rights that he has a ground for making his offering in his own innocence or even in his own good intention, is to stand outside of the divine Word. Such an argument is essentially inhuman because it contradicts that form of the human which God has ordained to be. This comes to full expression in the consequences of Cain's murderous action. Throughout the history of Israel the struggle is basically against election, a struggle between the stubbornness and rebelliousness of the human heart, which no longer has the freedom to be for God, and the gracious love and provision of God, who is for Israel as the object of his love. In this struggle Israel stands vicariously for all humanity. The particularism which represents

Israel's status over against the Gentiles belongs itself to the concept of election. Israel is chosen not to the exclusion of the Gentiles but on behalf of the inclusion of the Gentiles, as is already explicit in the original covenant with Abraham: "By you all the families of the earth shall bless themselves" (Gen. 12:3).

This, of course, is finally revealed in Jesus Christ. He is uniquely God's chosen one, the elect one, the "only begotten Son." Paul calls him "the firstborn among many brethren" (Rom. 8:29). Here, particularity reaches its narrowest point. And here we see election as the Word of God which is operative on "both sides" of the event of being human. Jesus is not only the God who "elects himself to be with and for the human person," but Jesus is the "man who is elected to be with and for God." But this election opens up the way for all human persons to experience the election of God. "I am the way, the truth, and the life," said Jesus (John 14:6). This is the elected way, the ordained way, the only way. By no other name under heaven can one come to know God, except the man Jesus Christ (Acts 4:12); but that way, in its absolute particularity, is totally human. There are no possibilities which belong to being human which are excluded in that divine election. The incarnation includes all that is human and brings it within the affirmation of God. Thus we are to have no fear of election, as though God "elects before he permits himself to love." Election is fundamentally human in its origin.

Once again we must make the point. Through the concept of election, we know that actuality precedes possibility with regard to being human. We can become human because we are in fact divinely determined to be human and *are* human. This challenges directly the existentialist concept that possibility exists before actuality. This challenges the fallacy that "in becoming I am." Rather, it insists that the "I am" precedes the becoming. The existentialist holds that human existence is a precarious point of balance between nonbeing and being. We tip the scales in that balance toward becoming human, and therefore have real human being, when we "decide" to be. When we actualize the possibility of our being, the existentialist argues, we are truly human. One who accepts this argument must follow it with an imperative on the possibility of self-actualization — *become, decide, act*; for the peril of not acting is nonbeing. Thus our "yes" to the possibility of existence actually determines our own existence as human.

In a sense, one could say that each person must thus "elect" or "speak" himself or herself into being. The human word becomes the original word. But we would counter that this would be a counsel of despair, fundamentally opposed to what Scripture teaches. Our own "yes" is an AMEN to God's original word, not the original word itself. True, there is an existential content to divine election. Adam did "decide," he did "act" with regard to the woman God brought to him. For the woman, however, Adam's "act" could never have been the actualization of her own being. She knew as well as he did that their own human response to each other was itself a result and not a cause. Thus, they did not live in dependence on either self-actualization or self-determination or even mutual affirmation. Instead, they were liberated to be for each other as an affirmation of the divine Word itself.

Election does exclude as well as include; it says No as well as Yes. What it excludes are possibilities foreign to our true humanity. Exclusion is the negative aspect of affirmation. The No does not stand independently as a divine decree. When God says, "Let there be light," darkness occurs as a possibility which only has its existence as a negation of light. To attempt to "live in darkness" is to take up existence in a way that is totally outside of God's Word (John 3:19-21). Election excludes the possibilities of the fruit of the tree of knowledge of good and evil: "in the day that you eat of it you will die" (Gen. 2:17). Just because the human person can eat of the tree does not mean that one can do that and still be authentically human. Not all possibilities open to human beings are "human possibilities." Eating fruit from the forbidden tree can never be affirmed as good, because God has not elected that it should be for the human good. Therefore, to resist this divine Word is alienation and death. What election thus excludes explicitly subsequent to the fall, is already excluded implicitly in the original affirmation — it is good.

"O that Ishmael might live in thy sight!" Abraham cried out (Gen. 17:18-19). But the answer from God was No. Isaac's election meant the exclusion of Ishmael. In one sense Ishmael had every right to claim the natural prerogative as Abraham's firstborn son. Yet this "right," argued on the basis of a human possibility, did not exist in the actuality of the divine Word. The case of Jacob and Esau teaches the same principle. Though both came from the same womb, Esau the firstborn is nevertheless set aside in favor of Jacob. Nor did Jacob receive the blessing because he outwitted Esau; remember that Rebecca the mother had been instructed by the Lord when she inquired about the meaning of the struggle in her womb: "The elder shall serve the younger" (Gen. 25:22-23). Jacob's deception and manipulation to secure the birthright was unnecessary. It was already his by divine election.

Certainly these cases must be considered as pedagogical rather than determinative of an eternal state of existence for either Jacob or Esau as individuals. It is for the principle of election that these events are recorded, as Paul himself recognizes (Rom. 9:6-13). God's salvation, which is being prepared through Israel and which will be completed in Christ, is not to be understood as the result of a human act of self-determination, but rather of a divine determination. Salvation, as an existential knowledge of one's own security of existence in this world and before God, rests on the affirmation which comes from God. It is by election, and it excludes all possibilities we might seek to insert which would leave us hanging on some human word or act. The concept of election cuts through all of the maze of human possibilities and excludes what does not belong to our humanity from the onset.

But election also includes every aspect of our humanity which has been broken off from the whole. Here is the positive aspect of affirmation. No matter how damaged our humanity has become, it has not fallen from grace as the object of a divine determination. God's original Word, which set forth the actuality of human existence, still stands; and it is the basis for our own existential possibility of healing and restoration to fellowship. Thus, when we are ready to judge ourselves as inhuman and unfit for consideration by either God or others, our judgment must be critically overruled by the judgment of election itself. We dare not call inhuman, whether in ourselves or in others, that which God himself has elected and chosen. His election does not include that which is only beautiful and bright and shining. His election includes that which has become marred and even disfigured. Why? Because it is human. We must never forget that no person can become so bereft of goodness as to lose his or her own humanity as one elected by God. So Barth can say:

> It is to this man, representing the rejected and to that extent suffering the divine rejection, that the witness of the community to the election of Jesus Christ is addressed. It tells him that he is erring, rebelling, fleeing, and hating, when everything points to the fact that he should not do so. It tells him also that he does it all in vain, because the choice which he thus makes is eternally denied and annulled in Jesus Christ, and because he for his part may deny and annul everything else by his own choice, but cannot possibly deny or annul the gracious choice of God. It is this very man, godless in his negative act, wantonly representing the rejected man, who is the predestinate.[2]

Election is the friend of the fallen. For the original word is not one of reprobation and rejection but of affirmation and restoration of all that is human. "Who shall bring any charge against God's elect?", asks Paul (Rom. 8:33). Who shall separate us from the love of God in Christ? This is the original Word and as such the actual Word which determines our answer to the question, "Who am I?"

COVENANT—RELATEDNESS OF THE SELF

A second fundamental need of human personhood is for belonging. This can be expressed as the experience of the relatedness of the self. Self-existence is

---

2. *Church Dogmatics*, II/2, 317.

a struggle between the reality of individuality and the reality of community. Because humanity is originally and esentially co-humanity, the fundamental affirmation of human existence is surely one of relatedness. "It is not good that the man should be alone" (Gen. 2:18). If election is the theological motif corresponding to the need for affirmation, covenant is the theological paradigm for co-humanity experienced as relatedness.

Although the word "covenant" (*berith*) does not appear in the Genesis creation account, the basic components of what will later be termed covenant are found there: the unilateral movement of the Creator toward the creature, calling human existence into relation through the divine Word; the unconditional response established as the presupposition for existence in relation to God; the divine initiative, both in the Word which summons the human being into existence and also in the Word which constitutes the human response. Human existence as co-humanity is not an accident of personhood which needs to be explained by sociological or psychological dynamics. Rather it is itself a social and psychical existence within the divine determination of covenant love. Barth says,

> What God created when He created the world and man was not just any place, but that which was foreordained for the establishment and the history of the covenant, nor just any subject, but that which was to become God's partner in this history, i.e., the nature which God in His grace willed to address and accept and the man predestined for His service. The fact that covenant is the goal of creation is not something which is added later to the reality of the creatures as though the history of creation might equally have been succeeded by any other history. It already characterizes creation itself and as such, and therefore the being and existence of the creature.[3]

One cannot say, according to Barth, that human being can have any other determination than the determination to exist in covenant relation with God, and therefore, to exist as covenant people, bound together by this structure of community. Covenant, theologically understood, is thus a way of talking about human relatedness from the standpoint of the individual's orientation to God and the other as a structure of being human. The covenant relation between God and Israel existed in several forms, but we are speaking here of covenant as the fundamental structure of humanity itself as co-humanity. "In this covenant," Barth says, "God gives to it what He undertook to give to it when He first gave it its being and nature. And God wills from it as a partner in this covenant only that for which He prepared and bound and pledged it when He first gave it its being and nature."[4]

---

3. *Ibid.*, III/1, 231.
4. *Ibid.*, p. 97.

This tells us something about the nature of human love. Love is the content of that which we recognize to be the core of human relatedness, even as divine love is the core of divine covenant. Theologically, we would say that there is a will to live that is more fundamental than unwillingness. This means that, though we experience ourselves as creatures who have a pervasive unwillingness deep within our being, which is at best stubbornness and at worst hatred, there is a deeper core to our being. That core is a "willing spirit," which can be renewed because it is an essential aspect of being human (Ps. 51:10-12). There is a will to love which is more essential than an unwillingness or even an incapacity to love. This will to love does not depend on our instincts, our emotions, our psyche, or even our human will. Love is fundamentally then not the result of our will, but it is that which enables and urges us to will what is for our good.

Paul's litany of ambivalence is familiar: "I can will what is right, but I cannot do it. For I do not do the good I want, but the evil I do not want is what I do" (Rom. 7:18-19). He can even conclude with the hopeless confession that "nothing good dwells within me!" However, hidden within this confession of inability is the confession of a more theological truth: "I delight in the law of God, in my inmost self" (7:22). Deeper and more fundamental than my failure to act in accordance with what I know to be good, Paul is saying, is the fact of my love for the law of God. This, of course, is more a theological statement than a psychological one. It is a statement based not on his present feelings but on a truth of his own being which is grounded in his knowledge of himself as a covenant partner with God. What Paul is claiming on his own behalf is the love which God himself has put within the human creature. It is not just that God loves him in some unfailing and ultimate sense, but Paul actually loves God in that same unfailing sense, because he knows himself to be a human person created in the divine image. While Paul also knows that he has compromised and confused that love for the law of God, he does not believe that he has destroyed it.

This helps us see the relevance of a theological construct of the self in overcoming self-contradictory feelings and experiences. Here we see the advantage of a theological paradigm of human personhood which posits the actuality of the self as the basis for possibility. Even if we need the assistance of a trained psychotherapist to sort out the confusion and conflict of the self, we know exactly what we can expect to find at the core of the self — a delight in the law of God. Michael Polanyi once wrote, "Our believing is conditioned at its source by our belonging."[5] For all of our brokenness and alienation, our fundamental condition is one of belonging. The "we" is prior to the "I." Personal

---

5. *Personal Knowledge* (London: Routledge and Kegan Paul, 1958), p. 322.

individuality is not an original given fact; it is achieved through the differentiation of the self within the structure of relation. The human person does not emerge by an act of individual self-consciousness with respect to all other creatures, but rather as a consequence of differentiation with regard to another human person.

"I need you to be myself," says John Macmurray. "This need is for a fully positive personal relation in which, because we trust one another, we can think and feel and act together. Only in such a relation can we really be ourselves."[6] In the conflict and struggle which results from the alienation of one from another, trust is replaced by fear, and the "I" precedes the "we." Even if we seek reconciliation with the other based on this contradiction, the most we can achieve, argues Macmurray, is a form of cooperation for such ends as each one has an interest in achieving. "But we will remain isolated individuals, and the co-operating between us, though it may appear to satisfy our need of one another, will not really satisfy *us*. For what we really need is to care for one another, and we are only caring for ourselves. We have achieved society, but not community. We have become associates, but not friends."[7] The inherent ideal of the personal as personhood existing in a structure of covenant love is "a community of persons in which each cares for all the others, and no one cares for himself."[8]

Love is the result of a good relationship, not the cause of it. A good relationship is one which acknowledges the fundamental structure of co-humanity as the core of personhood, and which values the other as constitutive of the self. In a good relationship, because it is structurally an aspect of our fundamental personhood, quite a high level of neuroticism and tension can be tolerated. The partners in a bad relationship (one which has self-interest as the basic motivation) have a low tolerance for neurotic or erratic behavior on the part of the other. This may help us see why stripping away the "character armor" of the self (to use Ernest Becker's language) does not ordinarily lead to a capacity for love. The source of love is not physical health, though distortion at this level can frustrate love. If the level of neuroticism becomes so high that the relation itself is obscured, then psychotherapy can be helpful in removing this hindrance to the relation.

I have often observed that married couples who manifest a rather trivial level of neuroticism but have a shallow relationship at the level of their core personhood have little tolerance for the neurotic behavior, because there is no structural form of covenant love on which the marriage is based. On the other

---

6. *Persons in Relation* (London: Faber and Faber, 1961), p. 150.
7. *Ibid.*
8. *Ibid.*, p. 159.

hand, I knew couples who would freely admit to a good bit of neuroticism, but have a basically constructive and healthy covenant relation and quite a secure marriage. Apparently, the structural reality of the essential "we" which constituted their relationship was premised on the mutual acceptance of each other as significant persons in terms of their own self-identity. If "character armor" (as Becker defines it) is really the fig leaves all of us wear to protect the self from existential anxiety in the face of life and death, then this protective element in our personality need not be stripped away as a presupposition for meaningful relationships.

We may need to wear such "character armor" when we go out in public, so to speak, because we are there exposed to humanity in general where the co-humanity aspect of our being has almost been totally suspended. However, in the more fundamental relationships in our lives, these personality traits which are psychologically necessary (so we feel) become more or less irrelevant. This "character armor" neither has to be stripped away nor taken seriously. To the degree that we can activate and live by the actuality of our co-humanity expressed through relationships rooted in our real being, we can relativize these frustrating and confusing aspects of our individual lives. This is one way of looking at what Paul was doing as he moved from Romans 7 to Romans 8. This does not imply that the psychical disturbances and frustrations to the self can be ignored in the hope that they will "go away." The point we are making is that each person is ontologically rooted in personal being in such a way that belonging is more fundamental and determinative of our being than existential estrangement or confusion. A theological anthropology informs us as to why we can be encouraged to believe this about ourselves despite the apparent contradictions at any given time in our life.

This gives us a perspective from which we can not only reorder our psychological state in accordance with actuality of being, but also seek more meaningful social relations. Because the social structure of personal being as co-humanity is more fundamental than our individual existence as discrete personalities, the covenant as a theological paradigm of personhood is the basis for human social relations. In the contemporary comic strip "The Wizard of Id," the midget king seeks out the wizard and requests a magic potion to help him get along better with the peasants. The wizard performs some incantations over the seething caldron and produces a steaming potion which the king drinks and promptly retches. Spitting it out, he turns to the wizard: "This is terrible! What in the world is it?" And the wizard responds, "It's the milk of human kindness."

On the other hand, Lucy complains to Linus in the comic strip "Peanuts," "I love mankind, it's people I can't stand!" Human strife, whether it is manifest in the form of indifference or violent hatred, is an ontological sickness and distortion. Though the civil rights movement eventually produced legislation which forced whites to give equal opportunity and status to blacks, the sickness remains. When even Christians defend the inhuman practice of segregation on the basis of color or race under the name of "property rights" or "neighborhood values," we know that the biblical concept of neighbor as brother or sister is not in view. Covenant means relatedness as a core value of human existence. Race, color, and social status are all accidental to our humanity, nor essential to it. Covenant as relatedness points to a fundamental "kinship" which is the presupposition of all human social institutions, whether marriage, the state, labor and management, or the church.

In Romans 1 Paul recites a litany of disorder and disease which is typical of the human race existing outside of and in denial of this fundamental truth. He says that people whom God has given up to themselves are foolish, faithless, heartless, and ruthless (1:31). The word "heartless" is *astorgos* in the Greek. *Storgē* is the love of kindred, the fundamental bond between those who share a common human womb, or at least filial unit. While there may be many levels of incompatibility and difference in temperament between my brother or my sister and myself, some part of me is at stake in their own life and death. I will respond to my brother out of *storgē* when he can't reach me through moral argument or logical persuasion. To be *astorgos* is to deny that fundamental connection of kinship. It is to surrender the other to the impersonal fate of being merely "human" in the abstract sense, and to value my own existence over his or hers. To deny my brother or sister is to deny the womb from which we both have come. It is to deny the common source and common dependence which we have for our own human existence. It is the inhumanity which comes to expression when we deny our paternity in God as his creatures, and which manifests itself in our denial of our brother or sister. When anyone asks, "Who am I?", it is at once a profoundly theological question. It is a question, not so much as to our destiny, but of our origin. It is not a question which means, "What will become of me?", but it is a question which means, "Where is the one to whom I belong, essentially and finally?"

SALVATION/ATONEMENT— HEALING OF THE SELF

Correlative to the need for restoration and healing as an existential aspect of human personhood is the biblical doctrine of reconciliation. The Greek word *sotēria* can mean either salvation or healing, and often, it is only the context that reveals which particular meaning the biblical author intended. The Psalmist's litany of salvation is also a litany of healing:

> Bless the Lord, O my soul;
>   and all that is within me,
>   bless his holy name!
> Bless the Lord, O my soul,
>   and forget not all his benefits,
> Who forgives all your iniquity,
>   who heals all your diseases,
> Who redeems your life from the Pit,
>   who crowns you with steadfast love and mercy,
> Who satisfies you with good as long as you live
>   so that your youth is renewed like the eagle's (Ps. 103:1-5).

Again, the Psalmist affirms, "He heals the brokenhearted" (Ps. 147:3). Speaking of the anointed one, the Messiah, Isaiah says, "With his stripes, we are healed" (Isa. 53:5).

In Jesus we see the correlation of forgiveness and healing. His first word to the paralytic is, "My son, your sins are forgiven" (Mark 2:5). Only subsequently — though inevitably to be sure — does he say, "Rise, take up your bed and walk." Health, then, is not the absence of sickness, but a positive orientation of the self toward the objective hope which results from God's initial intention. This objectivity of the divine Word, as that which constitutes both the origin and destiny of human personhood, correlates sin with sickness and atonement with healing. Christ is not merely a healer, he is the healed one. He took on himself the diseases and infirmities which inflict humankind and made an end of them in the resurrection from the dead. He is the source of health because he himself has been made health for us even as he was made sin for us.

This does not mean that sickness is a direct result of sin. Jesus answers that once and for all: "Master, who sinned, this man or his parents, that he was born blind?" Jesus responds, "It was not that this man sinned, or his parents, but that the works of God might be made manifest in him" (John 9:1-3). Jesus' reply is a warning that all must seek salvation through repentance, but if sin entails sickness, this is not reversible. The work of God made manifest in the healing of the blind man's eyes is God's reconciliation of the person in a final and eschatological sense. Salvation is healing because it is an eschatological act, and as such, forgiveness of sins includes the restoration of that which is human. Sin is inhuman, and sickness and death are both forms of inhuman existence. The atonement, as a vicarious death of Jesus Christ on the cross, is part of a larger context of reconciliation that stretches from Bethlehem to Calvary and the resurrection. When God assumed humanity as a form of being through the incarnation, he assumed an estranged humanity, under the judgment of death. Thus, reconciliation is the restoration of humanity to its true orientation through the new humanity of Christ. It is not another humanity, but the original one. Salvation is the historical work of God in Christ by which both the negative and the positive aspects of election are dealt with once and for all.

The doctrine of atonement therefore deals with much more than the religious aspect of the self. It is a community of reconciliation which both exorcises and edifies. The reconciliation of God expressed through Christ and in his continuing ministry through the church exorcises from the human community what is contrary to and destructive of humanity. It does this on the basis of election. Election, as the affirmation of the self, has its practical relevance precisely at this point. That which is inhuman is also demonic and ontologically contrary to God's intention for human personhood. That which is contrary to human community under divine reconciliation is denied the right to exist because it has no ontological existence in its own right. It is not and has never been affirmed by God. Thus, the basis for recognizing what is inhuman and denying it is not the community's ethical perceptiveness but an understanding of the theological anthropology which constitutes human community itself. There is an ordinary exorcism which is the constant and continual affirmation of the community as to its own true order as created and restored by the divine Word. The Christian community affirms its own health by the implicit affirmation and reaffirmation of the humanity of its members. Despite the contradiction, the community upholds members who experience sickness and even death as truly human. If the presence and power of the contradiction becomes outrageous and focused in or upon a single member of the community, there is apparently a form of extraordinary exorcism, which is noted in Scripture as the casting out of demons by Jesus.

However, the denial of that which is inhuman is only the negative side of election with respect to reconciliation. The positive side is edification of the body, building it up. The community practices edification when it seeks the good of each other. Jesus modeled both exorcism and edification when he confronted the demoniac who had suffered many years from the power of demonic oppression. Living naked in the cemetery, dragging the chains which once had bound him, he was confronted by Jesus, who drove the demons from him. And Luke tells us, "He who had been possessed of demons was found sitting at the feet of Jesus, clothed and in his right mind" (8:35).

When the original "we" is shattered, human personhood becomes divided and set in opposition to itself. Survival of the "I" becomes the project of existence, even at the expense of the other and as a final destruction of the self. When this occurred in the context of the original story of creation, "the eyes of both were opened, and they knew that they were naked, and they sewed fig leaves together and made themselves aprons" (Gen. 3:7). Knowing that they were naked did not imply that there was some deception in the original state:

this is not a case of the emperor's new clothes. The discovery of nakedness was not a move toward reality but a breaking of the unity of co-humanity. Adam and Eve "knew" in the Cartesian sense of viewing all else as objective to one's own "I." They knew each other in the abstract. The fig leaves were to cover themselves not for their own sake, but from the "I" of the other.

This also entails flight from the "I" of God, who is no longer viewed as a structure of "we" in covenant love. Instead of seeking refuge in the "we" of God, Adam and Eve seek refuge in the anonymity of the trees of the garden. They are now co-conspirators, whose only bond is survival as refugees. But this is an uneasy alliance, and left to themselves they will have no hope of recovering the original structure of co-humanity. When the Word of God summons them back from their hidden condition, the fig leaves are removed and God himself provides a covering, the skin of an animal. There is reconciliation, but one that is redolent of death, even though the promise is life. The primary modality of co-humanity is now reconstituted as the covenant becomes more and more explicit as the formation of a new community of God's people.

The fundamental problem of human personhood is thus shown to be ontological rather than behavioral. Sin is a division of personal being with the resulting estrangement and alienation of self with self. Reconciliation thus becomes the presupposition for therapy because it relates personality disorder and psychical disturbances to an order of being. This is what reconciliation expressed as *koinonia* means in the New Testament. Through the incarnation, the divine Word gathers up estranged humanity and binds it back into the fellowship God experiences within his own being. The modality of God's own being as Father, Son, and Spirit is a modality of fellowship, of community of being. That is why John says that the fellowship (*koinonia*) which we share with one another as reconciled sinners is the fellowship (*koinonia*) which exists in the relation of the Son to the Father (1 John 1:1-3). In this way, the primal act of salvation history, the incarnation and atonement, achieves the ontological foundation for all renewal and healing of persons. We do not first of all become "believers" and then "members of the community of Christ." Rather, in Polanyi's words, "our believing is conditioned at its source by our belonging." When one asks "Who am I?", the theological significance of the question may be expressed as "Where is my place of belonging?" Where is the place which promises my healing and which affirms my health as a person? Where is the "feet of Jesus," where I may be found, in my right mind?

ESCHATON—THE SIGNIFICANCE OF THE SELF

"Am I this or the other?", asked Bonhoeffer, "Am I one person today, and one tomorrow?" How can our personal lives have significance when we are subject to such contingency in life? How can I have continuity of my being when my place of belonging and my community of fellow human beings can be so impermanent and so transitory? All questions of personhood are fundamentally questions of ultimate significance. This was the insight of Paul Tillich, who saw the question of human existence as a series of questions of ultimate concern.

We have already argued that the divine Word which is the source of human personhood is a contemporary Word because it comes out of the future rather than merely out of the past. This Word is the original Word, because it was there too, but it is the final Word, because it is the *eschaton* of all creaturely being. However, the presence of the *eschaton*, or final Word, in our own temporal existence is never "at hand" in the same sense that other words and events are. In this sense we must be prepared to understand that the presence of Jesus as the *eschatos*, the "last one," is a truth emerging from the resurrection. The one who is present to us as the resurrected one is the same one who was "at hand" during his existence as Jesus of Nazareth prior to the crucifixion. But there was always something "tragic" about the presence of Jesus to the disciples before the resurrection. Even while he was present to them in the same tangible and temporal form as they were present to each other, an ontological discontinuity pervaded their relationship with him. There was a growing sense in which his presence was more of a foreboding of his absence than of presence itself. And when the absence became concrete and visible in the form of the crucified and buried body of the one who had been with them, their own being was shaken to the core. Their sense of community was broken and they scattered to the four corners of their own private worlds. The fact that the divine Word by which their own existence had meaning and significance was no longer present to them appeared to be the end of all purpose and hope.

In Arthur Miller's *After the Fall*, Quentin struggles to find some sense of absolute meaning for his life when it is collapsing around him. Finally, he says, "I am consigned to an endless argument with myself. A pointless litigation of existence before an empty bench." And as if to make his existential loss more profound by expressing it in theological terms, he says, "the string that ties my hand to heaven has been cut."

The theological paradigm of the *eschaton* as the final Word of God which gives meaning and order to all that precedes that final event is a constructive framework for a theology of personhood. In the quest for meaning and significance at the personal level, the presence of that final Word to us in the midst of the contemporary age is a source of comfort and hope. But in ourselves we have no capacity for that hope, as revealed by the disciples, even following the resurrection. Only when Christ's presence as the final Word of God came to them in the form of his Spirit did they rediscover the reality of their own lives as a community of being in which their own humanity was renewed. In a somewhat paradoxical sense, this eschatological presence of the divine Word is a "presence in absence." We live by faith, and not by sight, Paul tells us (2 Cor. 5:7). John Zizioulas puts it in a more complicated, yet insightful way:

> Personhood prefers to create its presence as absence rather than be contained, comprehended, described and manipulated through the circumscribability and individualization which are inherent in all creaturehood. Personhood thus proves to be *in* this word — through man — but not *of* this world. All this means that the ekstatic movement towards communion which is part of personhood, remains for man an unfulfilled longing for a presence-without-absence of being as long as there is no overcoming the space-time limitations of creaturehood. This situation implies that there is no possibility of the creature developing into something of an 'uncreated' being, and there is nothing that shows this more dramatically than this 'capacity-in-incapacity' which is implied in human personhood. At the same time, this reveals that there is a future, an *eschaton*, or a *telos*, a final goal in creation, which must resolve the problem created by personhood.[9]

Personhood as an existential phenomenon promises more than it can deliver. There is a reaching out for what is not present to us, yet in that reaching out we encounter a reality which becomes present to us. Surely this is what is meant by saying that Christ is present and with us through the Holy Spirit. The Holy Spirit, as the presence of Christ in the world, is a presence in absence. Precisely this eschatological presence of the Spirit enables the human person to reorient life to the final event which constitutes the present. Survival of the self, with continuity between the present experience and the future, is essential for healthy personhood. The resurrection of the body as the mode of personal existence determined by God is therefore a necessity if that survival is to take place. This is why the concept of the immortality of the soul as a form of eternal self-existence offers no real hope. It is personal communion in a structure of knowing relationships which constitutes the significance of personal human being. This means resurrection of the person (body and soul) as a person-in-relation.

All human love, which is the core of personal significance, reaches out toward the presence of the other without absence. There is something inherently tragic about the form of our present community of human love. We have presence to each other only through the present reality of discontinuity. No other person is ever totally "at hand" to us. Even if it should appear to be so

---

9. "Human Capacity and Incapacity," in *Scottish Journal of Theology*, XXVIII (1975), 420.

in any given moment, there is an inevitability of separation and distance which each person must traverse. Everyone experiences (if that is the correct word) death as an "I" and not as a "we." Even during extended and pervasive illness, this presence-in-absence becomes more acute. The concept of personal immortality through the resurrection of the dead is as much a truth and hope of human community as it is for the individual, if not more so. For co-humanity itself, as a fundamental structure of human being, is an eschatological reality which becomes present to us in provisional form in this life.

Being a human person is an actuality before it emerges as possibility in the form of existential response to life. We have set forth the theological paradigm for this assumption through such concepts as election, covenant, salvation, and *eschaton*. But concepts — even theological ones — do not exist as structures of the real world. Even Jesus Christ, as a primary concept, has no existence as such. If Christ exists at all in this world, Bonhoeffer wrote, he exists as community.[10] The theological paradigm for personhood must thus take place through the rituals and experiences which constitute the existence of the self in community. In and through these fundamental rituals of community actuality takes precedence over our own possibilities, and the eschatological reality which determines our personhood meets us as "bone of my bone and flesh of my flesh."

---

10. *Sanctorum Communio* (London: Collins, 1967), pp. 61f., 84f.

CHAPTER TWELVE

A LITURGICAL PARADIGM
FOR AUTHENTIC PERSONHOOD

COMMON TO ALL CULTURES ARE WHAT WE CALL "RITES OF PASSAGE," critical points in the life cycle of each person at which the community to which he or she belongs enacts a transition and confers status. "Men and beasts can be born," Karl Barth once said, "but men alone can be baptized."[1] Birth and death occur as creaturely events in the natural life cycle, but baptism would not occur except for the intentionality of community, in which individuals are grasped by the community itself in a ritual of initiation and participation in the event which constitutes the life of the community — the kingdom of God. Behind baptism lies more than a neurotic need to be sustained by an ecclesiastical mother. Whatever theological connotations baptism may have as a ritual of the church, for the individual it can have great significance as a reinforcement of authentic personhood.

In her short story "The Kingdom of God and the River," Flannery O'Connor describes the baptism of a young Southern boy in the river by an itinerant evangelist.

> "Have you ever been Baptized?" the preacher asked.
> "What's that?" he murmured.
> "If I Baptize you," the preacher said, "you'll be able to go to the Kingdom of Christ. You'll be washed in the river of suffering, son, and you'll go by the deep river of life. Do you want that?"
> "Yes," the child said, and thought, I won't go back to the apartment then, I'll go under the river.
> "You won't be the same again," the preacher said. "You'll count." Then he turned his face to the people and began to preach and Bevel looked over his shoulder at the pieces of the white sun scattered in the river. Suddenly the preacher said, "All right, I'm going to Baptize you now," and without more warning, he tightened his hold and swung him upside down and plunged his head into the water. He held him under while he said the words of Baptism and then he jerked him up again and looked sternly at the gasping child. Bevel's

---

1. *Church Dogmatics*, III/2, 359.

eyes were dark and dilated. "You count now," the preacher said. "You didn't even count before."[2]

When the boy returned to the apartment where he lived, he found the situation unbearable. In the neglect and alcoholic stupor of his parents he did not count. The preacher was right. There is only hope in finding the kingdom of God in the river. And so he returned the next morning by himself to the river. Wading in to his chest, he stood there for a moment.

> His coat floated to the surface and surrounded him like a strange gay lily pad and he stood grinning in the sun. He intended not to fool with preachers any more but to Baptize himself and to keep on going this time until he found the Kingdom of Christ in the river. He didn't mean to waste any more time. He put his head under the water at once and pushed forward.[3]

The power of O'Connor's writing is in the juxtaposition of the stark inhumanity of life with the promise of the gospel. The baptism of the boy had enacted a ritual of community which promised more than could be delivered. A life that had been miserable and unhappy now became intolerable. If the boy could only count by being part of the kingdom of Christ, and if baptism in the river was his initiation into that significant experience, better to let the river claim him than to live.

Baptism in this story illustrates what I mean by a liturgical paradigm that has some effect on our personhood. Our premise in this chapter is that the actuality of personhood as posited by the divine Word of God becomes actualized in our own lives through the experiences that may be called "rituals of reinforcement," which ordinarily take place through experiences of community. To be sure, these rituals may be secular or ecclesiastical, but from the perspective of personhood as an experience of the self in relation they may be considered liturgical in the broadest sense of the term.

"Liturgy" is usually associated with a particular form of ecclesiastical worship, but it has a deeper significance in the sense of "service." The Greek *latreia* means "service" or "divine service." *Latreia* is a particular offering to God of that which is appropriate to him. A *leitourgos*, "one who serves," is often translated "minister." In ancient Greece, the *leitourgos* served the state on the basis of his own resources. He devoted his life to public service and did not expect a wage for that.

In the biblical usage of the word, *leitourgos* is one who devotes himself or herself to the service of God. In ancient Israel the liturgical function is rendered

---

2. In *A Good Man is Hard to Find, and Other Stories* (New York: Harcourt, Brace, 1955), pp. 44-45.
3. *Ibid.*, pp. 51-52.

as service to God by those who are appointed to it. In a certain sense, however, Israel as the people of God renders a service to God on behalf of all the nations. Thus Israel is a *leitourgos*, offering up to God in the name of all human creatures that which properly belongs to him. But Israel, of course, must be saved herself; and thus Jesus Christ, as the one Israelite appointed and anointed for that service, renders to God the service that is appropriate. Consequently, Jesus is called the *leitourgos* (minister) who serves in the sanctuary of God (Heb. 8:2). He is the liturgist, who chooses the fields, the shops, and the streets as his sanctuary in which to render service to God. As the incarnate Son of God, he takes humanity and brings it back to its appropriate serviceableness to the Creator.

Looking at the life of Jesus, we can see three core aspects to his liturgy of reconciliation: restoration, renewed relation, and sabbath rest. Human beings are approached as sinners who need to be restored to the kingdom of God, and it is for that purpose that Jesus identifies with them in order to seek and find that which is lost. His own baptism was a liturgical act by which he identified with sinners and placed himself on the side of the estranged. In his baptism, there is the promise that those who have been rejected and despised will now count with God. The lost "children of the kingdom" will be restored; the covenant by which people can once more be related to God in loving fellowship will be renewed — and there will be a sabbath rest for the people of God — the *shalom* of God, in which hostility and hurtfulness will come to an end and joy and peace in the Holy Spirit will prevail.

In Jesus' ministry we often see the importance of the "ritual of reinforcement," which is at least one form of liturgical authentication of personhood. Confronted with the man who was blind from birth (John 9), Jesus "spat on the ground and made clay of the spittle and anointed the man's eyes with the clay." The words of healing were accompanied by tangible feel of moist mud on the blind man's eyes. The Word which became flesh continued to bind word to flesh for the sake of restoring a human being to serviceableness to God. In Mark 6 we are reminded that, after teaching all afternoon, Jesus would not permit five thousand people to leave with empty stomachs. When his disciples protested that they had enough to feed only themselves, Jesus insisted that they invite the multitude to share in that "liturgical" meal. Jesus knew that eating is a ritual of reinforcement with regard to personhood. The truths of the kingdom of God cannot be abstracted from the realities of our own existence as embodied souls and ensouled bodies. What the disciples had experienced through their own solidarity of labor, fellowship, and even hardship was now liturgically to be shared with others who "did not yet belong," but who were the lost sheep of the house of Israel. It is significant that this miracle did not occur during or as a result of Jesus' teaching, but during and as a result of the ritual of eating together. Hospitality is a greater miracle than teaching, for in it truth becomes actualized so as to effect new dimensions of personhood.

On at least one occasion, this liturgical significance of the incarnation was reversed. When a prostitute anointed Jesus' feet with her tears and wiped them with her hair (Luke 7), the Pharisees protested. Had Jesus only known what sort of person this was, they reasoned, he would never have permitted her to touch him. But Jesus was affected by those tears and by that liturgical act. Dare we say that she ministered to Jesus, and restored to him a sense of human solidarity that the Pharisees denied him? But in her ministry to him, she herself became whole. Such rituals are acts of reinforcement and the means for the recovery of authentic personhood.

THE EVENT OF COMMUNITY AS A LITURGICAL PARADIGM

The fundamental liturgical paradigm of personhood is community. We see glimpses of this in the gospel portraits of the "domestic" life style Jesus shared with the disciples, but it is made explicit at the end in what became known as the last supper. Although this meal was a repeat of earlier such occasions, it was heightened by the sense of impending death. Thus, Jesus takes what is ordinary and common and invests it with extraordinary significance. As Jesus broke the bread and poured out the wine and shared it with them, he communicated to his disciples the significance of this event of sharing in light of the breaking of his own body and shedding of his own blood. It was also a covenant with them that what they had experienced together would not be broken, but that there would be continuity between this reality and the reality of the new kingdom of God. Meeting them again after the crucifixion and resurrection, he breathed on them and said, "Receive the Holy Spirit" (John 20). Having touched his body and having seen his familiar features with their own eyes, they now feel his breath on them, and thus are led to experience the Holy Spirit as an intimate and familiar presence rather than as a strange and unknown power. The Holy Spirit would come charged with the familiarity of his own bodily breath and bearing to them the presence of his own person.

This sense of community as a solidarity of life together is a liturgical paradigm of personhood. Jesus himself has that community with the Father in the Spirit. Thus, liturgy takes place as a fundamental experience of God as a fellowship of being. Divine service takes place within the Godhead: the Son serves the Father, and the Father confers his own being upon the Son. This personhood of God himself, which is communal by nature, is itself the paradigm of all personhood. And what we call community is the liturgical expression of that personhood experienced as co-humanity. Community takes place, and personhood is enacted and re-enacted; it is reaffirmed, supported, and reinforced. The luturgical events which are intrinsic to community are rituals of reinforcement for human personhood. Community is more than a social event, it is the re-enactment of the personhood of Christ himself (his body), and the manifestation of his own service (*latreia*). This ongoing ministry of Christ through his humanity continues through the human community as his body. This is the ontological grounding of the church as the people of God.

This means that the community as the body of Christ exists as an eschatological reality. It exists as Jesus Christ himself exists in the world as the one who is also the "end" of the world, the *eschatos*. He is the one who brings restoration, renewal, and sabbath rest into the world. But it is brought into the world in such a way as to establish a tension between the immediate realization of that end and its final consummation.

Thus the community of Christ is never less than a human community of people who still live on "this side of the river." Brokenness and discord remain even though healing and peace are promised. For the boy in Flannery O'Connor's story, there was no mediating community between the kingdom of Christ in the river and the brutal inhumanity of his own home. The preacher in his fanatical desperation was right, but he was also wrong. In baptism into Christ, one now does "count." But baptism is not "into the river," but into Christ. There was no community of Christ to enact the liturgical significance of that baptism and make the boy feel and know that he counted. The significance of these liturgical events which belong to community can be found in the way in which they are not only signs of being in Christ, but they also effect authentic personhood through repeated acts of community life. This is why genuine liturgical acts in the life of community do not depend on novelty for their effectiveness. The act itself is more than a repetition of a movement, it is a re-enactment of a reality and therefore a present experiencing and knowing of that reality.

Restoration, renewal of relation, and sabbath rest are basically theological concepts, though they have personal and psychological connotations as well. To explore further the concept of community as a liturgical paradigm of personhood, we will elaborate these three core aspects from a more psychological perspective. This will enable us to see the integration of basic theological and psychological perspectives of human personhood. From the standpoint of the existence of the self, we can identify three core needs: (1) the integration of the self into a whole person, somatically, physically, and spiritually; (2) having value as a person, counting for something, for someone; and (3) survival, which is the need for immortality. Taking up each in turn, we will now see how community as a liturgical paradigm of personhood can work.

COMMUNITY AS A PARADIGM OF WHOLENESS

One way of expressing what it is to be lost and in need of salvation is to say that the self has disintegrated as a functional unity of being and the person experiences ambivalence and discord at the deepest level. The disintegration of the self can be viewed as a compartmentalization of the self into a physical self and a mental self; or it may be expressed as a fundamental conflict between instinctual drives and personal desires. There is also a fundamental disintegration of the self from other selves. Those who seek counseling or even psychotherapy often say that what they need is to "get my act together," or "to get my head together," or even "to become a whole person." Usually (though probably not in every case) what they also seek is the restoration of some relationship or of the capacity to enter into relationships. The root of the problem is an acknowledged breakdown in one's function as a person, which may have a variety of possible causes.

Because salvation is a term which includes both the concept of "being saved" and "being healed," it is quite natural for us to expect that one core aspect of reconciliation as a theological concept is the restoration of the self as a functioning, whole person. Thus, the rituals of community which express the reality of the ministry of Christ ought to lead to wholeness of personhood as a goal. Not that these rituals in themselves can cure or eliminate every pathological cause of psychical or physical disorder, but they ought to support rather than to hinder such healing. Community and its liturgical functions must be viewed as integrative rather than disintegrative experiences. And sometimes, where both medicine and psychotherapy fail, authentic rituals of community enacted as a means of restoring personhood may succeed.

One New Testament passage arouses our interest in this regard more than any other. Paul begins his first letter to the Corinthian church by addressing himself to the factions and forces which were creating problems there. Through his own personal knowledge of the situation and on the basis of first-hand reports, Paul writes a pastoral letter in the hope of stopping the disintegration of the body. The rivalry, jealousy, strife, and competitiveness between the members of the church are merely symptoms of a deeper disorder. The church is actually reinforcing these "diseases" in its liturgical life rather than reinforcing its health.

When the church gathers for the Lord's Supper, warns Paul, they are destroying themselves and one another.

> I do not commend you, because when you come together it is not for the better but for the worse. For, in the first place, when you assemble as a church, I hear that there are divisions among you; and I partly believe it, for there must be factions among you in order that those

who are genuine among you may be recognized. When you meet together, it is not the Lord's supper that you eat (1 Cor. 11:17-20).

The problem is not a deviation from correct polity or the use of unauthorized liturgical forms. The problem is a breakdown in the structure of community itself. "For in eating, each one goes ahead with his own meal, and one is hungry and another is drunk. ... What shall I say to you, shall I commend you in this? No, I will not" (11:21, 22). The body of Christ, in Paul's eyes, is not the bread, but the gathered assembly of believers in the name of Christ. The liturgical act of eating the bread and drinking the wine as a participation in the body and blood of Christ cannot be separated from the liturgical act of eating and drinking as brothers and sisters in Christ. In fact, Paul seems to be saying that it is not a liturgical event in which Christ is involved at all if it is not an event of recognition of each other as fellow members of Christ. By their actions they are saying to each other: "You don't count." But this nullifies the event, which is meant to convey the message that "you *do* count." Paul then warns:

Whoever, therefore, eats the bread or drinks the cup of the Lord in an unworthy manner will be guilty of profaning the body and blood of the Lord. Let a man examine himself, and so eat of the bread and drink of the cup. For any one who eats and drinks without discerning the body eats and drinks judgment upon himself. That is why many of you are weak and ill, and some have died (11:27-30).

This is not the easiest passage in the Bible to exegete. But I suggest that Paul knew very well that some of the church members had recently died and some were chronically ill. In making the strongest case possible, he might then have suggested that there is some correlation between their destructive practice and the sickness and death of some members. At the very least, he himself assumes some correlation between liturgical event and personal and physical health — in this case a negative one. By enacting a ritual that effectively destroys the bond of common fellowship in Christ at the personal and social level, they are destroying themselves. I do not mean to suggest a sort of magical, one-for-one correlation that endows a liturgical event with the power to kill. I am, however, suggesting a general correlation between wholeness of the body and the rituals by which the body enacts its own life together. Over a period of time, we can affect *sōma* (body) either negatively or positively through rituals that reinforce. There is, Paul says, a "demonic liturgy," or a *koinonia* which is demonic (1 Cor. 10:21). In all of the rituals we enact as members of community, we are reinforcing either that which produces wholeness and health or that which produces sickness and death.

Certainly there is sufficient evidence of psychosomatic illness to warrant the conclusion that physical effects can be created by mental or psychical images and energy. One could argue that the reverse is also true: there is at least a tendency toward wholeness and health which is the result of rituals of community which reinforce wholeness and health. I am not concerned here to make a case for physical healing and bodily health through the liturgical events of community (though there is no reason why such a case could not be made on the same grounds). My argument is more toward the point of becoming whole persons, where love replaces hate, self-acceptance replaces self-condemnation, hope replaces despair, communion replaces estrangement and aloneness.

Community as a liturgical paradigm of personhood has the power to restore wholeness to persons where there has been disintegration and fragmentation. This is the community in which Christ is present and active through the activity of the members. It is the place where there is no "other end of the table" where I am permitted to defy love through indifference and anger or to crave love in silent despair and hunger. Such community is the place where my aloneness is exorcised and my wholeness is enacted. It is the place where I leave more of a total person than when I entered.

There is authentic liturgical community when we are eating together with discernment and love, open to each other's humanity. It is when we are laughing together with freedom and without guile and rancor, when like children we actually have moments of play. That is authentic liturgical community, and it actualizes personhood as wholeness and health. My sickness is not a failure to the community, but it is not allowed to have final power over me. Even my death is not a failure to the community, but is itself an event of the community in which I am delivered over to another liturgical community. "I go to prepare a place for you," said Jesus (John 14:2). The healing function of the community is not to eliminate death, but to integrate the self even through this event; to sustain us, uplift us, uphold us, and to enable us to experience faith and hope and love.

This is why wholeness of personhood is the responsibility of the community, and not merely the responsiblity of the self. My own sickness and death disintegrate the unity of the self, but in the life of the community, my being is affirmed and restored by being related to the living one, Jesus Christ.

COMMUNITY AS A PARADIGM OF HOLINESS

One of the strongest biblical motifs which emerges through the teaching of Jesus is that of the value of the person. People do count for Jesus. In the parables of the lost sheep and the lost coin, Jesus portrayed his own search for that which is rejected and neglected. In his fellowship with sinners and tax-collectors, he enacted liturgically a fundamental paradigm of sanctification. That which has no value or holiness of its own becomes holy through sharing the life of the Holy One. Community as the body of Christ has a sanctifying aspect, but never at the expense of that which has no right in itself. Any concept of sanctification which has its core value in the devaluation of others is not of God.

Sanctification is first of all a positive liturgical act. It is the separation unto God, who is the Holy One, of that which is merely created and creaturely. The original sanctification, by which all creation received its true value, is expressed in the verdict the Creator himself rendered — it is good (Gen. 1). When creation became alienated from God through sin, the holiness of God appeared as a negative act. Now there must be reconciliation and restoration. To accomplish this, God came to his created world and among his creatures to create a new place of holiness, through which every created thing and person could receive the true value that God gives to their being. Holiness is goodness, considered from the standpoint that God is good.

Goodness is therefore not first of all an ethical value but an ontological value. For our personal life to have meaning and purpose is good; for it to be empty and meaningless is not good. To count for something or someone is good; not to count is bad. Those who make an ethical value out of religion gain this value by excluding those who don't count. This is what confounded the Pharisees in what Jesus did: he enacted the reality of the kingdom of God by restoring persons to full value in God's sight. He did this not by mere teaching, for that would have been a platitude, but liturgically. That is, he made his own life an event which included rather than excluded. He communicated the ontological value of his own person as the Holy One of God to those with whom he ate and all with whom he came in contact. The community as the body of Christ consequently carries with it this same ontological possibility through the actuality of its own being as the form of Christ in the world. Community then enacts personhood as a value by communicating its own being-in-Christ to those who have their being-in-community.

Paul appeals to this truth in dealing with the situation of marriage between a believer and an unbeliever (1 Cor. 7). No doubt some Corinthian Christians were arguing that an unbelieving spouse should be divorced on the grounds that this compromised the holiness of the church as the community of Christ. An unbeliever, this argument might have run, doesn't count as far as the community is concerned. Such a person cannot possibly have the same full value of personhood as a believer. Paul responds by giving his interpretation based on his understanding of God's act of reconciliation in Christ:

> To the rest I say, not the Lord, that if any brother has a wife who is an unbeliever, and she consents to live with him, he should not di-

vorce her. If any woman has a husband who is an unbeliever, and he consents to live with her, she should not divorce him. For the unbelieving husband is consecrated through his wife, and the unbelieving wife is consecrated through her husband. Otherwise, your children would be unclean, but as it is they are holy (1 Cor. 7:12-14).

This passage should be read alongside Paul's warning against being "mismated with unbelievers" (2 Cor. 6:14). One cannot draw from either of these texts a general "rule of marriage." Paul apparently does not feel that the situation he is dealing with in his first letter is one of being "mismated." There is "consent" on the part of the unbelieving spouse, which implies a participation in the life of the other without opposition or recrimination. This is supported by the argument Paul makes, based on the situation regarding the children of such a relation.

The point is that the liturgical life by which the community enacts its life as the body of Christ reaches into the life of its members so as to include all who participate, both directly and indirectly. Because the marital and filial bond is itself a liturgical enactment of personhood, the events of the community by which life with Jesus Christ is also enacted cannot be set aside as of another kind. Paul seems to be arguing from the incarnation itself. The disciples, for example, were "sanctified" through their association with Jesus prior to their "confession of faith." Jesus did not withhold from them any ritual of his own self-enactment as the Holy One of God. They gave their consent to this by their complicity in these events of his own life. They were accomplices before they became "believers."

Children, Paul argues, are accomplices in the liturgical events which constitute the value of the family unit as well as in those events enacted by the community as the body of Christ. The children count, and in the same way the unbelieving spouse counts, even though there is not yet a public confession of faith. As far as the church is concerned, baptism is the initiatory ritual which enacts belonging to the community. But the church itself exists as the human community which was already incorporated into the baptism of Christ, in his death and resurrection. There is a "priesthood" by which the community enacts the reconciliation of Christ prior to the ecclesiastical sacrament of baptism. One could say on the basis of Paul's teaching that the believing wife is the "priest" of the unbelieving husband. On behalf of the unbelieving spouse and the not-yet-believing children, the believer does what Christ himself did and continues to do — stand with sinners and incorporate them into his own self-enactment of communion with God.

This has significance for how we understand what Jesus meant by going into all the world and preaching the gospel, making disciples of all nations (Matt. 28:18-20). Ordinarily we take this to be the basis for the evangelistic mandate of the church. If a fundamental human need is not only to be made whole, but to have value, to count, then evangelism could best function as an extension of the liturgical event of community by which holiness is communicated as the ground on which belief becomes possible. Certainly Paul must have had eventual belief on the part of the unbelieving spouse and the not-yet-believing children in view. When will they really count? After they have made confession of faith and been baptized? That is often the case. The church only counts those members who thus qualify themselves. But this is quite different from the ministry of Jesus. The good news Jesus proclaimed was that publicans and sinners will enter the kingdom of God before self-righteous Pharisees, and that the "lost sheep" have as much value in God's eyes as those who are safely at home.

The original human condition is that of belonging. Our true origin as God brings us into being is not that of separateness and isolation, but that of belonging and being partakers of his covenant love. We do not first become believers, as those who have yet to find true value, and then belong in order to count. Rather, we are included by God before we include ourselves. Too often, evangelism takes place outside the event of community, where there are no rituals of reinforcement and no context of belonging. When conversion to Christ is understood first of all as a private and individual decision, incorporation into the community of Christ will become more of a religious or ethical duty. Now that you have been saved, the person is told, you *ought* to join a church, to become active in the body. It is not surprising that the liturgical events by which the community celebrates its own existence as the body of Christ are viewed rather diffidently by many people who come in by this route. However, for the person who has first of all experienced wholeness of person affirmed as a "gospel of belonging," enacted through rituals which reinforce this reality, growth in faith and knowledge will be supported and encouraged as a continuing event of this participation in community.

In my own pastoral ministry, I began to see the event of the Lord's Supper as the central event of the church's enactment of reconciliation to Christ, as an event of the body of Christ which is itself a threshold to the kingdom of God. Rather than restricting the communion service to those who were qualified by their own confession of faith, one could look upon it as a liturgical form of evangelism. Paul, as a matter of fact, did not address himself to the possible presence of unbelievers at the Lord's table. His warning was addressed to believers. Why should there be any danger to an unbeliever who participates in the liturgical event of Christ's death and resurrection as an enactment of the community's own life? And why should the presence of sinners destroy the value of the event — unless the value of the event comes by virtue of what it excludes, in which case it is typically Pharisaical.

When Jesus Christ is named as Lord of the community, and the one in whose name the grace and peace of Christ is offered to all who will receive, is this not the heart of the gospel itself? Certainly this event takes place in the context of the kerygmatic proclamation based on the Scriptures. But the Word has become flesh, and must not be made Word without flesh. The true order of Christ is one of reconciliation, which embraces and loves those who are estranged for who they are, not for what they have said or done to qualify for love. When John Wesley went on his preaching missions to the villages of England, he proclaimed the good news of Jesus Christ who came into the world to love and identify with sinners. Then he would set up tables and invite all to come and eat the bread and drink the wine that signified participation in the communion of Christ himself. Wesley called the Lord's supper a "converting ordinance." Surely it should be at least that!

Donald Buteyn tells of an incident when he was minister of outreach at First Presbyterian Church in Berkeley during the 1960s. In attempting to reach the thousands of young street people all around, the congregation discovered a fundamental distrust of the church as a religious institution. In attempting to bridge that credibility gap, the church established a house nearby which offered free lodging, food, and clothing to street people. Still, there was mistrust. The house appeared to be part of the "fortress" which the church represented to them.

Hoping for a breakthrough, Buteyn and some other local ministers planned an event on the church parking lot one Saturday afternoon. A rock band was brought in, and booths were set up offering free food and clothing. Hundreds of young people appeared. Toward evening the group of ministers appeared, dressed in the most extravagant ecclesiastical garb they could find, including lace sleeves and colorful vestments. Accompanying them were several young boys, serving as acolytes, carrying basins of water and towels. Walking over to the sound truck, they climbed on it and began to read from Matthew 25 about ministering to those in prison and those who were naked and oppressed. Then, releasing a large helium-filled balloon with a symbol of the Holy Spirit, they climbed down from the truck and approached the young people who were sitting and standing by in consternation at this somewhat ludicrous spectacle. Without a word the ministers, their elaborate ecclesiastical vestments trailing in the dirt, knelt and began to wash the feet of the young people at the front.

An incredible thing then happened, Buteyn reported. "The moment we took those dirty bare feet of the teenagers in our hands and began to wash and dry them, they began to break down and cry. Their defenses were penetrated by this tender and intimate touch. The mood was transformed from one of curiosity and jeering, to quiet and open interest. That marked the beginning of our ministry. They began to believe that we really cared about them as human beings."

Being a priest is precariously close to being a clown. Coming out dressed in such a way as to appear to be ecclesiastical clowns, the Berkeley ministers became priests when they took the dirty feet of the homeless youngsters in their hands. Far too often, in our attempt to be priests, we end up only being clowns. Holiness occurs in the street, not always in the temple. Wherever humanity finds itself, no matter how tattered and torn, no matter how lost and forlorn, is where liturgical acts should take place. For here there is vulnerability, here it counts.

COMMUNITY AS A PARADIGM OF IMMORTALITY

The church as the community of Christ enacts the immortality of the self in its basic liturgical drama of worship. Each person's deep existential need to survive this mortal life with continuity of the self is almost undeniable. To deny that is a form of despair. The celebration of the sabbath rest which comes to all who are reconciled to Christ is represented as the joy and hope which belongs to those whom God has created and loved. Karl Barth says:

> It is not man who brings the history of creation to an end, nor is it he who ushers in the subsequent history. It is God's rest which is the conclusion of the one and the beginning of the other, i.e., God's free, solemn, and joyful satisfaction with that which has taken place and has been completed as creation, and his invitation to man to rest with him, i.e., with him to be satisfied with that which has taken place through him. The goal of creation, and at the same time the beginning of all that follows, is the event of God's Sabbath freedom, Sabbath rest and Sabbath joy in which man, too, has been summoned to participate. It is the event of divine rest in the face of the cosmos completed with the creation of man—a rest which takes precedence over all man's eagerness and zeal to enter upon his task. Man is created to participate in this rest.[4]

Here is where the self is authentically placed within the actuality of immortality. The eternal life of God is not without content for the human person. It is the end that is held out before us in the beginning. Jesus says to his disciples, "You are those who have continued with me in my trials; as my Father appointed a kingdom for me, so do I appoint for you that you may eat and drink at my table in my kingdom, and sit on thrones judging the twelve tribes of Israel" (Luke 22:28-30). You will count, Jesus is saying to them. The significance of your own personal existence cannot be destroyed. You have

---

4. *Church Dogmatics*, III/1, 98.

continued with me in my trials; I grant you immortality as a pledge of my being yours. As I will live in my Father's presence, so shall you live in my presence and in the presence of one another. As I will be at that eschatological banquet, so I reserve a place for you. It is in the community of Christ on earth, and nowhere else, that this fundamental paradigm of personhood is authorized and enacted.

With respect to our individual lives, this means that the whole is greater than the sum of the parts. It will always be a mystery to us why we are persons at all, and why we are the particular kind of person that we are. The psychiatrist in Peter Shaffer's *Equus* says, in a moment of candor:

> "A child is born into a world of phenomena all equal in their power to enslave. It sniffs — it sucks — it strokes its eyes over the whole uncomfortable range. Suddenly one strikes. Why? Moments snap together like magnets, forging a chain of shackles. Why? I can trace them. I can even, with time, pull them apart again. But why at the start they were ever magnetized at all — just those particular moments of experience and no others — I don't know. *And nor does anyone else*. Yet, *if* I don't know — if I can never know that — then what am I doing here? And I don't mean clinically doing or socially doing — I mean *fundamentally*! These questions, these Whys, are fundamental — yet they have no place in a consulting room."

There is nothing more vulnerable in all of creation than a human self. It is vulnerable because it only exists as a self over against the mystery of its own creaturely being. It is vulnerable because the content of human personhood in terms of the person that we become is subject to great vicissitudes. Life experience is as much misfortune as it is fortune. There is nothing so fragile in life as the thin cord which binds the human self to its own existence in this temporal world. The borderline between sanity and insanity is always a thin line which we must walk. There is nothing more sensitive and vulnerable to destruction than the human person which the Word of God creates and sustains. Why is this? Because there is no permanent foundation in nature itself. There are no fundamental laws of nature, chemical or otherwise, which can ensure that a human brain will become a human mind, that a human life will sustain a human person. When God breathes into the human creature, that breath of life already knows of eternity, even though it has no power of its own to bring it about (Eccl. 3:11). When God calls Abraham out of Ur of the Chaldees, he makes Abraham vulnerable and exposes him to all the threats of a historical existence which cannot account for its own movements.

And yet, there is nothing more invincible, more lasting, more permanent than that which the Word of God calls into being. Why? Because it is upheld by the Word of God and will never pass away. When heaven and earth have passed away, as they surely will, that which is sustained as personal existence will never pass away, because the Word of God will never be destroyed (1 Peter 1:25). To say that there is such a thing as theological anthropology, is not to say that there are no horrors and nightmares in being a person. Like Abraham, who walks out on the old gods and is exposed to the merciless onslaughts of demons and false gods, we too in a sense are summoned to that wilderness.

But it is too late. The bush is already burning and is not consumed. We have breathed and been breathed upon. Someone has touched us. We are on holy ground. There is no backtracking, trying to find once again the entrance through which to escape. It is too late to run. Non-personhood is not an option. That holiness of God that created us as persons will kill us if we try to run. There is no safety in running. Take off your shoes, the ground on which you are standing is holy ground. Intimacy is a way of survival. Openness to the Word of God is life and joy and peace. And above all, we have been baptized — or are about to be.

CHAPTER THIRTEEN

A THEOLOGICAL PERSPECTIVE
ON THE CURE OF SOULS

ONE CAN APPROACH THE TASK OF MINISTRY IN TWO WAYS. THE FIRST may be summed up by the maxim "If it's working, don't fix it." In other words, don't tinker around with something that is running well enough to make you a success as its leader. The practical wisdom of this pragmatic approach to the mysteries of human behavior can be admired.

The other approach recalls a statement by Jesus of Nazareth — "Those who are well have no need of a physician, but those who are sick" (Matt. 9:12). At first glance this saying appears quite similar to the first. But its context makes clear that Jesus considered his own calling to be one of fixing what is not working. And if you study his life and teaching at greater length you could conclude with some justification that he considered nothing to be working, at least not in the way that it is intended to work. At the very least, this saying was an argument for his own commitment to people who were despised and rejected by the "healthy minded," but whom he considered in need of a message of good news, which had as much to do with humanizing their life into a community of love and acceptance as with the healing of their bodily afflictions.

Following Jesus, the Christian church has always understood its ministry to focus preeminently on what it called "the cure of souls" — a quaint expression which has given way, in our more sophisticated technical jargon, to the term "pastoral care." We have chosen this somewhat archaic concept as a focus for discussing the perspectives which both theology and psychology bring to the fundamental task of ministering the grace and good news of Jesus Christ to a humanity that could use some hope and healing.[1]

To speak of curing — rather than of caring — can be not only presumptuous, but dangerous. One can all too easily think of some purported cures which have been far more destructive, even demonic, than the original state. The

---

1. The word "cure" comes from the Latin *curare* (whence curate, curator), which means "taking charge of," "taking care of," "looking after." This is much more than merely "caring" in the modern sense of feeling concern for.

Reverend Jim Jones practiced the cure of souls according to his prescription, and the massacre of the innocents in Guyana is a stark reminder of another proverb quoted by Jesus — "Physician, heal thyself" (Luke 4:23). Many invitations to ascend the mount of transfiguration have resulted in disfiguration.

I suspect that as many pastors and theologians have done damage as psychologists. Both professions have their casualties as well as their trophies of healing. And yet, in the final analysis, the Rogerian technique of "doing no harm," applied either as a model of pastoral care or clinical counseling, may fail at precisely the point at which it offers to help: it produces no transfiguration and provides no radical cure. Nevertheless, before I place myself in the hands of one who has a cure, I want to know that the concept of health which informs the cure has the good of my person and the preservation of my own humanity in view. Accordingly, this is an attempt to set forth a theological perspective on the cure of souls.

The cure of souls, says Karl Barth,

> means a concrete actualization of the participation of the one in the particular past, present and future of the other, in his particular burdens and afflictions, but above all in his particular promise and hope in the singularity of his existence as created and sustained by God.[2]

This *cura animarum*, as the medieval church called it, is marked by a general concern for the individual in light of God's purpose for her or him. God is the one who is primarily concerned about souls. What we mean by soul here is the person in the totality of human being and individual personal existence. Even as God is concerned for "souls" in the sense that he purposely created, sustains, and continues to seek the good of those creatures which bear his image, so there is a cure of souls exercised by the mutual existence of persons in community. This was termed the *mutua consolatio fratrum*. Humanity is to exist fraternally, in mutual consolation, so as to nurture and sustain humanity in particular, not merely as a general principle. Hence, the cure of souls "provided confession with the promise of the remission of sins, and the invitation to the resultant amendment of life, not as an institution bound to certain clerical officials, but as an event."[3]

In certain extraordinary conditions of emergency and conflict, this included actions analogous to the healings and exorcisms which were part of the ministry of the apostolic church. These actions call for highly specialized endowments and training. Thus, Barth says, the cure of souls will not occur without the

---

2. *Church Dogmatics*, IV/3, 885.
3. *Ibid.*, 886.

conscious application of various forms of general or secular and therefore neutral psychology, psychogogics and psychotherapy. This does
not alter the fact, however, that the problems of the cure of souls
begin where those of a neutral psychology and the neutral art of
healing based upon it cease. It can thus understand the problems of
the latter and include them in its own discussions, but it cannot take
them over or try to solve them. This means that the community's
pastoral care must have such knowledge of its own modest and restricted function that it really knows what it is after and can the
better achieve it so far as there can be any question of achievement.[4]

Barth's attitude toward the "neutral" behavioral sciences, relegating their function to that of a lower order, may be somewhat condescending, but he is
entirely correct to say that the cure of souls as practiced by the church's
pastoral staff needs to acknowledge restrictions on its own dealing with the
complexities involved in the healing of persons. In the end Barth is calling the
church to acknowledge and practice its own specialty in the cure of souls; and
that includes a Christian understanding of God and the nature of human
personhood, which exists under divine calling and ordination. "Everything
depends upon its fidelity in doing what it does in this understanding," says
Barth:

> If it knows its own business and acts accordingly, there can be no
> fear of its becoming a superfluous religious duplication of the neutral
> science and art, and it will have both in its own narrower circle and
> in the world around the power of a sign of salvation and witness of
> the kingdom which only the community can set up.[5]

A THEOLOGICAL RATHER THAN
RELIGIOUS PERSPECTIVE

Why take a theological, rather than "religious," perspective on the cure of souls?
After all, is it not the business of religion to be concerned with the state of
the soul? A great deal of confusion can be created by trying to bridge the
supposed gap between theology and psychology by dissolving both into psychology of religion. There is a certain validity in studying the religious phenomena of human existence and even in seeking to interpret them in
psychological categories, but that is not what we mean by a theological perspective.

Barth himself takes great pains to show that the religious aspect of human
existence is phenomenological in character, and not theological. The "religious

---

4. *Ibid.*
5. *Ibid.*, 887.

a priori," which Reinhold Seeberg introduced into German theology, is not in Barth's estimation a point of contact for divine revelation, but only a phenomenological manifestation of the image of God which becomes human presumption. "From the standpoint of revelation," says Barth, "man's religion is simply an assumption and assertion ... and as such is an activity which contradicts revelation."[6] Barth clearly feels that the human person cannot escape being religious, because of the image of God, but this religious activity cannot be viewed as a positive aspect or as a ground for authentic theological existence:

> The religious relationship of man to God which is the inevitable consequence of his sin is a degenerate form of the covenant-relationship between the Creator and the creature. It is the empty and deeply problematical shell of that relationship. But as such it is a confirmation that God will not be mocked, that even forgetful man will not be able to forget Him. ... He has to bear witness to the Word of God and seal the fact that he cannot be without God in this way, in the form of religion.[7]

We should add that revelation for Barth not only negates false religion but establishes true religion. Thus Barth could never fully appreciate Bonhoeffer's attempt to speak of a "Christianity without religion."

Bonhoeffer was deeply influenced by Barth's absolute distinction between faith, based on revelation, and religion, based on the inverted divine image intrinsic to the creature. What Bonhoeffer wished to achieve in his life and thought was nothing less than a "religionless Christianity," a theme which emerges frequently in his *Letters and Papers from Prison*. "Not religion, but revelation," wrote Bonhoeffer, "not a religious community, but the church: that is what the reality of Jesus Christ means."[8] The fact that Bonhoeffer was not clear as to just what this meant in terms of what he called living in a "world come of age" is reflected by his informal comments from a prison cell to his friend Eberhard Bethge:

> What do a church, a community, a sermon, a liturgy, a Christian life mean in a religionless world? How do we speak of God — without religion? ... In what way are we "religious-secular" Christians, in what way are we the ekklesia, those who are called forth? ... What is the place of worship and prayer in a religionless situation?[9]

As the man closest to Bonhoeffer, Bethge clarifies what his friend meant by the term religion: on the one hand, metaphysics as an approach to knowledge of God, and on the other hand individual pietism as an approach to

---

6. *Ibid.*, I/2, 302.
7. *Ibid.*, IV/1, 483.
8. *Sanctorum Communio*, p. 112.
9. *Letters and Papers from Prison*, pp. 280f.

experience of God.[10] Bonhoeffer had as little confidence in one's psychological state of religious feeling (which he termed "methodism") as he did in speculative metaphysics as the formation of a "Christian world view."

To these two distinctive concepts of religion for Bonhoeffer, Bethge adds several others. The religious person divides life into sectors, says Bonhoeffer, of which religion accounts for only one, rather than encompassing the entirety of human existence, as he himself believed the incarnation demanded. In addition, the religious person seeks a privileged position in society, with the concept of the "chosen" leading to a spiritual elitism. In line with this, religion serves to keep the world under a "tutelage," preventing man from "coming of age," which Bonhoeffer described as experiencing the full powers of one's humanity as determined by the secularity of the incarnation. And finally, by religion Bonhoeffer meant dispensability. To the extent that faith becomes imbedded in a "religion," it becomes dispensable when history introduces a new age.

A theological existence, unlike a religious one, is always contemporary, with full assertion of one's own humanity, lived before God in faith, and embracing all of life. Thus revelation, as the presence of God in the world through Jesus Christ, provides a critical test for authentic existence. Because revelation does not emerge out of a creaturely possibility, but nevertheless comes to the creature in creaturely terms through the humanity of God in Christ, life can at every point be brought under the critical principle of a theological perspective. The religious life can never become that critical principle because it has already been compromised by allowing too much of a vested interest to determine its character on the part of the religious subject itself.

Without going into the differences between Barth's and Bonhoeffer's views of religion, we can note their unanimity in establishing a theological perspective as a critical principle for faith over against the phenomenon of religious experience. Because we believe that theology brings a principle of criticism to bear on human existence, we have chosen to discuss the cure of souls from this perspective. In this way, theology constantly calls for reconstruction of human thought and life in every age. Because the revelation of God through Jesus Christ is held to be contemporary through the living Christ, who is present in the church through the power of the Spirit, theology emerges out of what is objective to human experience. That is, a human anthropology, which knows only that there is a symptom of some disorder, can discover the true order of humanity through a theological anthropology. Because this dis-

---

10. See Eberhard Bethge, *Dietrich Bonhoeffer* (New York: Harper and Row, 1970), pp. 775ff.

covery can take place only in the context in which God's Word is heard and believed, divine revelation becomes the formal basis for the critical principle which theology brings to bear as a perspective. Now we must elaborate this formal basis for a theological perspective on the cure of souls more specifically in terms of the material content of such a ministry. We have chosen three core theological perspectives from which to explore the cure of souls: the christological, the ecclesiological, and the eschatological. Within each of these perspectives, we will look critically at the cure of souls as a ministry of bringing persons to wholeness and holiness.

A CHRISTOLOGICAL PERSPECTIVE

The relevance of a christological critique for the cure of souls is obvious. If one begins with the assumption that Jesus Christ constitutes not only the fulness of deity, but also the complete expression of true humanity, it is clear that humanity has been given an exceptional ontological status in the person of Christ. Not that Christ is any more or less human than any other human being; but his humanity cannot be attributed to an accidental or impersonal process of creaturely development. In Jesus Christ we discover that true humanity is rooted in personal being, and that is what is meant by ontological status.

To put it technically, the incarnation is the hermeneutical horizon for authentic personhood. All answers to questions about the nature of the human in terms of what it is to be a person must be derived from this event. One may not go beyond the "horizon" of the humanity of Christ to develop a speculative anthropology. We go to Christ to learn about Adam, Barth said, not to Adam to learn about Christ. It is not theologically irrelevant that Jesus Christ's humanity exists in solidarity with the human race begun in Adam. And as a state of creaturely being, Adamic humanity does determine the state of existence for Jesus. But a state of creaturely existence cannot provide an ontological status which it does not possess of itself. The qualitative distinction between human and non-human is an ontological one, not a phenomenological one. That is, behavior alone cannot establish a quality of being, nor can altered states of creaturely being constitute significant ontological determinations in being itself. Adam does appear to be a creature who has an orientation to a being not of his own order. But it is only through Jesus Christ that this orientation is given ontological status of a permanent order. And it is through Jesus Christ that humanity is anchored in permanence. Paul brings this christological critique to bear on the uncertainty and transitoriness of our creaturely being when he exclaims, "I am sure that neither death, nor life, nor angels, nor principalities, nor things present, nor things to come, nor powers, nor height, nor depth, nor anything else in all creation, will be able to separate us from the love of God in Christ Jesus our Lord" (Rom. 8:38-39).

In the cure of souls, this can become a tangible reality when the body of Christ speaks this with authority and hope to those trembling on the abyss of their own creatureliness. I have shouted it out at the funeral service of a woman who took her own life, but who belonged to the body of Christ. Certainly grief counseling was also necessary on that occasion as a function of pastoral care, but that could not "cure the souls" of her husband and children. Against all emotional fears of the worst and against all systems of religious thought which might teach otherwise, this theological perspective brings the revealed power and presence of Jesus Christ to bear in the tragic human situation in such a way that human existence itself is reconstructed and reoriented. This is the cure of souls.

The role of the Holy Spirit in the cure of souls is to be understood from this same christological perspective. The Christ who gave humanity ontological status through his own human being received the Spirit of God into his own personal, spiritual being. In Christ, Spirit and Word become a personal unity in such a way that Word can never be heard apart from Spirit, and Spirit can never be experienced except as Word. Because the fundamental orientation of the human soul is an orientation of spirit toward God as the source of personal being, personal health is also spiritual health. The Holy Spirit is the Spirit of Jesus Christ, the Holy One of God. The Spirit does not come to us as "naked" Spirit, to be clothed with our own subjective human feelings and possibilities. Rather, the Spirit comes to us "clothed" with the subjective feelings, experiences, and possibilities of Jesus Christ himself.

In a pastoral letter to the Corinthians Paul reminds them that God is "the Father of mercies and the God of all comfort." What is the source of this comfort which is surely an element in the cure of souls? Is it a depth of human compassion which the counselor brings to the client or the pastor to the parishioner at a time of suffering and grief? It is indeed that, but it is also more than that. This God of mercy and comfort, Paul goes on to say,

> comforts us in all our affliction, so that we may be able to comfort those who are in any affliction, with the comfort with which we ourselves are comforted by God. For as we share abundantly in Christ's sufferings, so through Christ we share abundantly in comfort too (2 Cor. 1:3-5).

This ministry, Paul reminds us, is a ministry "in the Spirit," for the Spirit gives life while the written code kills (2 Cor. 3:6). We are always "carrying in the body the death of Jesus, so that the life of Jesus may also be manifested in our bodies" (2 Cor. 4:10).

From this one could suggest that a ministry of the "healing of persons" also has an ontological status to the extent that it is grounded in the reality of the Spirit of Christ expressed through our own human lives. The cure of souls, while not indifferent toward techniques as instrumental in healing, makes available a resource of help and healing which goes beyond professional skill. A ministry of healing which understands itself as the cure of souls in this christological sense is nothing less than the continuing of Christ's own ministry through our lives as the Spirit of Christ lives and works in us. However, the Spirit of Christ is not an attribute restricted to the professional minister or practitioner of healing. Christ is on the side of the one who is in need of healing, not merely on the side of the healer. The assumption which must lie behind the task of helping persons is that one does not bring Christ to the other person, but one expects to meet Christ in the other person as the one who is the source of that person's healing and health.

This christological perspective on the cure of souls demands that such a ministry take place in a context of the body of Christ — not the body of Christ as a specifically religious institution but in a more incarnational sense. Through the incarnation, Christ has taken to himself all humanity as the horizon of his own being. No person exists outside of this horizon. Christ is the determination of the basic humanity of all persons, precisely because his presence in the world brings all humanity and each person under the determination of the cross, as sinful humanity.

This is why Paul can say that we always carry in our bodies the death of Jesus. "Everything would be ruined," says Bonhoeffer, "if one were to try to reserve Christ for the Church, and to allow the world only some kind of law, even if it were a Christian law. Christ died for the world, and it is only in the midst of the world that Christ is Christ."[11] Because Christ "emptied himself" and thus presented himself to the world in this "kenotic" sense, the ministry of the cure of souls also has a kenotic aspect. In taking our weaknesses on himself and in solidarity and identity with sinful humanity, Christ himself created the mandate for a kenotic presence and ministry in the world.[12] This led Bonhoeffer to say: "It is implicit in the New Testament statement concerning the Incarnation of God in Christ that all men are taken up, enclosed and borne within the body of Christ and that this is just what the congregation of the faithful are to make known to the world by their words and by their lives."[13] One can expect that Christ will be present where he has given himself to be present. Not the least of the occasions of Christ's presence in the world is his presence on both sides of the event of the cure of souls.

---

11. *Ethics*, pp. 205f.
12. For in-depth discussion of "kenotic" ministry, see Ray S. Anderson, *Historical Transcendence and the Reality of God* (Grand Rapids: Eerdmans, 1975), pp. 252-76.
13. *Ethics*, 206.

AN ECCLESIOLOGICAL PERSPECTIVE

A theological perspective may also be viewed as an ecclesiological critique. The cure of souls, as Barth pointed out, is a ministry and service of the Christian community. Whereas the christological critique provides human existence with an ontological status on which life can be reconstructed, the ecclesiological critique provides the proper "order" in which the cure of souls should take place. The body of Christ, as the social dimension of the theological community called the church, constitutes the true order in which faith and life are called to exist. This delivers the cure of souls from distortion by religious or pseudo-religious privatism. Here is a judgment on the "cult of personality" which turns transfiguration experiences into disfiguration. This critique delivers the true order of discipleship, as an attempt to reorient life into positive patterns of growth and fulfilment, from crippling enslavement to ideological, political, or even religious tyrannies.

This is not to say that any given historical church or fellowship will exemplify the true order of the Christian community. But even the imperfection of the church can be brought under the ecclesiological critique, as Paul clearly does in his letters to Corinth. The church becomes the specific and concrete occasion for experiencing, even if imperfectly, the true order of existence in fellowship. Belonging to this fellowship is not the prerogative of the healthy minded or the privileged or the successful. It is Christ himself who stands as the Lord of the church with his words of reminder, "Those who are well have no need of a physician but those who are sick." The true order of the church thus includes the cure of souls, and must therefore include those in need of cure.

On one occasion in my own pastoral ministry, I found it necessary to seek the services of a psychiatrist to treat a woman who exhibited serious psychotic symptoms which incapacitated her from functioning as a wife and mother. Through an extended hospitalization which involved a series of electric shock treatments, she recovered her mental and emotional stability; and when I called on her in the hospital, she indicated a readiness to resume her life responsibilities. Prior to her discharge, the psychiatrist, himself a Christian, told me that the prognosis for her continued healing depended on her involvement with a community of people who could love, accept, and support her. "I have only succeeded in altering her behavior," he told me. "The treatment she has received has no power to give her an orientation toward health. This can only come through the church." This, of course, is a highly idealized statement, considering the nature of the church; yet I found his distinction between an altered state of existence and an orientation toward true existence theologically meaningful and helpful in practice.

The ecclesiological critique is relevant for the practice of the cure of souls from a psychological standpoint. Whatever it means to be a Christian psychologist, it is surely not imposing a privatistic religious experience on a client for the sake of altering behavior. The therapist can bring the theological perspective by providing an orientation which holds true for both counselor and client. My psychiatrist friend could make the distinction, but provided no theological order for his patients. The context of his treatment had no ecclesiological dimension in terms of the cure of souls. Altered behavior patterns are a relative necessity in life, but a fundamental orientation to the true order of humanity through belonging to Christ's body is an absolute necessity. And it is available, if there is the theological courage to exercise it.

On the wall of my office is a linoleum block print made by a church member struggling with the problems of an active homosexual relationship. The picture is of a haggard, tormented woman squatting on the ground holding in her lap an emaciated, almost grotesque child. The caption on the print is, "The Bride of Christ." When he gave me the picture, he said, "This is the church, and that pitiable little figure is me — but I am in the church!" He knew that I believed this, too. In fact, he knew it because I believed it, and gave him reason to know it. Against the barrage of emotional and sometimes hysterical reactions to this particular behavior pattern, and in the face of religious systems of thought which teach otherwise, this theological perspective brings the revelation of God through Jesus Christ to bear in the critical human situation in such a way that reorientation is experienced and affirmed.

If a contradiction between patterns of behavior and the intended goal of human existence remains, it can be held within the true order of humanity as given in the Christian community — within certain practical limits. The cure of souls does not demand cures as a condition of acceptance; but, because there is orientation toward the true order of humanity as revealed in Christ, aberrations do not become normal or normative. And alteration of behavior does actually take place to the extent that it is possible. This is the cure of souls.

In the previous chapter we discussed at length the significance of liturgical events which enact on behalf of each participant authentic personhood. We suggested that the paradigm for personhood is the experience of community itself, as the body of Christ. And such liturgical events occur within the context of community. Technically, being a Christian does not entail membership in a religious body, as though only official members have a place within the body of Christ, but as a matter of actual experience the concept of a solitary Christian who never experiences community in Christ cannot be upheld as a paradigm of reconciliation and belonging to Christ. This is true not only because the Scripture teaches that Christ is present where "two or three" are gathered in his name, but because there would be no cure of souls in such a situation.

There would be no baptism and no communion (*koinonia*) by which the *mutua consolatio fratrum* could take place. The fraternal and mutual exhortation which upholds each member of the body of Christ is a bulwark against which the gates of hell cannot prevail (Matt. 16:18).

It is said that Martin Luther, one day when he was tormented by doubts and conflicts within and without, went to his writing table and, with a piece of chalk, wrote these words: *baptizatus sum* — I have been baptized! And then he promptly went about his work with the assurance that this was the final word concerning the state of his soul. The body of Christ dares to baptize that which is not yet whole and gives the bread and the wine to those who are not yet what they will be. This is what it means to say that we are justified by faith. Where this takes place, there is the cure of souls.

AN ESCHATOLOGICAL PERSPECTIVE

A third critique which a theological perspective makes possible is eschatological. Because the Word of God which summons creation and all creatures into existence is an eternal Word, it is always a present Word and always a Word which makes a critique of the present with its own presence. Human personhood, as a particular form of creaturely existence under determination of the divine Word, thus stands under the creative power of that which summons it into existence. In this sense, one might say that personhood as the essential mark of humanity is a goal and is determined by this goal as much or more than by its own event in history.

In the face of the apparent finality of that which is under the determination of nature and the temporal order, a theological perspective brings a liberating power which relativizes the past and the present to the future. While taking the present order of existence seriously, a theological perspective does not take it as the final word concerning our existence. This critique delivers human existence from the fatalism and determinism of "nature" as a given in which all possibilities are bound up. The *eschaton*, the ultimate Word concerning our existence, does not depend on the attainment of creaturely possibilities. The ultimate Word which determines human destiny is also the primal Word which is the source of our actual existence, and is thus the continued source of the possibilities of existence. This delivers the human situation from the doom of the absolute, as we tend to experience it in the apparently irrevocable events which take place in time.

This means that one who practices the art of the cure of souls need not possess the omniscience of God himself before daring to take up this ministry. The destiny of the human is not within my power. I cannot create the human, nor can I destroy it. Lacking infallibility, I will sometimes err in discernment and other times fail to act appropriately due to lack of faith. Have I missed a demon somewhere in interpreting aberrant behavior, and allowed the person to suffer what should have been cured through exorcism? Probably. Have I stopped short of a miracle of healing because I was uncertain whether God intended to deliver a person from physical bondage through divine intervention? Probably. But not intentionally or perversely, and not in the sense of ultimately dooming myself or the other. The cure of souls must be exercised under this eschatological critique in order that we might be delivered from either "playing God" with presumed omnipotence or copping out altogether and resorting to caring as a substitute for curing. We might also suggest that evangelism as an important aspect of the cure of souls be delivered from the "blood on my soul" syndrome. If I attempt to evangelize another in order to deliver my own soul, this desperation will intrude into the utter seriousness with which I must be concerned for the other soul. The cure of souls is a ministry seen "through a glass darkly," to borrow Paul's words. We know in part, but ultimately we shall know even as we have been known (1 Cor. 13:12).

But if all healing is provisional, does this mean that it is really not all that necessary? If alteration of behavior is only a relative good while orientation to God in living fellowship with his body is an absolute reality, is the alteration even necessary? This is an uncomfortably difficult question. Was it necessary for the demoniac to be exorcised so that he could actually experience his "cure" in this life and sit at the feet of Jesus (Luke 8:35)? Was it necessary for the paralytic to be healed in body if his sins were actually forgiven, which is itself the eschatological event (Mark 2:5)? Certainly it was not necessary as a presupposition for the forgiveness of sins. But it seems to be entailed as a consequence of the forgiveness of sins, though what Thomas Torrance calls an "eschatological reserve" is involved at this point. The resurrection of the body is necessarily involved with the cure of souls, but not instantaneously or immediately. In one important sense, the cure of souls stands within the eschatological reserve, with one hand on the present situation so as not to let it slip out of the grasp of the final healing Word, and one hand on the final Word itself, so as not to let it disappear from sight until it is consummated.

Some years ago at a church conference in the mountains near Los Angeles, the English evangelist Joe Blinco was leading the final service. It was a time of sharing, singing, and proclaiming the Word. At one point in the service, Joe suddenly stopped and advanced up the aisle to a man obviously suffering from Parkinson's disease. This was a man we all knew and accepted without making any particular reference to his affliction. It had become "normal" to us and, we assumed, to him as well. Pointing directly at the man, Joe said, "My brother, some day God is going to create for you a new body in the resurrection and you will sing and dance with us all!" It was a dramatic moment, and with a smile and nod of the head, the afflicted man gave his consent to this promise. But we were all summoned to acknowledge that promise, and we experienced the liberating effects of that stunning and authoritative, but altogether true, word.

Within six months Joe Blinco himself lay stricken with an inoperable and malignant brain tumor. A few days before his death Billy Graham, with whom Blinco had long been associated in crusades around the world, came to visit him. Joe said, "Billy, these are not tears of sorrow — I'm laughing! The Lord has given me great joy. I'm going ahead to get your room ready, and someday, before too long, you will follow me up there." This is the cure of souls: to dare to grasp what is out of order for the sake of orienting it to the true order.

Over against all other theories and practices, we have set forth a theological perspective as a critical principle in the cure of souls. We have developed this in terms of a critique in actual situations involving a ministry of healing and hope. Where uncertainty and anxiety about authentic human existence prevail, Jesus Christ establishes the ontological stability of humanity with permanence and assurance. In the face of conflicting claims and perverse powers which seek control over the souls of human beings, the true order of humanity is set forth in the church as the community of Christ's presence. In this community a fundamental orientation centers the person and relativizes contradictions to a secondary order. Finally, we have seen that the ultimate Word concerning our humanity delivers us from the tyranny of the necessary and frees us to grasp what is out of order for the sake of the true order.

The cure of souls, then, does not so much seek the normalization of pain and distortion for the sake of bearing it nobly, but delivers up pain and suffering to the reality of an actual healing which already is taking place provisionally and will most certainly take place finally.

APPENDIX A

BODY, SOUL, SPIRIT

B IBLICAL COMMENTARIES GENERALLY AGREE THAT THE CONCEPTS "BODY," "soul," and "spirit," as used in Scripture, do not express a clearly defined anthropology. Brunner says that these terms are used as more or less equivalent expressions which refer to the human person as a "whole."[1] However, this judgment should be accepted cautiously in light of the many specific references in Scripture which seem to imply a significant distinction in the terms. Perhaps Barth is closer to the mark when he says, ". . . we shall search the Old and New Testaments in vain for a true anthropology and therefore for a theory of the relation between soul and body."[2] The absence of a structured ontology of the human person in Scripture is the source of the ambiguity in the meaning of the terms as well as of some confusion in attempting to depict the nature of the human person as a combination of these concepts.

This fundamental ambiguity can be seen in the debate over the concepts of trichotomy and dichotomy in the history of doctrine. The "trichotomists" hold that the human person is composed of three elements: body, soul, and spirit. The "dichotomists" argue that there are only two components of the human person, a material aspect (body) and a nonmaterial (soul). While the debate is at least a symptom of a more fundamental problem in biblical anthropology, it cannot be ignored in setting forth a theological anthropology.

The early church was confronted with this issue in the christological debate with Apollinaris of Laodicea in the fourth century. Influenced by Platonic dualism, which posited a gulf between the worlds of body and spirit (*nous*), Apollinaris became convinced that the soul performed the function of me-

---

1. *Man in Revolt* (Philadelphia: Westminster; a reprint of the English translation published by Lutterworth in 1939), p. 363. For additional sources in this book pertaining to body, soul, and spirit, see pp. 362-89. For additional sources on this subject see Karl Barth, *Church Dogmatics*, III/2 (Edinburgh: T. & T. Clark, 1960), pp. 344-436; G. C. Berkouwer, *Man: The Image of God* (Grand Rapids: Eerdmans, 1962), pp. 194-233; John Pedersen, *Israel: Its Life and Culture*, Vols. I and II (London: Oxford U.P.); H. W. Wolff, *Anthropology of the Old Testament*, tr. by M. Kohl (Philadelphia: Fortress, 1974).
2. *Church Dogmatics*, III/2, 433.

diating between these two poles. This essentially Greek idea of a dualism between the intelligible and the sensible world can be seen as one base, at least, for the view of the human self as composed of three parts. For the soul could not be understood as either purely physical or purely mental. Theologians of the church thought this view would lead to a concept of two different souls, and therefore a splitting of the human self as subject into two centers; therefore, the trichotomous view was condemned as heretical at the Fourth Council of Constantinople in A.D. 869-70.[3] The idea of trichotomy, says Berkouwer, rests on the notion of Greek dualism. Thus, he argues, the resistance of the early church to this view of the human person was not because Scripture knows nothing of three substances, but because Scripture knows nothing of any dualism between spirit and matter.[4]

The church's attack on trichotomy was carried out in spite of the fact that Scripture uses expressions which seem to imply such a threefold division of the self. Hebrews 4:12 speaks of a "dividing of soul and spirit," and Paul prays for the preservation of "spirit and soul and body" (1 Thess. 5:23). The differentiation between spirit and soul as if both are in need of preservation seems to point quite clearly to a threefold essence of the person. However, if such a distinction is regarded as decisive, then it must be recognized that such a concept appears only here in Scripture. Likewise, in the passage in Hebrews, the implication cannot rightly be drawn that the spirit can be sundered from the soul in such a way that one stands on the side of God and the other on the side of the human person. This "dualism" is not expressed in Scripture otherwise, either directly or indirectly. Instead, in the use of the terms a parallelism is often involved in which a single truth of the self is being expressed, for example, when Luke quotes Mary: "My soul magnifies the Lord, and my spirit rejoices in God my Savior" (Luke 1:46-47). Here it is clear that there is a single subject which is expressed alike in the terms spirit and soul. This, of course, is not true in every case. The terms "spirit" and "soul" cannot be treated as exact synonyms. Neither, however, can one infer a dualism between a higher self and a lower self from the use of the terms. As Karl Barth well says, "Scripture never says 'soul' where only 'spirit' can be meant. But it often says 'spirit' where 'soul' is meant; and there is inner reason for this in the fact that the constitution of man as soul and body cannot be fully and exactly described without thinking first and foremost of the spirit as its proper basis."[5]

If, however, the basic dualistic premise which slipped in from Greek thought

---

3. *Ibid.*, p. 355.
4. *Man: The Image of God*, p. 209.
5. *Church Dogmatics*, III/2, 355.

is the fatal flaw in a trichotomous view, is a dichotomous view of human personhood any less suspect? We begin to suspect that the debate between the dichotomists and the trichotomists is based on a faulty presupposition, namely, that the human person is composed of two separate entities joined together in an uneasy alliance. This itself would destroy the unity of the human person which is at the heart of a biblical anthropology. Here we must make a distinction between a "duality" of being in which a modality of differentiation is constituted as a fundamental unity, and a "dualism" which works against that unity. Certainly, it is not because one speaks of two or even three aspects of the human person that the problem emerges. The problem emerges when the distinctions, as concepts, become determinative of ontology, that is, when the "being" of the human person is derived from an analytical determination based on metaphysical constructs. Duality becomes a dualism only when the inner order of being which is the basis of the unity of the self is destroyed. "Ontologically, man is a unity," says Brunner; "phenomenologically, mind and nature, and especially mind and body, are to be strictly distinguished."[6] It is our conclusion, therefore, that neither trichotomy nor dichotomy is an acceptable form in which to cast the ontological structure of the human person. The duality of the human person as a concrete experience of personal being that is also physical being is not identical to the metaphysical concept of dichotomy, nor does it exclude, as we shall see, the operations of body, soul and spirit, and heart, for that matter, in the event of personal existence.

The most common designation in the Old Testament for the "soul" is the Hebrew word *nephesh*. This word designates all that has life and breathes. When God created the world it became a swarm of "living souls." The term *nephesh* is applied both to human beings and to animals, separately as well as collectively (Gen. 1:12, 24; 9:10, 12, 15, 16). The Old Testament *nephesh* determines the content of the New Testament *psyche*. As contrasted with the Greek view, the soul (whether *nephesh* or *psyche*) is the concrete life of the creature. That is, it is the life of the body and therefore intimately belongs to the body. *Nephesh*, like *ruach*, means "breath"; but in the concrete sense it is the breath which comes and goes in a human throat, and which distinguishes the living being from the dead.

Since *nephesh* is bodily life, the soul can "long" and "be satisfied," or "hunger" and "be filled" (Ps. 107:9). It can also be chastened by fasting (Ps. 69:10) and polluted by forbidden food (Ezek. 4:14). Hence, to "save his soul" means simply to "go for his life" (1 Kings 19:3). Similarly, a man risks his soul, that is, his life, in a heroic deed (2 Sam. 23:17); a word can cost a man his soul, that is, his life (1 Kings 2:23). The soul can be "poured out" in death, be

6. *Man in Revolt*, p. 373.

devoured, or be killed (Lam. 2:12; Ezek. 22:25; Num. 31:19). The soul (the life) of the flesh is in the blood (Lev. 17:11); in fact, the soul (life) of all flesh is the blood (Deut. 12:23). In the New Testament, when the *psyche* (soul) is spoken of as loving, finding, preserving, gaining, saving, finding peace and prosperity, forfeiting, losing, perishing, being exterminated, and departing, there is no basis for thinking that anything different is meant than what we have already described in the Old Testament. Quite clearly, the soul is the "whole person," existing in a bodily form and state.

In the same way, "flesh" is spoken of as "crying out" for the living God (Ps. 84:2), and it is flesh that "longs for God" in a dry and thirsty land without water (Ps. 63:1). A man's bones can be vexed (Ps. 6:2), and they wax old when a man keeps silent about guilt (Ps. 32:3). When the prophet sees the destruction of his people drawing near, his "bowls are pained" (Jer. 4:19). This location of pain or compassion in the physical organs lies behind the Greek word for compassion, which also means bowels, or viscera. The language is obviously metaphorical to a certain degree, but one must see more than a figure of speech in this usage. An existential sense lies behind the words, in which the person is expressing in terms of both body and soul what is essential to himself or herself.

Karl Barth, more than any other contemporary theologian, has captured the remarkable union and differentiation which exists between body and soul when he says that the human person is "bodily soul, as he is also besouled body."[7] Therefore, the person is not simply a soul that "has" a body, but is "embodied soul." Soul would not be soul if it were not bodily soul. And body would not be body if it were not ensouled body. The soul is not an abstract concept which is located in a concrete place — the body. Rather, the soul is the life of that particular body, which is the person. If it were not the body of the soul, it would not be a body, but merely a material or even organic thing — a corpse. The body, says Brunner, is the extreme boundary of the soul as the life of the person existing in the world of time and space.[8] The soul has a particular "precedence" in its relation to the body; that is, there is an internal order to this relation by which the person exists as a "rational" creature. The *ratio*, or *logos*, of the person is manifested in the existence of the body as serving the soul and the soul as ruling the body.[9] This property of "rationality" is not a property of the soul as a "higher" principle of mind over the body, but is itself a property of the person who exists in the proper order of bodily soul and ensouled body.

7. *Church Dogmatics*, III/2, 350ff.
8. *Man in Revolt*, pp. 365, 374ff.
9. Cf. Karl Barth, *Church Dogmatics*, III/2, 418ff.

Out of this "order" emerges what is called "heart" (*leb*) as the center of the subjective self — that is, the person. What a person is in his or her heart is who that person is "body and soul." "With all my heart" necessarily means "with all my soul," and therefore, "with all my might" (Deut. 6:5). The heart does not constitute a third entity alongside body and soul. But the heart is the unity of body and soul in their true order — it is the person.

What then shall we say of spirit? Karl Barth stands quite alone here in his radical interpretation of the relation of spirit to body and soul. Spirit, says Barth, is not something which the person *is*, in the sense that a person is both body and soul. Rather, a person *has* spirit or, to put it another way, "spirit has him."[10] Spirit, Barth argues, does not belong to the human by virtue of creaturely being, such as soul and body do. Rather, Spirit belongs to God and is given to the human person as an endowment. Spirit, therefore, is immortal and, when the person dies, returns to God from whence it came.[11] Spirit is the operation of God on his creatures, in the broadest sense. Therefore, says Barth, neither soul nor spirit can be denied to nonhuman creatures. The distinction between the human and nonhuman is that the nonhuman soul has a spiritual determination which extends only to natural existence.[12] The human person has a "double determination," says Barth, in which one is determined the same as a nonhuman creature to be a creaturely soul, but in that determination is also determined to respond to God's Word and to share God's destiny of immortal existence. It is more than a little unclear as to precisely what this means. One suspects that Barth wishes to insert a radical principle of grace in his theological anthropology so that the distinction between the human and the nonhuman can be made only as a theological postulate, and not as an inference drawn from any phenomenological analysis.

Brunner, on the other hand, has less to say about spirit as such. Spirit, says Brunner, is more the mental aspect of personhood which comes into being when a person "rises" above mere psychical existence. The failure to exercise this possibility by rising above the equilibrium of a natural state of being is apostasy and self-alienation. This is so because it is a "revolt" against the command of God by which the human person is summoned into being and sustained as fully human.[13] Spirit, in this case, is the function of "mind" (*Geist*) by which the soul is "awakened" to its true responsibility of perceiving and responding to God. However, Brunner will not tolerate the independent existence of the mind over and against the soul as an abstract principle of rationality. This is a false use of freedom. Thus, the mind must be "renewed"

---

10. *Ibid.*, pp. 354ff.
11. *Ibid.*
12. *Ibid.*, p. 361.
13. *Man in Revolt*, p. 364.

and take up its task of integrating the self in its relation to creation as well as in obedience to the Word and will of God. Faith then, concludes Brunner, is itself the integration of mind and soul.[14]

Some mediation between these two positions may well be the best view to take. Both Brunner and Barth agree that spirit should not be construed as a third dimension of the self alongside soul and body. This appears to be the consensus of most contemporary theologians, Berkouwer included. It is doubtful that one can follow Barth in positing spirit as an immortal dimension to human existence. This would evacuate the human person of a truly human, mortal spirit. It might be construed as a form of Apollinarianism, where the divine Spirit takes the place of a human spirit. However, it would also be a mistake to posit spirit as a potentiality of will, as Brunner tends to do. For this would mean that the "spirituality" of the human person is a matter of one's own capacity and intention. Spirit, we conclude, might be considered the life of the soul (the person) as an orientation toward God, summoned forth by the divine Word and enabled by the divine Spirit. When the prophet tells Israel that a new heart will be given to them, and a new spirit put within them, it means that the soul of the people will be of quite a new kind and of a new power, which will produce new responses (Ezek. 37:14; Jer. 31:31-34).

To say that a person has "life" is to assert a single truth which is qualitatively distinguished from that which does not have life. Yet this "life" is at the same time a bodily life, a life of the soul, and a spiritual life. It could not be a life of the spirit if it were not for the fact that body and soul in their interconnection constitute a living person. Because there is a precedence which the soul exercises with respect to the body, the soul becomes the primary orientation of the spirit in this life. This permits us to posit a basic duality of personal being, where the body represents the material aspect of life while the soul (and the spirit) represents the nonmaterial aspect of life. But even here we must not permit this to become an abstraction. For one cannot speak of body apart from the soul which gives it life. The creaturely soul experiences the effects of spirit as life in its primacy, and thus the creaturely soul of the human might be said to be a "spiritual soul."

There is, however, an intimation that the creaturely body is also the life of spirit; thus there will also be a "spiritual body" (1 Cor. 15:44). This eschatological reality answers to the dilemma of the soul (the person) when it is confronted with the "dreadful" possibility of a "disembodied" existence. Paul contemplates death for the Christian as being "absent from the body" but "present with the Lord" (2 Cor. 5:1-5). But he immediately feels the unnaturalness of this state, and says that we "sigh with anxiety" at the prospect of

---

14. *Ibid.,* p. 372.

being "unclothed," longing with greater expectation of being "clothed." Whether it is better to be "at home in the body" and absent from the Lord, or to be present with the Lord and absent from the body, Paul does not know, though he himself longs to be present with the Lord (2 Cor. 5:8). Nonetheless, he is persuaded that the power of God in Christ will not let him suffer disintegration and alienation. He appears to resolve the problem by simply trusting in the God who raises the dead and who will summon all people before the judgment seat of Christ.

The so-called "intermediate state" between death and personal bodily resurrection is a hypothetical one. The closest Scripture comes to speaking of this is in 2 Corinthians 5. From the standpoint of the theological anthropology which has been developed, it would appear that the concept of a disembodied personal existence which experiences duration and extension in time is difficult if not impossible to hold. The eschatological tension between this present age and the age to come may well resolve this difficulty. From the perspective of the personal life of one who experiences death as an immediate experience of presence with God, the resurrection of the body may well be part of that immediate experience. From the perspective of this age, one can only "see through a glass darkly," and, like Paul, speak in human terms of "being absent from the body" and present with the Lord.

In summary, it is clear that Scripture treats the body and bodily organs of the human person as the visible and objective life of the soul. That a human being lives and moves, experiences good and ill, is healthy and sick, and in the end dies, is not a matter of mere body. Rather, all these things are experiences and actions of the human subject, and therefore the soul of the person. The only interest biblical anthropology has in the body is that it is an ensouled body. In the same way, the fact that a human person has aspirations, that it grieves and rejoices, remembers and forgets, hopes and fears, is not itself primarily the affair of the soul, but of the person as body. The only interest biblical anthropology has in the soul is its bodily state, both in this age and in the age to come. This unity of the self, despite the tensions inherent in the duality, comes to expression as a power of spirit. It is a human spirit precisely because it is so determined and enabled to be that by the divine Word and Spirit. Biblical anthropology defies any systematic consideration of the various dimensions of human life, either as a metaphysical or a psychological structure of being. The interconnection of body and soul will forever remain an insoluble enigma, says Brunner.[15] Yet it is precisely in discovering this interconnection as an existing person that one's own personal identity and wholeness of self

---

15. *Ibid.*, p. 375.

emerge. When one is a whole person, one's whole self is healthy — body, soul, and spirit. While this remains an eschatological reality, it nonetheless gives us an orientation toward seeking health for ourselves and others during this present life.

IMAGO DEI

A NY DISCUSSION OF THE *IMAGO DEI* MUST TAKE NOTE OF THE FACT that this doctrine does not play a very important part in the Bible.[1] That is to say, the biblical texts which have to do with the general state of human origins and the specific language which speaks of "image and likeness of God" are few in number and clouded with ambiguity. Nonetheless, there is no more important issue for Christian theology than the question of the nature of human being. It is not the purpose of this brief appendix to survey the entire history of interpretation and thought with regard to the concept of *imago Dei*, but rather to elaborate more fully on some specific aspects of the doctrine of a more technical nature than was done above in Chapter Six.

The doctrine of the *imago Dei* is explicitly stated in the Old Testament in three texts: Genesis 1:26f.; 5:1; 9:6. To these texts, we might add two references in the apocrypha: Wisdom ii.23 and Ecclesiasticus xvii.3. In all of these passages, a special quality of life is attributed to the human creature as against the nonhuman, described either as being created in the image of God (*tselem*) or after the likeness of God (*demuth*) — or both, as in Genesis 1:26. The *imago* is also mentioned in the New Testament in a similar sense in two passages: 1 Corinthians 11:7 and James 3:9. The "man," representing the human

---

1. Cf. E. Brunner, *Man in Revolt* (Philadelphia: Westminster; a reprint of the English translation published by Lutterworth in 1939), p. 499. The key portions of Brunner's book which speak to the doctrine of the *imago Dei* are pp. 82-113, 168-211, and 499-515. For additional sources on the doctrine, see Karl Barth, *Church Dogmatics*, III/1 (Edinburgh: T. & T. Clark, 1958), 183-206; G. C. Berkouwer, *Man: The Image of God* (Grand Rapids: Eerdmans, 1962); Dietrich Bonhoeffer, *Creation and Fall* (London: SCM Press, 1959); W. Eichrodt, *Theology of the Old Testament*, Vols. I and II (Philadelphia: Westminster, 1975); Joseph Fichtner, *Man the Image of God: A Christian Anthropology* (New York: Alba House, 1978); Carl F. H. Henry, "Man," *Baker's Dictionary of Theology*, ed. by Everett F. Harrison (Grand Rapids: Baker, 1960); Reinhold Niebuhr, *The Nature and Destiny of Man: A Christian Interpretation*, Vol. I (New York: Scribners, 1943); John Pedersen, *Israel: Its Life and Culture*, Vols. I and II (London: Oxford U.P.); N. W. Porteous, "The Nature of Man in the Old Testament," *The Interpreter's Dictionary of the Bible*, ed. by George A. Buttrick, Vol. 3 (New York: Abingdon, 1962); H. Renckens, *Israel's Concept of the Beginning* (New York: Herder and Herder, 1964); T. C. Vriezen, *An Outline of Old Testament Theology* (Oxford: Blackwell, 1958); H. W. Wolff, *Anthropology of the Old Testament*, tr. by M. Kohl (Philadelphia: Fortress, 1974).

person, whether a believer or not, is a bearer of the "image and glory of God" (1 Cor. 11:7) and for that reason should never be "cursed" (Jas. 3:9). Paul, in his message to the Athenians, even summons the Gentiles as witnesses to this relation with God which characterizes all human beings — "in him we live and move and have our being" (Acts 17:28).

In addition to these explicit references to the human person as created in the image of God, there are other important New Testament references which add significantly to the concept of the *imago*. Among them are the following: Romans 8:29; 2 Corinthians 3:18; Ephesians 4:24; Colossians 3:10. In an even more general sense, one might say that Christ reflects this *imago* in his own divine sonship, which becomes the basis for becoming "children of God" and being "like him" (1 John 3:2). In the New Testament, the *imago Dei* as the formative concept of the Old Testament for an understanding of human being is "torn out" of its structural or morphological rigidity and molded to a more dynamic understanding of the *imago* as being-in-the-Word-of-God.[2] The basis for this is the "loss" of the *imago Dei* as a positive orientation of life toward God through the Fall, and the renewal of the *imago Dei* through the whole work of Jesus Christ as the incarnate and thus the original *imago*. "He is the image of the invisible God," says Paul, "the firstborn of all creation ..." (Col. 1:15).

Our purpose in this discussion is twofold: first, to identify key points in the history of interpretation of the concept of the *imago Dei*; and second, to say something about the present state of theological thought concerning this doctrine.

The core text for a concept of the *imago Dei*, from which all others seem to take their departure, is Genesis 1:26: "Then God said, 'Let us make man in our image, after our likeness; ...'" Genesis 1:27 restates this: "So God created man in his own image, in the image of God he created him; male and female he created them." Here the word "image" alone is used. In Genesis 5:1 we read: "When God created man, he made him in the likeness of God." Here, only the word "likeness" is used. The third text, Genesis 9:6 (a warning against murder), reads: "Whoever sheds the blood of man, by man shall his blood be shed; for God made man in his own image."

The earliest significant commentary on the concept of the *imago Dei* was done by Irenaeus (ca. 140-202). In a somewhat dubious exegesis of Genesis 1:26, Irenaeus posited a twofold character for the *imago* based on a distinction between the words image (*tselem*) and likeness (*demuth*). Etymologically, these words can mean, respectively, representation and imitation. Thus, image was construed to be the basic natural *form* of the human, while likeness was

---

2. Brunner, *Man in Revolt*, p. 501.

taken to mean the supernaturally endowed *function* of existing in right relation to the Creator.[3] The "image" represents the ontic imprint of God on the human character, typically reason or conscience. The "likeness" is the *iustitia originalis*, the original state of God-likeness which was lost in the Fall. While Irenaeus was willing to allow that the body itself had some place in the *imago*, along with the soul, in his definition of the *imago* he localized it chiefly in the human reason.[4] To protect himself against the rationalist implications of *imago* as reason alone, Irenaeus argued that the "likeness" (*similitudo*) is a mediation of righteousness through the divine Spirit. This is posited in Adam as spirit as in a child. It is not yet fully developed, but through growth and maturity will become the true state of the human person. With the Fall, this development was stopped, and only through Christ is it restored. Thus, Adam could not lose the *imago* but could lose the *similitudo* because this was only a "seed" or a "promise" of that mature state which is posited by God for him.

With Augustine (354-430), there is a continuation of the distinction between image and likeness, but with a correction in the thought of Irenaeus. Augustine affirmed an original state of perfection, contrary to the concept of "immaturity" which Irenaeus posited for Adam. The *similitudo* and the *imago* were present as both a perfect form and a perfect function of the human person as rightly and spiritually related to God. Augustine attempted to overcome the dualism implicit in the thought of Irenaeus by arguing, on the basis of the doctrine of the Trinity, that the human person is centered in the spirit, which is increasingly molded in accordance with the image of God. If the human spirit truly loves God, then the self-love of God expressed in trinitarian form becomes the form in which the human *imago* is to be understood. Thus, for Augustine, the Fall could virtually extinguish the *imago Dei* with the loss of this true knowledge of God through love. Augustine's unique contribution to the doctrine of the *imago* is this emphasis on the God-directed character of the image. While the image is essentially a part of the being of the human person, it is also a capacity for relation with God. Experienced as sinful humanity, the *imago* has no positive contribution to make, but becomes a hunger for God, an internal appeal for fulfilment from and in a transcendent other.[5] Despite Augustine's tendency to create a dichotomy between the rational soul as a lower order of knowledge (*scientia*) and the spiritual soul as a higher order of knowledge (*sapientia*), he does succeed in overcoming the dualism

---

3. For a discussion of these distinctives, see K. Barth, *Church Dogmatics*, III/1, 197ff.; E. Brunner, *Man in Revolt*, pp. 504ff.; and G. C. Berkouwer, *Man: The Image of God*, pp. 67ff.

4. See Irenaeus, *Against Heresies*, III.xviii.6; cf. also Brunner, *Man in Revolt*, pp. 504f.

5. Cf. Reinhold Niebuhr, *The Nature and Destiny of Man*, I, 156.

of Irenaeus through his mystical concept of the *imago* as the single expression of the person in love and knowledge of God. Brunner sees in Augustine's concept of the *imago* as love of God a positive and unique contribution to the doctrine of the *imago Dei* that is somewhat similar to his own concept of the *imago* as being-in-the-Word-of-God.[6]

Scholastic theology, and particularly the thought of Thomas Aquinas (1225-1274), did not introduce any radical change in the doctrine as developed by Irenaeus and Augustine. However, Aquinas did add significant elaborations. Drawing upon Aristotelian concepts of human nature. Thomistic theology divided the *imago Dei* into three stages: a natural endowment enabling knowledge of and love for God; actual conformity to the image in knowing and loving God; and complete perfection in the love and knowledge of God.[7] "The first state of the image then is found in all men, the second only in the just, and the third only in the blessed" (*Summa*, I, xciii, 5). There is an image of creation, an image of re-creation, and an image of likeness. In a certain sense, Aquinas intensified the dualism of Irenaeus and lost the unifying concept of Augustine through his distinction between the *imago* as *anima rationalis* (rational soul) and the *similitudo* as *donum superadditum supernaturale* (a supernatural addition to human nature). Through the Fall, the *imago* survives, even though it carries with it an element of concupiscence, while the *dona superaddita* is lost. The *imago* as an ontic imprint on the character of the human person is indelible, and even in its estrangement from God is capable of "natural reason"; thus it continues to be responsible to know and seek God. For Thomistic thought, there was a bestowal of creaturely being as a "being-in-kind" with divine being. But this is only an *analogia entis*; the connective tissue which links human being with divine being is not a matter of identity, but of proportion. The formation of a natural theology and a natural ethics in Thomistic theology is premised on this concept of the *imago Dei*. Likewise, the possibility of free will (and human responsibility) as well as of good works apart from special grace is entailed in this concept.[8]

With the Reformation, a radical break with the scholastic tradition ensued through the thought of Luther and Calvin. Both Luther and Calvin returned to Augustine for their anthropological assumptions, even though each contributed a special emphasis. Luther wrote a scathing indictment of the ontic formulation of the *imago* in scholastic theology: "If the *imago* consists in that power of the soul (*anima rationalis*), then it follows that Satan too would be formed according to the image of God, since in him these natural qualities are far

---

6. *Man in Revolt*, p. 506.
7. James Childs, *Christian Anthropology and Ethics* (Philadelphia: Fortress, 1978), p. 21.
8. Brunner, *Man in Revolt*, p. 507.

stronger."[9] Luther argued that the *imago* is the same as the *iustitia originalis*. Following Augustine's lead, he posited a unified concept of the *imago* as existence in the true knowledge of God. With the Fall this knowledge is lost, and there remains no "rational soul" by which the sinner can continue to have free will and from which a natural theology can be developed. With an ambivalence characteristic of Luther at times, he argued for a total loss of the *iustitia originalis*, and therefore of the *imago*, while at the same time positing a survival of a "relic" of the *imago*. Yet on this little relic is based the total possibility of the sinner's public existence as one who continues to bear the *humanum*. In the Fall, the "private" *imago* of righteousness is lost, but the "public" *imago* of dominion and of rudimentary knowledge of God survives. The aspect of *iustitia civilis* survives the Fall and becomes the bearer of the *humanum*.[10] Here we can see how Luther's anthropology provided the basis for his concept of the "Two Kingdoms," the state representing the rule of Christ over non-Christians through the *iustitia civilis*, and the church the rule of Christ through the gospel of justification by faith through grace.

While Luther argues that the *imago* is destroyed for all practical purposes as far as an individual's theological existence before God is concerned, Calvin argues for a sovereign preservation of the individual in a state of "common grace" despite the total "defacing" of the *imago*. While the reason, which belongs to the *imago*, is defaced, it is not totally destroyed. Positing a formal aspect to the *imago* in the sense that *imago* equals *humanitas*, Calvin was able to attribute to the sinner ideas of justice, integrity, and honesty. The distinction between the human and the nonhuman is due to the fact that the formal aspect of the *imago* is present. Nonetheless, there is the same ambivalence here that we find in Luther. Reason belongs to the *imago*; the *imago* is destroyed or at least defaced; yet we remain rational creatures. The solution to this can only be to argue, as Calvin does, that the higher the reason aspires, the more it errs. Like Augustine, he does not believe that there is any basis in the sinner for a knowledge of God apart from enlightenment from above through the grace of God.[11]

While the Reformers center the *imago* primarily in relation to God rather than in an autonomous and individualistic possession of a natural reason, they are not free from what has become the central issue for a doctrine of the *imago Dei*. That is, how is the loss of the *imago* as *iustitia originalis* to be combined with the recognition of the fact that the *humanum* which has not been lost (freedom, reason, conscience, language, etc.), belongs to the *imago*

---

9. *WA*, 42, 46; cited by Brunner, *Man in Revolt*, p. 507.
10. Brunner, *Man in Revolt*, p. 508.
11. *Ibid.*, pp. 509f.

Dei? The Reformers rejected both the exegetical conclusions drawn by Iren-aeus as support for a dualistic view of the *imago* and the philosophical spec-ulations of scholastic theology. To this extent, they were no further ahead than Augustine, though they did develop a more christological understanding of the *imago* as a relational reality established through "being in Christ."

The theology of the post-Reformation period did not contribute anything significant to the doctrine of the *imago Dei*. Rather, there developed a ten-dency to return to the scholastic conception of the *imago* as a rational soul (*anima rationalis*), with the Aristotelian notion of reason the formal basis for the *humanum*. Through the influence of biblical criticism and with the de-velopment of historical and scientific criticism, the matter of the primitive state of the human prior to the Fall became moot. Concepts of sin as originating in a personal corruption of being were replaced by more impersonal concepts of evil, with a positive view of human nature coming to the fore as a result of the humanism taught by the Enlightenment. In response to this, and as a result of an unqualified identification of the human spirit with absolute Spirit (Hegel), Kierkegaard introduced a more existential and dialectical view of hu-man being as the existence of the self in tension between sin and grace. Existential anthropology made a clean break with the more traditional cate-gories, which only served to reinforce certain attempts to return to a more rationalistic and individualistic concept of the *imago* as a reaction.

Turning to the present state of theological thought concerning the *imago Dei*, several things can be said by way of establishing some general assump-tions. With the possible exception of the doctrine of the *imago Dei* as taught by the Eastern Orthodox Church, theologians today generally agree that at-tempts to establish a dualistic view of the *imago Dei* based on exegetical conclusions drawn from the distinction between image (*tselem*) and likeness (*demuth*) in Genesis 1:26 are without foundation. Berkouwer says that at-tempts to continue this distinction in contemporary theology are isolated and generally unsuccessful.[12] The two terms, "image" and "likeness," are used with no apparent consistency in the Bible. In addition, regard for the typical struc-ture of parallelism in Hebrew literature suggests that the two words are used to reinforce a single idea. That is, a correspondence between the Creator and the human person is denoted with no clear indication as to the nature of this correspondence in terms of human nature itself.

In general, there is no clear and consistent track orthodox theology has taken in over nineteen hundred years of theology in regard to the doctrine of the *imago Dei*. Unlike the christological controversies of the first six centuries, discussion of the *imago Dei* did not seem to touch the nerve of theological

12. *Man: The Image of God*, pp. 68ff.

orthodoxy in the same way that concepts of the person of Christ did. And yet it is clear that soteriological conclusions are as much determined by anthropological assumptions as by christological ones. It is also noteworthy that the doctrines of Christology and soteriology were taken over by the Reformers from the medieval church virtually intact. On the other hand, a radical break was made with scholastic theology in terms of the anthropological assumptions which lay behind the doctrines of grace, sin, and the Christian life of faith. So then, having said that there is no clear track by which one can trace orthodox concepts of the *imago Dei*, we must also admit that two rather clear alternatives have been at work during this period, interacting with one another. If one wished to identify these alternatives by some form of typology, then the first would be Augustinian, and the second Aristotelian or even Thomistic. The first (Augustinian) represents a stress on the unity of the *imago* through orientation to God as its source and determination. This view of the *imago* subordinates the ontic aspect to the functional or relational. The second (Aristotelian) represents a concern for the formal grounding of the *imago* in the *humanum* as a basis for the continuity of human being through the Fall, and as a basis for human freedom and responsibility *vis-à-vis* the grace of God in the gospel of Christ. This view of the *imago* subordinates the relational aspect to the ontic. Within each of these typologies, extreme views can be found that appear to be of another kind altogether. However, as a general basis for understanding the contemporary situation, these two tendencies will be found in the prevailing concepts of the *imago Dei*.

Within the tradition of Reformed theology, the concepts of Emil Brunner, G. C. Berkouwer, and Karl Barth represent the most significant contribution to the doctrine of the *imago Dei* in modern theology. All would share the general assumptions which have been set forth above, though with sharply defined areas of disagreement. Brunner argues for the basic position of Calvin as more helpful than that of Luther because it attempts to deal more consistently with the reality of the presence of the *imago* as a formal component of the *humanum*, both in the unregenerate person and in the Christian. Brunner's earlier depiction of this formal basis for the *imago* as a "point of contact" for the Word of God has been modified following his debate with Barth. He now wishes this formal notion of the *imago* to be understood as a dialectical relation between the *imago*-origin and the humanity-of-the-sinner.[13] Thus he renounces the term "formal *Imago*," though he avers that the *humanitas* does actually exist in the sinner as that which the Word of God presupposes when it addresses the sinner.[14] Brunner wishes to be understood as teaching a doc-

---

13. *Man in Revolt*, p. 513.
14. *Ibid.*, p. 514.

trine of the *imago Dei* as a unified "theological" human nature. From the perspective of God, Brunner argues, *humanitas* continues to be the foundation of the divine predication of human existence, in the sinner as well as in the regenerate Christian. What Luther meant by "relic," Brunner holds to be a significant, though spiritually impotent, aspect of each human person. Rejecting the concept of a primitive state of righteousness prior to a historical Fall, Brunner thus does not have to deal with the question of *iustitia originalis*. This is not a historical concept, argues Brunner, but rather an eschatological one.

Berkouwer, on the other hand, while beginning also with Calvin, stresses the "hermeneutical" method of seeing the *imago* through its restoration in Christ rather than as an anthropological datum.[15] He argues that Calvin was more concerned with our *knowledge* of the *imago* through Christ (Eph. 4:24; Col. 3:10). Thus, Berkouwer stresses the relational aspect of the *imago*, but not as a mere abstract possibility. The *imago* exists concretely in conformity to the character of God. This is first of all a christological statement, but it does not evacuate the anthropological statement in Genesis 1:26 of all meaning. The ontic conformity of Christ to God in his own *humanitas* is presupposed by the *humanitas* of Adam before the Fall which exists as conformity to the character of God. The corruption of the *imago* through the Fall is thus horizoned for Berkouwer by these two events. What remains uncertain is the nature of the *imago* as *humanitas* in the sinner. On the one hand, says Berkouwer, the human person without this concrete relation to God is a mere abstraction, and does not exist as such in his or her own right. But on the other hand, this abstraction resulting from the Fall does not bring an end to basic human relationships.[16] It is in relationship between persons that evidence of the preservation of the *imago* can be seen, argues Berkouwer. This appears to give ontic stability to the *imago* even where there is no relation of conformity to the character of God. Perhaps this is what Brunner means by his dialectic of *imago*-origin and the humanity-of-the-sinner. The concept of "intersubjectivity" as the ontic content of the *imago* is an advance on the thought of Augustine, as well as of Calvin. With certain qualifications, both Brunner and Berkouwer offer a relational concept of the *imago*, though each is still somewhat uneasy when it comes to explaining how it is that the human person as sinner "loses" the *imago* and yet continues to possess it.

Karl Barth cuts this Gordian knot with an innovative thrust of the sword. While Barth in his earlier writing followed Luther more closely than Calvin in positing a total loss of the *imago* through the Fall, he modified that view in

---

15. *Man: The Image of God*, pp. 87ff.
16. *Ibid.*, pp. 179, 197f.

his later writings by insisting that the human person could not lose the *imago* because it never possessed it in the first place. "We certainly cannot deduce from this that man has lost it through the fall, either partially or completely, formally or materially. . . . What man does not possess he can neither bequeath nor forfeit."[17] Arguing that the human person is not created to *be* the image and likeness of God, but rather created *in* the image of God, Barth makes a distinction between the *humanum* as such and the *imago*. One might see here a correspondence between Barth's concept of covenant as the internal basis of creation and the *imago* as the internal basis of the *humanum*. Without the *imago*, there would be no *humanum*, even though the *humanum* exists only because it bears the *imago*. For Barth, covenant is the concrete and historical basis for the existence of the human as creature. Creatureliness is abstract humanity while being-in-relation is concrete and actual humanity. The difference between Barth's and all other concepts of the *imago* can now be seen more clearly. To a certain extent, the *imago* has been considered the abstract and formal element, and the *humanum* the concrete and material element of human existence. This seems to be true for both the Augustinian and Thomistic concepts, and it underlies the views of both Brunner and Berkouwer to some extent. Thus, with Barth we are not permitted to discuss the doctrine of the *imago Dei* as a problem of uniting the ontic and the relational (or the formal and the material). The human person actually exists before it knows how it exists. And therefore it must know itself in terms of its concrete existence. Because this existence of the *humanum* is always creaturely, and is always in a polarity of sexual being, Barth argues that the statement in Genesis 1:27 is an exegetical and theological commentary on Genesis 1:26. "In the image of God he made him; male and female he made them." This intersubjectivity is not merely a function of the *imago*, based on a formal possibility. Rather, co-humanity is itself the *imago* as humanity under the determination of the divine Word. This daring assertion is justified by Barth as the consequence of an even more radical and daring assertion made by the apostle Paul, that the man Jesus, who is the Messiah, a man who was crucified and who died in Jerusalem, is himself the *imago*.[18] It is this radical assertion of New Testament Christology that gives Barth his theological clues for his exegesis of Genesis 1:26-27. Only because Jesus is himself the *imago Dei*, not merely a creaturely expression of it, can one understand that all humanity, from the very beginning, and even through its disobedience and sin, exists under this determination. Therefore, the Fall, argues Barth, cannot take away what only God has determined to be the case. As sinner, the human person

---

17. *Church Dogmatics*, III/1, 200.
18. *Ibid.*, p. 202.

is under the determination of the *imago* in an even more penetrating and excruciating way. The judgment, including the pain and alienation from the face of the Father which Jesus experienced, reveals this fact in unmistakable fashion.

Barth's view, of course, is not without its critics. Berkouwer charges Barth with doing theological construction or even speculation, rather than doing sound biblical exegesis.[19] In answer to Barth's thesis that we participate in Jesus' human nature, not he in ours, Berkouwer responds by saying that the presupposition of the incarnation is that Jesus "became like us" (Phil. 2:7-8; Heb. 2:14, 17).[20] Granting that Barth unites the ontic with the relational in a manner not unlike his own, Berkouwer nonetheless takes Barth to task for his *method* more than for his conclusions. This critical issue in Barth's methodology we will leave for others to judge. What is of significance for us is that Barth's theological anthropology and his concept of the *imago Dei* as concrete human existence in the form of co-humanity so that the ontic *is* the relational represent the most radical, if not the most important, advance in the doctrine of the *imago Dei* since Augustine, including the Reformers. No discussion of the doctrine can take place from this point on without taking his views into consideration. This fact alone gives him a significant place in the theology of the church.

We have discussed the concepts of the *imago Dei* from within the tradition of Reformed theology today. Despite the differences among the three theologians we have discussed, all might well be said to hold a concept of the *imago Dei* which we have identified as Augustinian. The emphasis has been on the unity of the *imago* as the orientation of the person toward God as the source and determination of existence as a human being. While each affirms in some way that the *imago* is a determination of the human person, and thus an ontic reality, all three stress the relational aspect of the *imago* as primary. Relation with God entails the intersubjectivity of relation with other persons as the content of the *imago*. There is also consensus among the three that the total person is affected by sin in such a way that no aspect of the human person continues to bear the *imago* as a natural and positive orientation toward God. Thus all are agreed that the renewing grace of God is necessary for both a noetic and ontic restoration of relationship to God.

Because it is not our purpose to investigate all of the contemporary options with regard to the doctrine of the *imago Dei*, we will not take up other concepts of the *imago* which share most of these assumptions, such as those of a strongly existentialistic character (Reinhold Niebuhr) or from a Lutheran

---

19. *Man: The Image of God*, pp. 72ff., 93-97.
20. *Ibid.*, pp. 95ff.

perspective (Helmut Thielicke). Instead, we will examine briefly a representative of what may be called the Aristotelian, or Thomistic, view of the *imago Dei*. Here again, we will set aside consideration of the Roman Catholic position today (Karl Rahner) as well as the Anglo-Catholic view represented by someone like Eric Mascall. It is of more significance for this discussion to examine the concept of the *imago Dei* which shares the same Protestant and Reformation tradition as theologians like Brunner, Berkouwer, and Barth, and yet reacts strongly against the Augustinian orientation held by these three.

Within contemporary theology of a conservative evangelical orientation, Carl F. H. Henry represents the concern of many when he rejects all relational motifs in the doctrine as inherently existential and subjective. In his view, such an emphasis on "intersubjectivity" and the "response-oriented" character of the human self sets aside the essential faculty of human reason as the primary activity of the *imago*. Through the intellect as a divinely endowed capacity to apprehend the revelation of God as truth, the human self is oriented toward God both formally in man's personality (moral responsibility and intelligence) and materially in his knowledge of God and his will for man.[21] Gordon Clark agrees with Henry when he says: "The image must be reason or intellect. Christ is the image of God because he is God's Logos or Wisdom. This Logos enlightens every man that comes into the world. Man must be rational to have fellowship with God."[22] Henry's concern is to offset what he feels is a tendency of "neo-orthodoxy" to exaggerate the transcendence of God to the point of denying the concreteness of the *imago*. Because he sees both the material and the formal aspects of the *imago* as located in the intellect, Henry is able to do what Augustine and the Reformers had difficulty in doing, keep a unified *imago* intact through the Fall. While both aspects are defaced, neither is destroyed or totally lost. That the sinner continues to exercise reason and moral perception is the basis for human responsibility for sin, argues Gordon Clark. If these human characteristics and capacities had been lost, a person could not be a sinner.[23]

In contrast to the Augustinian orientation of the Reformers, Henry and Clark build on the more Aristotelian notion of a rational soul as the locus of the *imago Dei*. Consequently, the *imago* is both an abstraction from the concrete world of co-humanity and an individualistic correspondence with truth as an order of being. Because the *imago* has become identical with the *humanum* as a formal principle of reason, from which issue freedom and moral responsibility, it must survive the Fall with sufficient potency to posit

---

21. Carl F. H. Henry, "Man," *Baker's Dictionary of Theology*, p. 341.
22. Gordon Clark, "Image of God," *Baker's Dictionary of Christian Ethics* (Grand Rapids: Baker, 1973), p. 313.
23. *Ibid.*

a human life, albeit as a sinner. This view has certain similarities to that of Thomas Aquinas, although those who know Thomas aver that he was more cautious when it came to positing such outright claims for the identity of the *imago* with human thought itself. Henry is more of a scholastic than a Thomist, and draws more from the well of Aristotelian logic than from the wellsprings of the Hebrew soul.

Again we are reminded that one's anthropological commitments in terms of a concept of the *imago Dei* strongly determine epistemological and soteriological conclusions. Where the *imago* is essentially rational, and where reason and moral responsibility are grounded in the *humanum* itself as a presupposition for hearing and responding to the Word of God, metaphysical categories of truth and reality will govern both revelation and ethics. The unregenerate person is capable and therefore responsible to know the truth about God and to live by the moral law. Special revelation as the work of God through Christ is not denied as a necessary operation on the *imago* to give it a material content of faith and love for God, but this "subjective" function of the *imago* is clearly subordinate to the "objective" essence of the *imago* as *anima rationalis*. The line seems rather clearly drawn at this point between the Augustinian and the Aristotelian concept of the *imago*.

It is my judgment that those theologians who continue to explore the significance of the *imago Dei* along the lines of the Augustinian approach are tacking closer to the shoreline of the Hebrew concept of the soul than those who have the clear-sighted vision of Aristotle. If there is no longer a mystery connected to the *imago*, if the divine Word is first of all comprehended as abstract, timeless truth before it can be made operational in human lives and relations, then we have indeed lost more than we knew.

> When ... the author of Genesis 1 says that man is the image of God, he is indeed truly saying something unheard of. He is attempting to express a truly overwhelming mystery, a mystery which for the Israelite is the source of a holy awe of himself and of his fellow man, and which reveals to him that he owes everything that he is and has more to Jahweh than to himself, and that in this life he has a task to fulfill and a responsibility to bear. ... 'Covenant' and 'image of God' are parallel realities, for both express God's nearness. Just as Jahweh commits himself to his people Israel, so the Creator commits himself to the human race.[24]

---

24. H. Renckens, *Israel's Concept of the Beginning*, p. 116.

BIBLIOGRAPHY OF WORKS CITED

Anderson, Ray S. *Historical Transcendence and the Reality of God*. Grand Rapids: Eerdmans, 1975.

Balthasar, Hans Urs von. *A Theological Anthropology*. New York: Sheed and Ward, 1967.

Barth, Karl. *Church Dogmatics*. 4 Vols. Edinburgh: T. & T. Clark, 1936-1962.

Basil, St. *St. Basil's Letters*. Vol. IV/9. Loeb Classical Library.

Becker, Ernest. *The Denial of Death*. New York: Macmillan, The Free Press, 1973.

Berkouwer, G. C. *Man: The Image of God*. Grand Rapids: Eerdmans, 1962.

Bethge, Eberhardt. *Dietrich Bonhoeffer*. New York: Harper and Row, 1970.

Bonhoeffer, Dietrich. *Creation and Fall*. London: SCM Press, 1959.

_____. *Ethics*. New York: Macmillan, 1955.

_____. *Letters and Papers From Prison*. New York: Macmillan, 1972.

_____. *Sanctorum Communio*. London: Collins, 1967.

Branson, Roy. "Is Acceptance a Denial of Death? Another Look at Kübler-Ross," *The Christian Century*. May 7, 1975, pp. 464-468.

Bromiley, Geoffrey. *God and Marriage*. Grand Rapids: Eerdmans, 1980.

Brunner, Emil. *Man In Revolt*. Guildford, England 1939; rpt. Philadelphia: Westminster Press, 1979.

_____. *Love and Marriage*. Selections from *The Divine Imperative*. London: Collins, The Fontana Library, 1970.

Buber, Martin. *I and Thou*. Trans. Walter Kaufman. Edinburgh: T. & T. Clark, 1979.

Burns, J. Patout, trans. and ed. *Theological Anthropology*. Philadelphia: Fortress Press, 1981.

Carey, George, *I Believe in Man*. Grand Rapids: Eerdmans, 1977.

Childs, James. *Christian Anthropology and Ethics*. Philadelphia: Fortress Press, 1978.

Clark, Gordon. "Image of God," in *Baker's Dictonary of Christian Ethics*. Ed. Carl F. H. Henry. Grand Rapids: Baker, 1973.

Clark, Stephen B. *Man and Woman in Christ*. Ann Arbor, Mich.: Servant, 1980.

Crane, Richard. "Problems of the Homosexual in Relation to the Church." Diss. Fuller Theological Seminary, 1977.

Eccles, Sr. John. *Facing Reality*. London: Heidelberg Science Library, 1970.

_____. *The Human Mystery*. Berlin, Heidelberg: Springer-Verlag, 1979.

Eichrodt, W. *Theology of the Old Testament*. Vols. I and II. Philadelphia: Westminster Press, 1975.

Fichtner, Joseph. *Man the Image of God: A Christian Anthropology*. New York: Alba House, 1978.

Forell, George W. *The Protestant Faith*. Englewood Cliffs, N.J.: Prentice-Hall Inc., 1960.

Henry, Carl F. H. "Man." In *Baker's Dictionary of Theology*. Ed. Everett F. Harrison. Grand Rapids: Baker, 1960.

Jewett, Paul K. *Man as Male and Female*. Grand Rapids: Eerdmans, 1975.

Kierkegaard, Søren. *Fear and Trembling and The Sickness Unto Death*. Princeton: Princeton U. P., 1954, 1969.

_____, *The Concept of Dread*. Princeton: Princton U. P., 1944.

Kübler-Ross, Elizabeth. *On Death and Dying*. New York: Macmillan, 1969.

_____. *Questions and Answers on Death and Dying*. New York: Macmillan, 1974.

Macmurray, John. *Persons in Relation*. London: Faber and Faber, 1961.

Menninger, Karl. *Whatever Became of Sin?* New York: Hawthorne Books, Inc., 1973.

Miller, Arthur. *After the Fall*. Middlesex, England: Penguin Books, 1964.

Miskotte, Kornelis. *When the Gods are Silent*. London: Collins, 1967.

Mowrer, O. Hobart. *The Crisis in Psychiatry and Religion*. Princeton: Van Norstrand Press, 1961.

Mühlen, Heribert. *Sein und Person nach Johannes Duns Scotus*. Werl, West Germany Dietrich-Coeldle-Verlag, 1954.

Niebuhr, Reinhold. *The Nature and Destiny of Man: A Christian Interpretation*. Vol. I. New York: Charles Scribner's Sons, 1943.

O'Connor, Flannery. "The Kingdom of God and the River," In her *A Good Man is Hard to Find and Other Stories*. New York: Harcourt, Brace, 1955.

Pattison, Mansell. "Women's Role and Status in Western Society: A Psychological Perspective," an unpublished paper delivered at the Second Annual Conference On Contemporary Issues, Conservative Baptist Seminary, Denver, ca. 1973.

Pedersen, John. *Israel: Its Life and Culture*. Vols. I and II. London: Oxford U. P., 1973.

Pelikan, Jaroslav. *Fools for Christ*. Philadelphia: Muhlenberg Press, 1955.

Polanyi, Michael. *Personal Knowledge*. London: Routledge and Kegan Paul, 1958.

Porteous, N. W. "The Nature of Man in the Old Testament," In *The Interpreters Dictionary of the Bible*. Ed. George A. Buttrick. Vol. III. New York: Abingdon, 1962.

Renckens, H. *Israel's Concept of the Beginning*. New York: Herder and Herder, 1964.

Shaffer, Peter. *Equus*. New York: Avon Books, 1974.

Small, Dwight H. *Christian: Celebrate Your Sexuality*. Old Tappan, N.J.: Revell, 1974.

Thielicke, Helmut. *The Evangelical Faith*. Vol. I. Grand Rapids: Eerdmans, 1974.

_____. *The Ethics of Sex*. Grand Rapids: Baker, 1964.

Vriezen, T. C. *An Outline of Old Testament Theology*. Oxford: Basil Blackwell, 1958.

Wolfe, Thomas. *Look Homeward, Angel*. New York: Random House, 1929.

Wolff, H. W. *Anthropology of the Old Testament*. Trans. M. Kohl. Philadelphia: Fortress Press, 1974.

Zizioulas, John. "Human Capacity and Incapacity", *Scottish Journal of Theology*, 28 (1975), 401-448.

INDEX OF SUBJECTS

INDEX OF NAMES